Corporate Fraud: Prevention and Detection

Corporate Fraud: Prevention and Detection

Julia Penny BA FCA
Director of Training, Chantrey Vellacott

Members of the LexisNexis Group worldwide

United Kingdom	LexisNexis Butterworths Tolley, a Division of Reed Elsevier (UK) Ltd, Halsbury House, 35 Chancery Lane, LONDON, WC2A 1EL, and 4 Hill Street, EDINBURGH EH2 3JZ
Argentina	LexisNexis Argentina, BUENOS AIRES
Australia	LexisNexis Butterworths, CHATSWOOD, New South Wales
Austria	LexisNexis Verlag ARD Orac GmbH & Co KG, VIENNA
Canada	LexisNexis Butterworths, MARKHAM, Ontario
Chile	LexisNexis Chile Ltda, SANTIAGO DE CHILE
Czech Republic	Nakladatelství Orac sro, PRAGUE
France	Editions du Juris-Classeur SA, PARIS
Hong Kong	LexisNexis Butterworths, HONG KONG
Hungary	HVG-Orac, BUDAPEST
India	LexisNexis Butterworths, NEW DELHI
Ireland	Butterworths (Ireland) Ltd, DUBLIN
Italy	Giuffrè Editore, MILAN
Malaysia	Malayan Law Journal Sdn Bhd, KUALA LUMPUR
New Zealand	LexisNexis Butterworths, WELLINGTON
Poland	Wydawnictwo Prawnicze LexisNexis, WARSAW
Singapore	LexisNexis Butterworths, SINGAPORE
South Africa	Butterworths SA, DURBAN
Switzerland	Stämpfli Verlag AG, BERNE
USA	LexisNexis, DAYTON, Ohio

© Reed Elsevier (UK) Ltd 2002

A CIP Catalogue record for this book is available from the British Library.

ISBN 0 7545 1298 3

Typeset by Action Publishing Technology Ltd, Gloucester
Printed and bound by Bookcraft, Midsomer Norton, Bath

Visit Butterworths LexisNexis *direct* at www.butterworths.com

Foreword

Fraud has become one of the greatest threats to the UK economy, not only in terms of its impact on our major corporations and key financial institutions but also its effect upon smaller companies and ultimately the wider public who indirectly pay for the losses through increased costs of goods and services.

Many organisations fail to recognise that fraud can prove to be even more catastrophic than other forms of critical incidents such as terrorist attack, fire or flood. Events of that nature may cause serious disruption to the business but rarely are they insurmountable. However, a significant fraud against the company not only undermines financial stability, it can ultimately result in such damage to the reputation and loss of investor confidence that it proves irreparable.

It is often for these reasons that company directors write-off losses to fraud under the general heading of 'bad debt' rather than admit that there has been a failure to implement proper safeguards or managerial negligence in applying appropriate levels of oversight to routine business processes where company cash and assets are at risk.

Julia Penny's book is primarily designed to help company directors to establish a culture of fraud awareness and to develop preventative measures to minimise the risk of loss through a form of crime that, although repetitive in type, is nonetheless constantly evolving with the development of new forms of information technology.

Julia has also focused on areas of business where fraud is most commonly found and provides invaluable practical advice on how to respond when it is discovered. In doing so she has drawn on her experience as an accountant and auditor as well as the insight she has gained from working with police officers and public and private sector investigators dedicated to the task of tackling fraud.

Ken Farrow
Detective Superintendent
Head of the City of London Police Fraud Squad

Preface

The trouble with getting organisations to take fraud seriously is that most of us are optimistic and do not want to believe that fraud will affect us or our organisations. However, with UK fraud estimated at between £12–£16 billion per annum, it is likely that our businesses will, at some stage, be victims.

The aim of this book is to act as a catalyst for organisations who have decided to take the risk of fraud seriously. I hope that the book will provide not only important information to enable an understanding of fraud and its prevention, but also practical help in identifying and implementing the necessary polices and procedures. The appendices should be particularly useful in this respect, as they include a model fraud response plan, a reporting checklist and many other practical tools.

I cannot complete this preface without saying that I am extremely grateful for the help given by the following people and organisations: Philip D'arcy and his colleagues from Blandy & Blandy solicitors, who reveiwed and contributed to the section on civil recovery procedures; Detective Sergeant Lee Dinnell of the Hampshire Constabulary, for his contribution on steps to take when a fraud is suspected; and Graham Dowling of the Metropolitan Police service, for statistical information on fraud and steps for fraud prevention.

Thanks also to all of my Chantrey Vellacott DFK colleagues for their help with ideas, and especially the following who contributed material for the book: Mark Kinsella, David Chitty, Stephen Hill, David Ingram, Iain Birrell and Sally Kirby.

Julia Penny
June 2002

Contents

		Page
Foreword		v
Preface		vii

		Para
1 Introduction		
What is fraud		1.5
The impact of fraud		1.7
Causes of fraud		1.11
Corporate fraud		1.25
2 Directors' duties and role in fraud prevention		
Corporate governance		2.4
Requirements of the Listing Rules on corporate governance		2.6
3 Risk factors		
Illustrative examples		3.6
Assessing risks in your organisation		3.18
Next steps		3.25
Preventing fraud – internal controls		3.27
Management fraud		3.35
4 Procurement frauds		
Examples of fraud		4.2
Bribery		4.2
Backhanders		4.4
Supply frauds – underdelivery		4.9
Dummy invoices		4.10
Stock theft and cover up		4.16
Double invoice fraud		4.17
5 Debtor fraud		
Teeming and lading		5.2
Bad debt write-offs		5.4
Credit note fraud		5.5
Long firm fraud – the disappearing act		5.6
Forged credit rating		5.10
Invoice factoring fraud		5.11
6 Payroll and expenses fraud		
Payroll fraud		6.1
Expenses fraud		6.6
Agency staff fraud		6.8

		Para
7	**Sector fraud**	
	Hotel sector	7.2
	Retail fraud	7.6
	Manufacturing frauds	7.14
	Charity frauds	7.16
	E-business fraud	7.26
	Public sector fraud	7.52
	Professional firms fraud	7.62
	Insurance fraud	7.81
8	**Investment frauds**	
	Investment scams online	8.2
	Prime Bank frauds	8.3
	Pyramid investment schemes	8.5
	Advance fee fraud	8.6
	Terminology	8.10
9	**Insolvency fraud**	
	Phoenix companies	9.2
	Recent developments in dealing with insolvency fraud	9.5
	Steps to prevent becoming a victim	9.6
10	**Money laundering**	
	Primary legislation	10.3
	Secondary legislation	10.4
	How does it work?	10.6
	What to watch for?	10.10
	Methods of laundering	10.12
	Cyberlaundering	10.24
	Legal responsibilities for accountants and other professionals with regard to money laundering	10.25
	Steps required	10.27
	Future developments	10.28
11	**Technology for fighting fraud**	
	Biometrics	11.1
	Signatures	11.4
	Checking identity for access to computer systems	11.6
	Data mining	11.7
	Surveillance technology	11.11
	Developments in fighting fraud	11.12
12	**The external auditor's role**	
	The auditor's work on fraud	12.6
	Non-audit companies	12.25

		Para
13	**The internal auditor's role**	
	Risk review output	13.2
14	**What to do on discovering a fraud**	
	Contingency plans	14.1

	Appendices	*Page*
A	The Turnbull Report – a summary	203
B	Charity Commission – Strategic Risk Management Framework	207
C	SAS 110 – Fraud and Error	219
D	Example of an external auditor's inherent risk assessment	243
E	Example of an internal audit testing schedule	247
F	What to do if you suspect a fraud	251
G	Criminal offences which may be appropriate for cases of fraud	259
H	Organisations that help with the pooling of data	261
I	Fraud healthcheck	263
J	Example fraud policy and response plan	269
K	Model Fraud Policy Statement: Short Version	299
L	Model Fraud Policy Statement: Long Version	301
M	Useful websites and bibliography	307

| **Index** | | 317 |

Introduction 1

1.1 Fraud? – why do I need to know about fraud?, you may ask. The simple answer is that fraud is estimated to cost the UK economy £16bn per annum, about £650 for every household (survey by the Association of British Insurers, 1999). Not all of that fraud affects businesses, but a lot of it will. This book will look at the key areas that you need to know about to help protect your business or organisation (or those of your clients) from the consequences of fraud.

1.2 The book first covers matters of general importance in understanding fraud and then looks at how to tackle the issue of fraud within your organisation. Prevention and detection of fraud is obviously key, but in order to achieve this, knowledge of the types of fraud that exist is necessary. The book sets out examples of frauds that can affect almost any type of organisation and then looks at frauds that are specific to a number different sectors. For each type of fraud a list of internal controls that can help prevent the fraud is set out. The controls are provided in a table with a space for marking if the control is in place in your organisation. You may find that you do not have the particular control mentioned, but that you have a different control that will fulfil the same objective.

1.3 As well as knowledge of the types of fraud that exist, it is helpful to understand your responsibilities with regard to fraud. A section on directors' responsibilities covers this area, including the role of non-executive directors. There is also a section on the internal auditors, discussing the role that they play. The section on the external auditors describes their responsibility with regard to fraud and the requirements of the relevant auditing standards.

1.4 Overall the aim of the book is to ensure that something is done to improve the way that you or your organisation deals with the risk of fraud. By completing the various checklists you will begin to build a record of the work that has been done to tackle fraud. If you are reporting to the board this could form the foundation for a summary of the work done and the work yet to be tackled.

What is fraud?

1.5 There is no offence of fraud so any prosecution will be under more specific offences such as those under the theft act (see Appendix G). The elements in a crime that help define it as fraud in a general sense are:

- an illicit financial gain for the fraudster or loss for the victim; and
- deception.

For example, if someone takes money from the petty cash tin with no authority the action is a simple theft. If the theft is covered up by a false voucher, saying that the money was spent on office refreshments, then we would say it is fraud.

1.6 There has been a lot of pressure in recent years from those fighting fraud for a specific offence to be introduced. However, many in the legal profession believe that this is unnecessary and the current offences are adequate to achieve convictions for those guilty of fraud.

The impact of fraud

1.7 It can be very difficult to judge the level of fraud from statistics based on prosecutions, convictions or even reports to the police of fraud, because there is a large element that goes unreported. Companies, in particular, are not always keen to report fraud for fear of the repercussions it may have on their business. This may include trading partners being less willing to use the company, investors not wishing to invest in the company and a general fall in the company's reputation. There have been a number of studies that set out to determine the level and impact of all fraud, including that which goes unreported. The extracts below give an indication of their findings.

Research by Ernst & Young

1.8   The research by Ernst & Young found that:

- More than half of companies had been defrauded in the last year.
- 30% had suffered more than five frauds in the last five years.
- 84% of the worst frauds were committed by the company's own employees, half of whom had been with the company for more than five years.
- Only 13% of loss due to frauds had been recovered (including insurance recoveries).
- 87% of respondents felt that the incidence of fraud would increase or at least remain static over the next five years, but less than half of these had done as much as they cost-effectively could to protect their business against fraud.
- Only a small percentage of companies believed that their directors had a good understanding of treasury and computers.
- Virtually everyone surveyed felt that their company was vulnerable to fraud in the computer area.

Survey by KPMG

1.9   A survey by KPMG of 100 British companies indicated that:

- 30% of companies had reported a fraud of over £50,000 and 24% a fraud of over £250,000 in the previous two years.

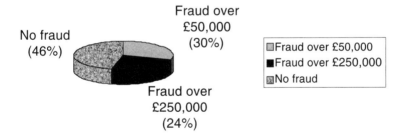

- One third of companies had suffered a fraud, but had not reported it.
- 62% of companies believed that fraud had become much more common over the previous five years.

2000 Survey conducted by Euromonitor Consultancy on behalf of Cybersource (a leading provider of risk management and electronic payment solutions)

1.10 The following graph summarises some of the key findings of the report, which questioned on-line businesses.

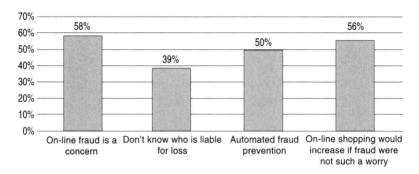

These findings highlight that whilst fraud is regarded as a big and possibly growing threat, most organisations remain unprepared. In particular many companies are unsure about their ability to tackle computer fraud even where they sell on-line.

Causes of fraud

1.11 The Specialist Crime Unit at the Metropolitan police authority compiled the figures shown in the chart at the top of page 5 in 2002.

Notice that 42% of frauds could have been prevented if the internal controls that a company had designed had actually been properly applied. A further 21% could have been prevented if internal controls had been put in place. That suggests that a total of 63% of frauds are preventable through the proper design and application of internal controls. Many managers think that internal controls are only something that the accountants and auditors of this world need to worry about. It may be a vital area for them to deal with in their work, but if everything is left to just one person in an organisation you will usually find that the response is not as effective as if a number of people are involved. It is especially important that fraud is taken seriously at all levels within an organisation starting with the board of directors or equivalent, as this helps to send the right message that fraud and its prevention is taken seriously.

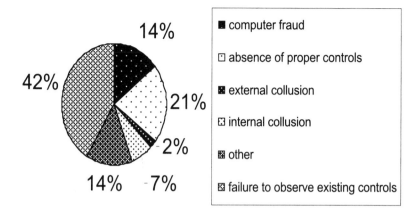

1.12 Some organisations take the view that if fraud happens they will report it to the police and that will be that. But bear in mind, apart from the fact that police will need input from the organisation about the fraud, the successful prosecution of a criminal is difficult to achieve. The graph below shows statistics (again supplied by the Metropolitan Police) about the percentages of convictions achieved for all crime – not just fraud.

Attrition in Criminal Justice System

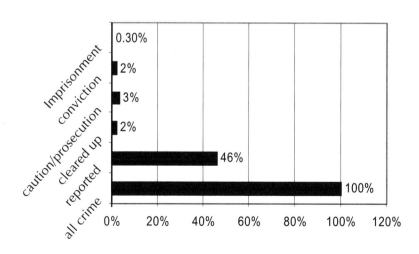

1.13   Crime prevention officers talk about the Ten Points of Crime Prevention. It is worth considering these and how they might be relevant for your organisation:

1   Target hardening;
2   Target removal;
3   Reduce the payoff;
4   Remove the means;
5   Access controls;
6   Surveillance and monitoring;
7   Environmental design;
8   Rule setting;
9   Increase the chance of getting caught;
10 Deflecting offenders.

So what do these mean?

Target hardening

1.14   This means making the asset (or target) that the fraudster might set their sights on harder to get to. This involves, for example, ensuring that the computer system has a sufficient level of security built into it.

Target removal

1.15   Take steps to limit the amount of valuable assets held in a risky situation. For example, only allow a limited number of cheques to be on the premises. Don't allow large numbers of staff to be cheque signatories where it is not necessary.

Reduce the payoff

1.16   Set appropriate authorisation levels, for example, as this will help to ensure that even if a fraud is committed the amount lost should be limited. A disaster recovery plan and a civil recovery programme will also help to limit the amount of loss.

Removing the means

1.17 Stopping the fraud taking place by, for example, having adequate separation of duties such that collusion will always be necessary to commit a fraud. Although still possible, it will always be much more difficult to commit a fraud if you need someone to collude with. Imagine going up to a colleague and saying 'hey, do you fancy committing a fraud with me?'. It is clearly a high risk strategy as they may report you to management or the police.

Access controls

1.18 This covers physical controls such as locks, alarms and security staff as well as adequate supervision to ensure that the controls are maintained.

Surveillance and monitoring

1.19 Regular internal audits and clear supervisory regimes help to deter the fraudster.

Environmental design

1.20 Knowing who is or has been in the building and having an open plan environment where it is difficult for staff to do things in privacy are helpful steps. There are many types of security system available that can help to keep track of staff and visitors' movements; some of them are discussed later in the book.

Rule setting

1.21 A fraud policy statement will help everyone to appreciate the organisation's attitude to fraud. In addition, a balance must be struck between the desire to encourage and reward performance and proper risk management. Too much emphasis on meeting targets at any cost will encourage employees to meet the targets fraudulently.

Increase the chance of getting caught

1.22   A good fraud response plan that details what should happen as soon as a fraud is suspected will increase the chance of catching the perpetrator. If everyone is aware of the policy it may also act as a deterrent. It is important though, that the plan will actually work and is not full of the names of ex-employees or old telephone numbers. An example fraud response plan is given in Appendix J.

Deflecting offenders

1.23   Sometimes it is more desirable to manage the risk associated with the loss of particular assets, rather than try to deflect the criminal's attention away from those assets. This is because you may deflect them towards a more valuable target. Action to prevent and detect fraud must always be taken as part of an overall assessment of the risk of loss and the impact of that loss as well as a consideration of the cost of prevention. Spending vast amounts of time checking expense claims, for example, may be of little use if it means that there is no proper attention to the computer systems.

(The above was adapted from a paper provided by DC Graham Dowling, SO6 fraud prevention officer of the Metropolitan Police.)

1.24   By considering all of these areas your organisation will have a better chance of understanding the risk areas and implementing appropriate controls.

Corporate fraud

1.25   For the purposes of this book, corporate fraud means the fraud that affects companies, businesses and other similar organisations. To better understand the types of fraud possible we will begin by discussing three categories of corporate fraud:

• Management fraud;
• Employee fraud;
• External fraud.

Management versus employee fraud

1.26 Surveys on fraud often distinguish between management and employee fraud. The reason for this is usually that the tactics for dealing with each type of fraud is different. Management fraud can often only be tackled from outside the organisation, or at least by bodies such as audit committees, which we shall look at later. Employee fraud can usually be dealt with by the management of the company.

Management fraud

1.27 Management fraud in this sense means the fraud committed by the top levels of management, such as the board of directors. Fraud at management level covers not only the direct misappropriation of funds but also the manipulation of the accounts of the entity. Such manipulation usually also results in a financial advantage for the perpetrators. Such advantage may be by them retaining jobs that they would have lost had the entity's true performance been known, or getting a loan or other contract for the business that would not have been agreed to had the accounts been accurate. This type of fraud is often more difficult to detect, because internal controls can often be overridden by members of the board. It is important though, particularly for listed or public interest organisations such as charities, that the risk of this type of fraud is taken seriously and that controls exist to try to prevent and detect such fraud. The Turnbull Report on the control issues of corporate governance deals with this to some extent and we will come back to this in Chapter 3.

Example: Resort Hotels

1.28 Events at Resort Hotels helped trigger concerns about corporate governance after it emerged that Robert Feld, managing director, had used his control of the company to forge documents relating to profitability.

The forgeries perpetrated by Mr Feld misled shareholders who subscribed £20.6m for a rights issue in 1992. Discrepancies were discovered in Resort's finances the following year and it eventually went into receivership.

Mr Feld was sentenced to eight years for the fraud in 1997, reduced to six years by the Court of Appeal.

(Financial Times, 22 March 2001.)

Example: Queens Moat House – misstatement of accounts

1.29 In March 1993, QMH's listing was suspended at the company's request. Its market capitalisation at that date was £728m. Under new management, the accounts for that year reported a loss of £1,040.5m. Later, investigators from the JDS (joint disciplinary scheme) found 67% of the company's profits for 1990 'could not be justified on a true and fair basis'.

In this case, the company accounts were found to have been misstated, primarily in connection with a number of property trans-actions being recognised earlier than allowed by accounting stan-dards.

On the civil side, the English Court of Appeal upheld a decision of the High Court to award the sum of £26,700,000 to the company Queens Moat Houses plc against three of its former directors, in connection with payments of dividends to the directors in the year's in which the accounts have been found to be misstated. Although the decision is being appealed it seems unlikely that it will be reversed.

Employee fraud

1.30 Employee fraud means the fraud committed by all other employees apart from top management. The reason for the distinc-tion is partly that employee fraud is an area that is often more easily dealt with by the common types of control than management fraud.

Example

1.31 An employee, James, worked in a hotel and had responsibili-ties for paying temporary staff (in cash), doing the bank reconcilia-tions, keeping payroll records and for managing the other staff who assisted with these areas. James made out false payroll records, requiring payment for various (non-existent) temporary staff. The cashier was presented with the records and duly handed over the money. James took the money for his own use, but covered up his theft by destroying the list of supposed temporary staff and recording the payment of money as various other items that would not be noticed. The fraud was only discovered by chance, when he was off sick and unable to remove the false payroll information. The information then went to Head Office where it was realised that there was a problem.

1.32   This type of fraud is simple to commit when there is a lack of proper controls over procedures as is the case here. In particular, James had responsibility for too many areas, allowing him to cover his tracks.

External fraud

1.33   In addition to the split between management and employee fraud, there is a further class of fraud that companies need to be concerned about and that is external fraud. Many of the risk factors and indicators of fraud are the same regardless of whether the fraud is employee, management or external and an understanding of these indicators will assist the organisation in planning its defences against fraud.

Example

1.34   A fraudster sends out several documents that look like invoices for an entry in a trade directory. Each invoice is for only £20 so many companies pay it, believing it is genuine. In fact, there is no directory and the fraudster gets away with however many lots of £20 as are paid.

1.35   A variation on this theme is where there *is* a directory, but only a single copy is printed. The invoice says in the small print that 'by paying this invoice you are authorising us to make an entry in the trade directory mentioned'. In this situation it can be more difficult to prove a fraud, as there is an argument that a genuine service has been provided.

Directors' duties and role in fraud prevention 2

2.1 If you are the director of a company, what are your duties with regard to fraud? The Companies Act sets out very little with regard to a director's duties, except in terms of specific duties such as disclosing interests in shares or transactions. Your duties as a director come primarily, therefore, from the fiduciary position that you hold. This essentially means that you have a duty to the company and its members to act for their benefit. It should be noted that the Companies Act does extend this by adding that the directors should have regard to the interests of employees as well as members.

2.2 A useful summary of directors' responsibilities is probably that given in an auditing document, Statement of Auditing Standard (SAS) 600, which is as follows:

> 'Company law requires the directors to prepare financial statements for each financial year which give a true and fair view of the state of affairs of the company and of the profit or loss of the company for that period. In preparing those financial statements, the directors are required to:

> - select suitable accounting policies and then apply them consistently;
> - make judgements and estimates that are reasonable and prudent;
> - state whether applicable accounting standards have been followed, subject to any material departures disclosed and explained in the financial statements;
> - prepare the financial statements on the going concern basis unless it is inappropriate to presume that the company will continue in business.

The directors are responsible for keeping proper accounting records which disclose with reasonable accuracy at any time the financial position of the company and to enable them to ensure that the financial statements comply with the Companies Act 1985. *They are also responsible for safeguarding the assets of the company and hence for taking reasonable steps for the prevention and detection of fraud and other irregularities.'*

2.3 The italicised section is the one most relevant for our purposes. It does not give us much of a clue as to how the directors should go about meeting that responsibility. For this we need to delve a little deeper. The primary way in which directors and others in an organisation can safeguard assets, and hence reduce the risk of fraud, is to recognise the factors that increase the risk of fraud and set up and operate appropriate internal controls.

Corporate governance

2.4 Further information on the responsibilities of directors is contained within the various corporate governance requirements, now included in the Listing Rules of the London Stock Exchange and also applied to not-for-profit and public sector bodies.

Principles of corporate governance

2.5 Corporate governance is all about trying to ensure that companies are run in a proper manner. Many of the requirements of the current corporate governance rules have come about as a result of scandals. For example, issues such as 'fatcat' pay have prompted rules on directors' remuneration and contracts, issues on fraud and other losses have prompted rules on internal controls and appointment of non-executive directors.

Requirements of the Listing Rules on corporate governance

The Cadbury Report

2.6 The Cadbury Report was published in December 1992. The Report presented a code of best practice that companies should adopt for good corporate governance. The Code was incorporated into the Stock Exchange Listing Rules together with a requirement to disclose certain information with respect to corporate governance in the annual report and accounts.

2.7 The Code of Best Practice included the following (those items in bold are the points particularly relevant to fraud prevention and detection):

General requirements

- **Audit committees to be established for all listed companies.**
- Directors' service contracts should not exceed three years without shareholder approval.
- Directors' total emoluments and those of the chairman and highest paid UK director should be fully disclosed and split into salary and performance related elements.
- Executive directors' pay should be subject to the recommendations of a remuneration committee of wholly or mainly non-executive directors.

Disclosures in annual report

- A statement of the directors' responsibility for the preparation of the financial statements.
- A statement describing how the Principles of Good Governance have been applied.
- **A statement of compliance with the Code Provisions of the Combined Code.**
- Statement on the going concern status of the company.
- A description of other features of the company's corporate governance arrangements.

Auditors are required to give a separate report on these disclosures, but only to the extent that the disclosure requirements have been complied with.

Directors

- **Executive and non-executive directors should have the same duties under the law.**
- **The majority of non-executive directors should be independent**

and, to be effective, should make up at least one third of the membership of the board. This applies to all sizes of company.
- The separation of the roles of chairman and chief executive should not be a firm rule, but separation is to be preferred. Companies should justify a decision to combine the roles.
- **There should be a lead non-executive director other than the chairman, who should be identified in the annual report.**
- Companies should set up a nomination committee to make recommendations to the board on all new board appointments.
- All directors should submit themselves for re-election at least every three years and companies should make any necessary changes in their Articles of Association as soon as possible.

Accountability and audit

- The audit committee should keep the nature and extent of non-audit services under review.
- **Auditors should report on internal control privately to the directors. This allows for an effective dialogue to take place and for best practice to evolve in preference to prescription.**
- **Directors should maintain and review controls relating to all relevant control objectives and not merely financial controls.**

Code provisions

2.8 The requirements summarised above are intended to help ensure the proper running of the company. There are a number of more detailed points contained within the code, some of which are relevant to the task of preventing fraud. They include the following points:

- The board should meet regularly.
- The board should have a formal schedule of matters specifically reserved to it for discussion.
- There should be a procedure agreed by the board for directors, in the furtherance of their duties, to take independent professional advice if necessary, at the company's expense.
- All directors should have access to the advice and services of the company secretary, who is responsible to the board for ensuring that board procedures are followed and that applicable rules and regulations are complied with. Any question of the removal of the company secretary should be a matter for the board as a whole.

- All directors should bring an independent judgement to bear on issues of strategy, performance, resources (including key appointments) and standards of conduct.
- Every director should receive appropriate training on the first occasion that he or she is appointed to the board of a listed company, and subsequently as necessary.

2.9 It may seem that little here impacts on fraud, but of course if there is a strong element of independence, an ability to get independent advice at the company's expense and a need for training of directors, it is much more likely that a culture of fraud prevention will prevail and the board will question any transactions or actions which seem dubious.

Internal control

2.10 One of the other areas which is clearly very important from the viewpoint of fraud prevention are the provisions in the code in relation to internal controls and the audit committee. The following section sets out a little more detail on these requirements.

Principle

2.11 The board should maintain a sound system of internal control to safeguard shareholders' investment and the company's assets.

Code provisions

2.12 The directors should, at least annually, conduct a review of the effectiveness of the group's system of internal controls and should report to shareholders that they have done so. The review should cover all controls, including financial, operational and compliance controls and risk management.

2.13 Companies which do not have an internal audit function should from time to time review the need for one.

Audit Committee and Auditors

Principle

2.14   The board should establish formal and transparent arrangements for considering how they should apply the financial reporting and internal control principles and for maintaining an appropriate relationship with the company's auditors.

Code provisions

2.15   The board should establish an audit committee of at least three directors, all non-executive, with written terms of reference which deal clearly with its authority and duties. The members of the committee, a majority of whom should be independent non-executive directors, should be named in the report and accounts.

2.16   The duties of the audit committee should include keeping under review the scope and results of the audit and its cost effectiveness and the independence and objectivity of the auditors. Where the auditors also supply a substantial volume of non-audit services to the company, the committee should keep the nature and extent of such services under review, seeking to balance the maintenance of objectivity and value for money.

Unlisted companies and other organisations

2.17   Although the Combined Code is only compulsory for listed companies, its principles are still good practice for smaller companies and other types of organisation. Indeed the charity Statement of Recommended Practice (SORP) 2000 incorporates many of the points of the combined code, particularly with regard to risk assessment and internal controls, and other regulated entities are often covered by equivalent requirements.

2.18   In order for the board as a whole to be able to tackle the issue of fraud from a company or group-wide perspective, it is necessary for board members to have an appreciation of risk factors and types of fraud that could exist within their company. As discussed above, it is not just the executive directors who have a responsibility to protect the company against fraud – the non-executive directors have the same responsibilities and should not take them lightly. You only have to consider cases like Enron to realise the potential result of not taking an active enough interest in how the company, of which you are a director, is acting.

Risk Factors 3

3.1 When considering fraud as an issue within your organisation it is important to understand the factors that may increase (or reduce) the risk of fraud. Whilst there are many factors that affect this risk, some of them dealt with elsewhere in this book, the list below gives examples and explanations of some of the major factors. Further examples of factors affecting risk are given in Appendix C.

3.2 Personnel risks:

- Dominant/autocratic Chief Executive Officer (CEO).
- Low staff morale.
- Staff not taking holidays.
- Staff retaining tasks on promotion that would normally have been left for the more junior staff members.
- Staff with an expensive lifestyle not supported by their salary level.
- Lack of support for controls at board level or elsewhere.
- Controls only implemented when convenient – if staff are pressed they will ignore controls to concentrate on other tasks.

3.3 Organisational risks:

- Treasury controls not implemented or understood by board.
- IT controls entirely delegated to IT department with no board involvement.
- Performance related pay.

3.4 Structural risks:

- Complex structure, particularly if no apparent business reason.
- Lots of subsidiaries or branches with wide geographical spread.
- Special purpose vehicles with unclear association to main entity.

3.5   Cultural risks:

- 'Results at any cost' type culture.
- No code of conduct or anti-fraud policies.
- Relaxed attitude to legislation generally.

Illustrative examples

Dominant CEO

3.6   Robert Maxwell must be the most obvious example of the problems that can arise with a dominant CEO, although this is of course at the extreme end of the spectrum. Maxwell was able to move funds about between various companies, and of course the pension fund, to try and hide the business's severe lack of cash. It appears he was able to do this because there was a lack of anyone at a similar level of authority to question the transactions.

Low staff morale

3.7   A manager defrauded a major airline of several thousands of pounds because he felt he had not been properly paid, or otherwise rewarded, for his efforts.

Staff not taking holidays

3.8   Many frauds will require the fraudster to be constantly present in order to cover up the fraud. If a teeming and lading fraud is in operation (see **5.2**), the fraudster will be unable to leave their task without someone to assist them with the fraud.

Staff keeping tasks when promoted

3.9   Some years ago, the accountant for the Dodgers (a Los Angeles baseball team) was promoted gradually to the level of finance director. Throughout his time at the company he always dealt with the payroll himself, even returning from holiday to complete it on occasions. It was eventually discovered, when the finance director was off sick and couldn't return to do the payroll, that he was the perpetrator of a major payroll fraud. He had colluded with employees to pay them way over the odds, splitting the difference with them, and he had created a number of entirely fictitious employees whose salary he was collecting.

Staff with an expensive lifestyle not supported by their salary

3.10 A purchase ledger clerk being paid £16,000 per annum but who comes to work in a new Porsche and is always very generous with buying drinks on a night out may raise suspicions of fraud. Of course it may be that the car is the result of a windfall gain, such as a lottery win, or perhaps the clerk's spouse or family are very wealthy, but it pays to be vigilant.

Lack of board support for controls/controls only implemented when convenient

3.11 If the board of directors do not take controls seriously, it is unlikely that other staff will. They are not going to be recognised or rewarded for carefully carrying out control procedures if their bosses do not consider this important. Such an attitude reduces the effectiveness of controls and also sends a message to potential fraudsters that they are more likely to get away with it.

Treasury or IT controls not understood

3.12 There is a danger that the board of directors has little expertise in certain areas, such as treasury or IT. If this happens they may entirely delegate controls to these departments. Clearly this creates a risk of fraud, because the people in these departments then know that nobody else understands or is overseeing the work they do. The board need to ensure that they have sufficient expertise (or there is an internal audit department with sufficient expertise) to judge the controls and performance of all areas of the business.

Subsidiaries or branches with wide geographical spread

3.13   Many frauds have, over time, been committed at remote locations of larger businesses. Sometimes controls are not operated properly at these locations, or staff feel isolated and unable to report a suspicion to head office. There may be pressures to meet targets in order to keep the location open, giving an incentive to manipulate results.

Complex structure, particularly if no apparent business reason

3.14   Where there are lots of subsidiaries, and there is no apparent business need for them, it may be because they have been set up to try and hide fraudulent transactions or money laundering. Entities set up in jurisdictions known for their secrecy are particularly at risk.

Special purpose vehicles with unclear association to main entity

3.15   Separate companies or partnerships may be set up to limit the risk that an organisation suffers. From an accounting point of view these can only be excluded from the accounts if the organisation has genuinely transferred the risk to another party. Special purpose vehicles raise the possibility that liabilities or losses of the company are being 'hidden' or that complex transactions are being used to hide other types of fraud. At time of writing it appears that Enron may be an example of this type of manipulation.

Results at any cost/performance related pay

3.16   Driving staff to achieve certain targets, whether by paying bonuses based on performance or in any other way, provides an added incentive for fraud. The manger who is not going to hit his sales target may create a false sale, move a sale from next year into this, or make a sale to someone that is known to be a bad credit risk. Whilst performance related pay can be a great motivator, you must bear in mind the incentive to falsely meet targets.

Lack of anti-fraud policy

3.17 A stated policy, which all staff are required to read and acknowledge, setting out what the company will do in respect of fraud or suspected fraud can be a strong deterrent. If all members of staff know that suspected fraud will always be reported to the police, they may think twice before committing such an act. Similarly, if staff know that the company takes fraud seriously they will be more likely to report their suspicions of both internal and external fraud (the policy should make it clear to whom reports should be made). Lack of such a policy increases the risk of fraud seeming an easy crime to get away with. A general attitude of laws not being important will give the message to staff that all law-breaking will be regarded in a fairly relaxed way and that even if the fraudster is caught there is not likely to be a heavy sanction or any report to the police.

Assessing risks in your organisation

3.18 We have talked about the above risks as if they are company wide. It may of course be that some of the risks affect certain departments only – maybe the sales department is the only one with performance related pay for instance. You will need to consider the various risks for your own organisation, focusing on the assets that you have that are most at risk. You will find it helpful to have studied the rest of the book before doing this as it will help to ensure that you are considering a wide range of potential frauds.

3.19 To identify these areas, it is often helpful to have a brainstorming session, with other members of staff and the management team. A grid like the one below can help to identify your priorities.

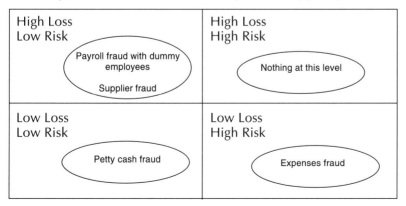

High Loss Low Risk	High Loss High Risk
Payroll fraud with dummy employees / Supplier fraud	Nothing at this level
Low Loss Low Risk	Low Loss High Risk
Petty cash fraud	Expenses fraud

25

If a senior representative from each department is asked to think about the risks to the company's assets (including reputation), you can build up a picture of the fraud risks that the company has. You can then use this a basis for planning an anti-fraud strategy.

The practicalities of risk assessment

3.20 Think of the areas where you could suffer loss and place them in the grid according to the potential level of loss and the relative risk level – the items above are just examples, what goes in each box will depend entirely upon your own organisation. For example, if you know you have good controls in the payroll department, then the risk of loss may be low. However, be careful not to kid yourself – even if you have good procedures laid down in an accounting manual, for example, this doesn't mean that the controls are effectively operated. You must also be careful to distinguish between controls that will be effective for fraud and not just errors. The table below gives just a few examples of common controls that will not necessarily be effective against fraud.

Examples of how effective controls may be against fraud

Control	Effectiveness against fraud
Passwords for computers	Only effective if: • kept to yourself (not taped to the computer or given out to any member of staff asking for it); • difficult to guess (many people's passwords use a favourite footballer or even the default password such as manager or letmein); • changed regularly and always when the system may have been compromised. Even if the above rules are followed passwords can often be obtained by hacking into the system or watching over someone's shoulders.

Control	Effectiveness against fraud
Signature authorising expenditure	Often payments to be made are authorised by a manager signing the appropriate invoice. This is only of limited use in preventing fraud, as signatures are generally easy to forge. This problem applies to credit card payments received by a company and has become such a big problem that the banks now plan to use a PIN number instead of a signature.
Matching documents prior to recording in the records	Usually in business, related documents, such as a purchase order, goods received note and invoice, will be matched with each other to give assurance that the company has been billed only for those items it ordered and received. However, documents are increasingly easy to forge, especially with the help of a scanner or a word-processing package and decent printer. A determined fraudster could create genuine looking documents in order to get false invoices approved.

3.21   Do not think that just because of the type of problems listed above, there is no point in putting these controls in place – although they are not foolproof they will still act as a deterrent, perhaps making the potential fraudster think twice. Almost all frauds could have been prevented or discovered earlier, if adequate controls had been put in place.

3.22   Assessing the risk of fraud is often best carried out as part of an overall risk review of the organisation with the creation of a risk register. An extract from a risk register is given below. It distinguishes between the gross risk, ie the risk before taking into account any controls or other mitigating factors, and the net risk after these are taken into account. The impact and probability of the risk is given in terms of high (H), medium, (M) or low (L). This helps the organisation to prioritise. The further action/date for review column should help to ensure that the exercise leads to improvements where desired, but also to a periodic review where no immediate changes are considered necessary. Finally, the responsibility column is there to be completed when it has been decided who will take responsibility for the area in question. It may require a fair amount of pessimism to come up with a comprehensive risk register and many organisations find it helpful to make use of a professional to assist them with the review.

Extract from a risk register

3.23   The examples shown opposite just show sections relevant to fraud. Although the biggest risks for many organisations may not be fraud it is still an important area of risk.

Mind-mapping

3.24   Another methodology that can help with determining the risks of fraud is that of mind-mapping. The principle here is that the central thought is noted in the middle of a page and then each new idea regarding a possible fraud is noted in terms of its connection with the other ideas on the page. This does not rank the items at all, but allows the mind to run more freely, quickly generating new ideas, without having to stop the thought process by considering the level of risk at that point in time. An example might start like the one below: further information including mind-mapping software can be found at www.illumine.co.uk

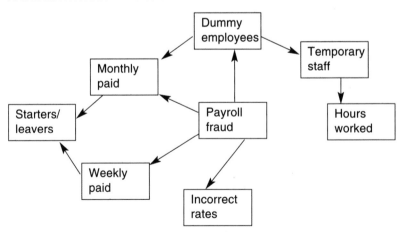

Extract from a risk register

Gross risk	Controls/mitigating factors	Residual risk		Further action/ Review date	Responsibility
		Impact	Probability		
Lack of control over charitable donations leading to potential theft or fraud	Management board aware of this risk	H	M	Very difficult to implement controls in this area – risk remains	
Inability to budget and control spending in branches	Improved monitoring of delegated powers Official books of account for each branch maintained by Director of administration	M	L	Budgets to be created for branches Branch accounts to be reviewed to ensure spending within budgeted figures	
Misappropriation of cash by staff. Reliance on single member of staff to deal with cash	Reduce cash transactions by using BACs etc wherever possible. Suitable recruitment procedures were used when accountant appointed	M	L	Review when staff changes take place. Review periodically to check if safer methods of operation are available	

Next steps

3.25 Once the risk of fraud has been considered and the risks identified have been documented, it is important that something is done
to tackle them. One clear area will be to introduce controls that will
help to prevent or detect the fraud risks identified. If you have used
the mind-mapping technique to set out possible fraud risks you will
need to consider their relative importance for the purposes of putting
controls in place to prevent or detect such frauds. However, designing controls to prevent fraud is only a part of the issue. You also need
to create an anti-fraud culture in your organisation if one does not
already exist. It can be very difficult to change culture, after all
culture is the very thing embedded in the way we work and the
beliefs we have. Steps can, however, be taken to change the culture,
although it must be accepted that this cannot happen overnight.

Changing culture

3.26 One of the main tools in changing culture is training. You
should aim to train all your staff to understand the impact that fraud
has (or can have) on an organisation. This training can often be done
as part of the induction process and periodically be updated there-
after. A necessary part of this training will be to instil in employees
the expectation that they will report any suspicions of fraud that they
have. They should understand that the company will give protection
to any such 'whistle-blowers' – particularly important if the suspicion relates to a more senior employee. The degree to which you
train employees in the types of fraud and the warning signals for that
fraud will depend on the nature of the role that they have in the
organisation. Those with responsibility for areas of finance or with
authorisation duties should normally have a good awareness of fraud
types and indicators. The only danger here is that a company may
feel that by training staff in methods of fraud they will be more likely
to commit the fraud. Whilst this is possible, the chance of this
happening is very much reduced if:

- there is a wide knowledge of fraud techniques and indicators
  across the organisation;
- there are good internal controls; and
- there is a policy that encourages all staff to report suspicions.

Whistle-blowing

3.27 With so much fraud perpetrated from within the organisation, whistle-blowing policies and precedures are a vital part of the tools to prevent and detect fraud. All staff should know that they are encouraged to report their suspicions and that reports can be made in the strictest of confidence. Ideally a telephone helpline number will be widely advertised, which will allow the caller to speak to someone independent of the organisation. This may be the entity's auditor, if they are willing to operate such a service, or a member of the audit committee where there is one. It should be remembered that e-mail is not a secure way of sending messages, unless it is a specially designed system. Staff should be aware that this is the case.

Preventing fraud – internal controls

3.28 As stated in Chapter 1, 63% of frauds occur due to a lack of internal controls or because controls are not operated as set out in the organisation's policies. The concept of internal controls is a simple one; think of something that could go wrong, such as petty cash being taken, then think of a method to help prevent the problem – that method is an internal control. Internal controls are the company directors' main weapon in preventing and detecting fraud. Whilst some of you will already be familiar with the concept of internal controls, it is still useful to revisit these, but with fraud as the thing foremost in our minds rather than error. For those of you to whom this topic is new we will start with an example to explain the nature of internal controls.

Example of internal controls

3.29 A company keeps petty cash and is aware that there is a risk that it will be taken by staff and used for their own rather than the company's benefit. To reduce the risk the company takes the following steps:

- Keeps the cash in a locked tin to which only two people hold the key;
- Requires staff to fill out a voucher detailing what the cash has been spent on;
- Requires staff to attach the receipt or bill for the payment to the voucher;

- Requires a signature on the voucher (from one of the staff with the key) authorising payment from petty cash;
- Requires a weekly check (by a manager without access to the key) to make sure that the balance of the vouchers and the cash in the tin is the level of the cash float held.

3.30   All of the steps above are internal controls of various types. If you are to understand how to prevent fraud wherever possible, you will need to understand the nature of internal controls. Below is a list of the main types of internal controls to help you do this:

Control Type	Description
Organisation	Clear lines of responsibility including someone to whom concerns can be reported.
Personnel	Taking care with recruitment of staff, including taking up references. Training staff properly and allowing them sufficient time to the job.
Physical	Keeping assets locked away, using alarms etc.
Supervision	Supervising the work done to ensure that it is being done properly (this does not mean watching every single minute, but providing adequate supervision).
Authorisation	Authorising expenses, new staff, new suppliers etc. Almost everything with a monetary implication can and should be authorised.
Separation (or segregation) of duties between: • Initiation • Authorisation • Execution • Custody • Recording	The key stages of a transaction should be split between different people wherever possible.

Control Type	Description
Arithmetic	Checking additions and other calculations on documents or in records.
Management	This includes a whole range of things such as: • checking actual to budgeted information; • setting up and using an internal audit function; • using your knowledge of the business and staff to notice when something seems odd; • carrying out reconciliations of balances.

Separation of duties

3.31   This area is worthy of a more detailed description as it is perhaps the one most likely to contribute to fraud if it has not been properly applied. In large organisations there is no excuse for not properly segregating duties attached to different stages of a transaction. As mentioned above the five key stages of a typical transaction will be:

• Initiation;
• Authorisation;
• Execution;
• Custody;
• Recording.

So what does this mean in practice? If we take the example of a transaction to purchase a fixed asset, say a car, we can see the following stages:

A decision is made that the organisation needs a car and the transaction is initiated, perhaps by a requisition form being completed. In order for the transaction to proceed it needs authorisation. Clearly you do not want the same person authorising the transaction as has requested the item, so typically a senior manager may authorise the transaction.

Next the transaction is actually executed, ie a purchase order is made out and sent to the supplier. Ideally this will be done by someone different from the people so far involved, as they can then check the appropriate details, such as authorisation, before placing the order.

When the car is delivered the custody should ideally be with the warehouse department or some other specified person. The person receiving the item can then check it is as ordered and that the order has been properly authorised.

Finally, someone needs to record the purchase of a new fixed asset. This will usually be in the hands of the accounting department and again all the details on the requisition, order, delivery note and invoice can be checked for agreement and authorisation.

If this level of segregation is achieved it becomes much more difficult for a manager, or other employee, to order, collect and keep the car for themselves, recording it as something else in the records in order to hide their tracks.

3.32 In small organisations this level of segregation is unlikely to be possible. This doesn't mean that no effort to separate duties should be made. If the custody of the asset and the recording of the asset can be kept separate, that provides an important distinction in roles and makes any fraud much more difficult. The fraudster wants the asset, but needs to access the records in order to cover his/her tracks. Segregation means that collusion is necessary.

3.33 If we go back to our example of the petty cash tin we can see where some of the controls fit into the above list.

Control	Nature of control
Keeps the cash in a locked tin to which only two people hold the key.	Physical control.
Requires staff to attach the receipt or bill for the payment to the voucher.	Part of authorisation, as the record will allow the person to decide whether authorisation should be given.
Requires a weekly check (by a manager without access to the key) to make sure that the balance of the vouchers and the cash in the tin is the level of the the float.	Management controls (reconciliation of cash and vouchers to records).

Control	Nature of control
Requires a signature on the voucher (from one of the staff with the key) authorising payment from petty cash.	Authorisation.

The above is a simple example of how a business can put controls in place to help protect its assets. In reality though, something like petty cash is unlikely to be top of your list in terms of fraud prevention, unless you hold or use large amounts of it.

3.34 As mentioned earlier, the Turnbull Report sets out the requirements for listed companies in respect of the corporate governance issues relating to internal controls. A summary of the report is given in Appendix A but the essence of the requirements is that directors must consider the significant risks that their company faces and ensure that appropriate controls are implemented and properly operated. Although the requirements are only compulsory for listed companies, they are also indicative of best practice for all types of company.

Management Fraud

Manipulation of accounts

3.35 The issue of manipulation of accounts is a very wide one. Such manipulation may or may not actually involve fraud, but fraud is usually considered as an option where it becomes apparent that the view given by the financial statements is not entirely what might have been expected. A recent example, albeit with an American group, is Enron. At the time of writing the debate about what happened at Enron has only just begun, and so it would be premature to suggest that the collapse was due to fraud. However, some aspects of the collapse suggest that there was a manipulation of the accounts to make the company look stronger than in fact was the case.

The Enron case

3.36 The following extract highlights how company failure, particularly on a grand scale, can start leading to thoughts of fraud. It is taken from an article on the BBC website (www.bbc.co.uk).

'The collapse of energy giant Enron is the largest bankruptcy and one of the most shocking failures in United States corporate history.

In just a little over 15 years, Enron grew into one of the US's largest companies. It embraced new technologies, established new methods of trading in energy and seemed to be a shining example of successful corporate America.

But the company's success was based on artificially inflated profits, dubious accounting practices, and – some say – fraud.

In 2000, it is believed that Enron began to use sophisticated accounting techniques, including a partnership that owned certain special purpose entities, to keep its share price high, raise investment against it own assets and stock and maintain the impression of a highly successful company. Enron could also legally remove losses from its books if it passed these "assets" to an independent partnership. Equally, investment money flowing into Enron from new partnerships ended up on the books as profits, even though it was linked to specific ventures that were not yet up and running. One of these partnership deals was to distribute Blockbuster videos by broadband connections. The plan fell through, but Enron had already posted some $110m venture capital cash as profit.

The current situation

In January 2002 the US Justice Dept announced a criminal investigation into the affair of Enron. Internal investigations have already revealed massive misrepresentation of the accounts. Andersens, Enron's auditors are now considering whether to file for chapter 11 insolvency protection in the US. There is also talk of the firm being rescued by other top accountancy practices.'

3.37 Enron was a massive, global corporation. It supplied energy to a vast array of customers, but also enterted into derivative contracts. One of the accounting methods used to try and reduce the level of gearing (ratio of debt to equity) on the balance sheet was to use special purpose vehicles (SPVs) that under US accounting rules were not consolidated. This meant that the group accounts that were presented to investors and others excluded a large amount of debt that the company appeared to still have obligations in respect of. It appears that these hidden obligations may be behind the collapse of this giant corporation.

3.38 Under UK rules it would be much more difficult for this type of SPV to be left off the group balance sheet as an accounting standard, FRS

5 'Reporting the Substance of Transactions', requires the economic substance of a transaction to be considered, rather than just its legal form.

3.39 Other corporate disasters have occurred over time with the question raised as to whether there was fraud or manipulation of the accounts. In many cases the accounts have been presented in a rather too favourable light – but only because the accounting standards of the day permitted it. For this reason UK standards have gradually been tightened up to try and ensure that there are no loopholes for the creative accountant to sneak through.

UK accounting standards

3.40 Before discussing this type of fraud any further it is necessary to give a brief overview of the accounting regulations in the UK.

There are, at present, two types of accounting standards:

- FRSs (Financial Reporting Standards);
- SSAPs (Statements of Standard Accounting Practice).

3.41 Financial Reporting Standards are issued by the Accounting Standards Board (ASB). The ASB has a further committee that also issues documents – these are known as Urgent Issues Task Force (UITF) abstracts. The UITFs cover areas of abuse or misunderstanding that require rapid action.

3.42 The second type of standard is the Statement of Standard Accounting Practice, which were issued by the Accounting Standards Committee, the predecessor of the ASB. They are gradually being replaced by FRSs.

3.43 It should be noted that the EU intends to require all listed companies within its boundaries to use International Financial Reporting Standards (formerly known as International Accounting Standards) by 2005. Many of these standards are similar to UK Standards and efforts are currently being made to eliminate the remaining differences.

Types of manipulation

3.44 Set out below are a number of the methods that have been used in the past for such creative accounting together with details of any changes in accounting rules or regulations that have sought to limit that type of manipulation.

Method of manipulation	Rules preventing this
• Overstating of gross profit by treating some of the cost of sales as administrative or overhead expenses which therefore leaves them out of the gross profit calculation. This doesn't affect the overall profit but can have an impact on the view given by the accounts, as gross profit is regarded as a key ratio when analysing a company's accounts.	• This is covered by the general requirement to give a true and fair view.
• Profit can be increased by capitalising some expenses as fixed or current assets rather than showing them passing through the profit and loss account.	• The fixed asset standards, SSAP 13, FRS 10 and FRS 15, give strict definitions of what can be treated as a fixed asset. • In addition UITF 24 on start up costs gives further guidance as to when costs may be shown as an asset rather than an expense.
• Overstating of sales by manipulating the 'cut-off' through including sales from the next accounting period or recognising orders that have yet to be delivered as sales. • Recognition of profit early in contract which lasts for several months or years.	• All items shown in a set of accounts must relate to the period in question. • SSAP 9 deals with the rules on accounting for profit on certain long-term contracts. However judgement is still needed as it requires an assessment of the likely outcome of the project. • Areas of doubt creep in where complex contracts exist. In this case it may be difficult to judge in which period an item of income should be recognised. There is as yet no accounting standard in the UK that covers revenue recognition although a discussion paper on the matter has been issued.

Method of manipulation	Rules preventing this
• Understating purchases by similar deliberate 'cut-off' errors.	• See above.
• Overstating purchases, if management wish to reduce profits, by including orders for goods which have not yet been received.	• See above.
• Setting up large provisions to reduce the profits in good trading years. In future years when the trading environment is less favourable, these provisions are found to be too large and profit is increased by reducing the unnecessary provisions.	• FRS 12 was introduced in 1999 to severely limit the occasions when a provision could be set up. It is now not possible to set up a provision just because profits this year are large and expected to be lower next year. There must be a genuine liability as a result of a past event before a provision is allowed. • This is still a very judgmental area, however, and so is at greater risk of manipulation.
• Off balance sheet finance: this can take various forms, for example, taking liabilities off the balance sheet with the aim of making the business appear to have less debts and improving the gearing ratio. These techniques may include transferring assets (and the liabilities associated with them) to a 'friendly' third party or by the 'application' of the accounting rules for leased assets. • The use of Special Purpose Entities (SPEs) to try to keep liabilities off the balance sheet.	• FRS 5 'Reporting the substance of transactions' and SSAP 21 'Accounting for hire purchase and leasing' both seek to limit the occasions when assets and liabilities can be left off the balance sheet. • FRS 5 in particular is a very strong standard as it is based on principles rather than detailed rules. The principle is that if an organisation has control of an asset it should be on the balance sheet. If an asset is shown then any related liability must also be shown. • This is still a complex area, however, and so preparers of accounts may still seek to keep items off the balance sheet by using complex corporate structures.

Method of manipulation	Rules preventing this
• Manipulating the way that the cost of stock or the basis for determining the provisions for old or unsaleable stock are calculated.	• There are a number of ways that stock can be valued according to the accounting standard on the subject, SSAP 9, including first-in-first-out or weighted average. A company should choose the method that is most appropriate for its circumstances. Within these rules there is still quite a large degree of judgement required, so this may be an area that is used to try and manipulate the accounts.
• Increasing trade debtors by ignoring debts which are not recoverable.	• A certain amount of judgement is required to assess the level of bad and doubtful debts included within the balance sheet and so this may be an area where attempts are made to alter the view given by the accounts.
• Increasing cash balances by including cash received in the days following the period end or by ignoring expenses paid before the period end.	• This type of manipulation should be picked up relatively easily by looking at the bank account balances and cash book records.
• Misstating creditors in the same way as purchases.	• If manipulation of accounts is desired it is often easier to suppress the existence of creditors rather than change the figures for items already in the accounts. • Although this is obviously prohibited it may still be possible to achieve this kind of misstatement without it being noticed.

Method of manipulation	Rules preventing this
• Hiding the fact that certain transactions are with related parties and possibly not at fair value. (The Maxwell case had a large number of related party transactions, the significance of which was not realised until it was too late.)	• FRS 8 'Related party transactions' was introduced as a standard after the Maxwell affair, in order to help ensure that transactions with parties that have a special relationship with the company or its key managers are disclosed in the financial statements. • SAS 460 deals with the auditing of such transactions, but it is worth noting, however, that this is still a difficult area to check up on due to management's ability to hide the true nature of a transaction.

3.45 A body, the Financial Reporting Review Panel, looks at the accounts of large private and listed companies in order to check for non-compliance with accounting standards. Where the panel is unhappy with the interpretation or non-application of a standard it can require the company to restate its accounts. Their reports can be found on the web at www.frrp.org.uk

Illustration of accounts manipulation

3.46 It can be difficult to detect manipulation of accounts if it has been carried out by management, as they usually have access to all the correct documentation and signatures to make a document look genuine. However, one very powerful tool that can help to show that manipulation has taken place is analytical review. This means comparing actual ratios for the business (or relationships between the numbers) with what is expected. An auditor may set out their expectations based on their knowledge of the business, or the board of directors or non-executive directors may consider the ratios or relationships that they expect to see and compare them with what they actually see. The example below sets out a simplified version of that process.

3.47 Set out below is a summary profit and loss account and balance sheet. In Version 1, £100 is added to sales in these accounts. An alternative, and perhaps not so serious adjustment, is to move expenses from one section to another. To illustrate this, in Version 2, £50 is moved from expenses to cost of sales.

Summary profit and loss – original

	£	Ratios
Turnover	1,000	
Cost of sales	(700)	
Gross profit	300	30%
Expenses	(220)	
Net profit	80	8%

Summary balance sheet – original

	£	£	Ratios
Fixed assets		350	
Current assets			
Stock	180		
Debtors	29		11 days
Cash at bank	22		
	231		
Current liabilities		(160)	
Net assets		421	
Shareholders' funds			
Share capital		380	
Retained profit		41	
		421	

Summary profit and loss – version 1

	£	Adjustment	£	Ratios
Turnover	1,000	100	1,100	
Cost of sales	(700)		(700)	
Gross profit	300		400	36%
Expenses	(220)		(220)	
Net profit	80		180	16%

Summary balance sheet – version 1

	£	£	Adjustment	£	£	Ratios
Fixed assets		350			350	
Current assets						
Stock	180			180		
Debtors	29		100	129		43 days
Cash at bank	22			22		
		231			331	
Current liabilities		(160)			(160)	
Net assets		421			521	
Shareholders' funds						
Share capital		380			380	
Retained profit		41			141	
		421			521	

Summary profit and loss – version 2

	£	Adjustment	£	Ratios
Turnover	1,000		1,000	
Cost of sales	(700)	(50)	(750)	
Gross profit	300		250	25%
Expenses	(220)	50	(170)	
Net profit	80		80	8%

In the above example, the effect of this simple manipulation is a very stark change in key ratios for the company. This type of misstatement should therefore be easy to notice if the company is audited and if the ratios for the company are normally fairly constant and do not already include the effect of fraud. However, a clever fraudster could choose adjustments that were a lot less noticeable, particularly if they were aware that management and auditors used certain key ratios to judge the company's performance.

3.48   In order to make full use of this technique, those carrying it out must have a good understanding of how the business operates and the state of the industry and economy in which the business is being run. It is much more effective if there are detailed management accounts setting out the expected figures, including ratios, for the business. Its effectiveness is also considerably improved if information from outside the financial records is used to help detect possible fraud. For example, in a hotel forms filled in by the cleaners to show which rooms have been occupied can be checked to the records showing which rooms have been billed for. In a taxi company the number of miles travelled by the taxi can be used to get a rough idea of the income that the taxi should have generated.

3.49 Some companies may subscribe to a benchmarking service. Such services collect key financial data from their members and collate it to provide a picture of key performance indicators. Whilst the purpose of the service is to provide information to management on areas such as efficiency or inefficiency it can also be very useful in identifying possible areas of fraud. Any performance which is much better, or much worse, than other companies in the same sector should give rise to concerns that a fraud or error could be present. Both auditors and the board as a whole should want to see such information where it is available. Information can be found on benchmarking from sites such as www.benchmarking.co.uk

3.50 Similar information will be available for a business with a number of similar branches. If there is a careful study of any unexplained differences between branches there is a much better chance of fraud being detected.

Procurement frauds   **4**

4.1   There is the potential for a large amount of procurement fraud, in many different types of businesses. All businesses need supplies in order to operate, even if it is only stationery, so there is the risk of fraud. Clearly the risk is greater where levels of procurement are high. This means that manufacturers, retailers, construction companies and many public sector bodies are particularly vulnerable. Set out below are some examples of the higher profile fraud cases that have arisen in recent years. You may think that your business is not of the size to suffer such a fraud, but that does not mean there is no risk. Consider the types of fraud which are possible, look at the suggested controls and complete the section to show whether the control (or an equivalent control) is in place, adding any comments that you feel are relevant. This will help in making decisions about the risk of fraud in this area for your organisation and the steps needed to reduce that risk.

Examples of fraud

Bribery

4.2

'A British engineer built a golden lifestyle by cheating the sheiks of Dubai out of £15 million. Stephen Trutch worked his way up from being an apprentice joiner with construction firm Langs to become manager of the Dubai government's Engineers Office.

He used his powerful position to take bribes from firms wanting contracts and to secretly set up or invest in other companies from which he took a profit.

He was jailed for nine months at Winchester Crown Court by judge Robert Pryor, QC, who told him: "I regard these offences as serious. It is quite plain, and particularly Mr Trutch has admitted, that he made a number of false assertions in the course of proceedings."'
(The Express, 9 November 2001.)

4.3　There is always the possibility of bribes being paid to company officials in order to gain contracts. You need to consider the risk that your organisation could have members of staff who accept bribes in order to allocate work to particular suppliers.

Backhanders, frauds and bribes

4.4　Companies, or individuals within a company, might want a contract but not be confident of their ability to land it through the normal commercial routes. Instead, they resort to paying backhanders, or bribes, to employees at the company that needs the work done, in order to ensure that they get the work. This fraud is common in all sorts of industries, and indeed in the public sector, where many lucrative contracts are available if only they can be won.

4.5　This type of fraud may at first seem to lack a victim – after all, someone has done the work, issued a bill and been paid, so does it matter that they wouldn't have got the contract without giving a backhander to staff at the company? It does matter and can indeed be critical, because part of a company's normal procedures before accepting an order would be to check on the quality and timeliness of the contractors' work. If the process is being distorted it is much more likely that substandard work is done, that deadlines are missed, or that the price charged is greater than the normal market price. In the case of some work, a lack of quality could be very dangerous – a building may be constructed inappropriately, electrics may be dangerous, etc. It is therefore very important that companies take steps to try to prevent their employees accepting backhanders in return for awarding contracts or other favours.

4.6 Steps to prevent/detect this type of fraud in a tendering situation:

Control	In place?
Identical conditions and specifications given on the same day to all firms invited to tender	
All tenders logged on receipt	
All tenders received are opened at the same time by the tender opening committee.	
Keep records of any tendering process you use including: • who was asked to tender; • who actually tendered and for what price; • who won the tender (not just the company name, but the directors and/or owners of the company).	
Ensure that tenders are only seen by the people who **must** see them and that the opening of tender documents is controlled.	
Regularly review the results of tendering to check if any particular patterns emerge that are unusual – for example a certain company always fails to tender, or two companies tendering are actually owned by the same people. If you have lots of contracts that go out to tender, it may be worth considering using software to analyse the pattern of the tendering process. Software such as i2 (www.i2.com) can be used to help in all aspects of procurement.	

Control	In place?
If possible, rotate the staff that deal with tenders so that they are less likely to develop a relationship with a supplier that includes receiving bribes.	
Always carry out checks on new companies that are being invited to tender, including a credit check and finding details of who owns and/or runs the business. Companies House services are available on-line at www.companieshouse.gov.uk and include the accounts of companies and details of their directors. Credit agencies such as Graydon (www.graydon.co.uk) provide a comprehensive credit rating and company information service.	
Ensure that there is someone to whom reports can be made if members of staff have concerns that fraud is taking place.	
If the lowest tender is not accepted, are the reasons set down in a report to the relevant committee.	

4.7   Steps to prevent backhanders in other procurement situations:

Control	In place?
A small number of senior employees should have the responsibility for agreeing contracts for work needed.	
Suspicions should be aroused if a contractor will only talk to one employee – staff should be trained to notify this to a more senior manager.	

Control	In place?
Responsibilities for particular types of contracts should be rotated periodically (if practical) in order to help prevent too good a relationship between the employer and the contractor.	
A system should be in place to ensure that a number of quotes are sought for each job over a specified value.	
Checks on the quality of a potential contractor should be made, either by referring to reports on previous work done for the company or seeking references from other companies that have used their services.	
Staff and management should be trained to be aware of the signs of fraud, such as an individual appearing to have more money than can be explained. They should know to whom this should be reported.	
Checks on the individuals behind a company should be made to see if there is any relationship with an employee: • same name; • same address; • Same telephone number; • employee used to work for the company.	
Details of contracts awarded should be regularly reviewed by a senior manager outside the buying department to check for reasonableness and whether there is any indication of only certain firms being used. The records kept should include all offers received to do the work, including prices, and the reasons for the choice of contractor.	

4.8   The example below is taken from the Serious Fraud Office's 2000/2001 annual report and shows how a major fraud of this nature can be carried out and also how information on computer media storage (a floppy disc in this case) can hold vital evidence. Remember that even if the user of a computer believes that information has been deleted from a computer, it is often possible to recover it with specialist techniques. The police can be brought in to deal with this type of situation or an external specialist may sometimes be appropriate. Always make sure that if someone is suspected of fraud all of the computer equipment that they may have used is checked for evidence.

'Cash for contracts in cable-laying industry

The construction industry witnessed a boom in television and telephone cable-laying during the 90s. New ventures sprang up to meet an expanding market. It was a potentially lucrative business if contracts could be won, but, in a growth industry, competition was fierce. This is a case where senior executives awarded contracts in return for "backhanders". Top marque cars in the drive, Rolex watches and a Spanish villa were amongst the accruals from illicit payments. The rotten scheme was blown wide open by a taped conversation and the discovery of an incriminating disk left in a laptop carrying case.

In 1988, an American company named Jones Intercable entered the UK cable industry and set up its head office in Watford. By 1994, after a merger, it became Bell Cablemedia plc. The company operated on the basis of being awarded franchises to install television and telephone networks in different parts of England, acting as a main contractor, managing the whole project and employing various sub-contractors to undertake different parts of the work. One element of the work was the "civil build"; digging trenches, usually in roads or pavements, and laying duct piping in them, the cable would then be pulled through, the trenches in-filled and the surface made good. Individual properties could then be connected to the network. Bell Cablemedia would engage sub-contractors at an agreed rate per metre of trench dug. The rate would take into account the relative ease or difficulty of digging trenches in various types of ground. It was a competitive industry and the main contractor could drive a hard bargain with sub-contractors. This contract mechanism lay at the heart of a web of corruption that spanned 1994 to 1996.

The individuals

Four defendants were convicted. Two of them, Michael Simmons and Barry Falconer were senior employees of Bell Cablemedia. Simmons had the more senior position. He had been Group Director of Construction since 1990 and had oversight of all the company's contracting operations in the UK. Barry Falconer joined the company in 1994, initially to manage the Leeds franchise but later to include contracts in the Norwich and Peterborough regions. The case against them was that they both abused their positions of responsibility in order to extract from sub-contractors financial inducements for the award of contracts.

The other two convicted defendants were David Hutchinson, a director of a Loughborough based sub-contracting business called Cable Connect Ltd, and Daniel "Danny" Thomas, an agent who represented sub-contracting firm M&N Contractors Ltd of Cardiff. He also acted as agent for Cable Connect Ltd. They were charged with making corrupt payments. All four admitted their guilt.

Captured on Tape

The undoing of the corrupt foursome was the unwillingness of another sub-contractor, May Gurney Ltd, to play ball. May Gurney was already digging cable trenches for Bell Cablemedia and the unravelling started in November 1995 with a telephone call to the company's contracts manager. Negotiations had opened for the following year's contract and May Gurney wanted to increase the rate per metre from £24.40 to £25.50. The May Gurney contracts manager received a telephone message that Bell Cablemedia was sympathetic to the request and would be prepared to discuss an increase but that the detail needed to be hammered out with Michael Simmons. During the resulting discussion with Simmons, the May Gurney contracts manager was told that any deal would have to include a payback in cash. When he reported this approach to his superiors he was instructed to feign interest in order to obtain incriminating evidence.

On the basis of that instruction, the May Gurney representative told Simmons in a subsequent conversation that in order to accommodate the payback arrangement, the rate would have to be increased to £27 per metre. A number of reasons to justify the increased rate in their bid for the contract was discussed by Simmons. At a meeting in a hotel bar before the official tender negotiations, Simmons suggested that the sub-contractor put in a price of £27.15 which would enable him, in a show of negotiation on behalf of Bell Cablemedia, to knock down to £26.75. This discussion was secretly taped by the May Gurney man, as were subsequent conversations, during which Simmons sought a commitment that £1 of the rate per metre would be kept back for him. He even bragged about similar arrangements with other sub-contractors. It was, he said, to help him with his pension. May Gurney subsequently won the contract at £26.75 as pre-arranged and in January 1996 submitted its first invoice to Bell Cablemedia for nearly six and a half thousand metres of civil build.

When the corrupt offer was brought to the attention of top management at Bell Cablemedia, Simmons admitted his complicity. Falconer claimed that, although he was aware of some deal being worked out involving payment, he was not part of it. He later admitted to an act of corruption. They were both dismissed and the matter was subsequently referred to the Serious Fraud Office. The investigation, which was supported by the West Yorkshire Police, opened shortly afterwards.

Incriminating Evidence on Disk

May Gurney's whistle blowing prised the lid off this dishonest practice, but what really sealed the fate of the fraudsters was the discovery of a computer disk inadvertently left by Simmons in his company-issue laptop. On his dismissal from Bell Cablemedia, Simmons' laptop was returned to the company. The disk, found in a pocket in the carrying case, was to provide the basis of the direct evidence against him as well as supporting evidence. It contained records of corrupt agreements made with fellow defendants Hutchinson and Thomas. It detailed Simmons' Swiss bank account and payments made to him as well as details of anticipated payments and where they would come from. The disk also contained records of stage payments required for the purchase of a villa in Spain – the "El Paradiso". In all, his prediction of illicit gain was in the order of £800,000. Simmons admitted he was the author of the disk.

The Simmons disk also contained reference to business dealings with Cormac Byrne, a director of an Enfield sub-contracting firm, Cable Network Systems. He was also prosecuted. He denied the charges against him and was acquitted on 23 June 2000.

Hutchinson admitted his guilt in the corrupt scheme. He had kept micro-cassette tape records of his dealings with Simmons.

The recordings included conversations involving him, Simmons and Falconer. These, and other incriminating evidence, were seized by police officers when they searched his home. The evidence against Hutchinson revealed that he would arrange for Simmons to receive shares in his firm, Cable Connect, or a subsidiary company. He also arranged payment of £10,500 to pay a firm of chartered accountants to establish an offshore company with Simmons as the beneficial owner and a bank account for the corrupt payments that Hutchinson would arrange through Cable Connect.

Danny Thomas also was incriminated by details on the disk from Simmons' laptop. It was to show that he was involved in arranging cash payments to Simmons. Some of these were paid into Simmons' account in Zurich from a company in Gibraltar. It was an off-the-shelf company acquired by Thomas for £500. He was the beneficial owner and was able to channel payments to Simmons through the company's Gibraltar bank account.

Trappings of Luxury

Evidence gathered showed that Simmons was enjoying a lifestyle beyond his legitimate income. In addition to acquiring a villa in Spain, he had made a number of cash payments over a two-year period. These included £46,000 on a Porsche; over £23,000 part payment on a Ferrari; around £13,000 on two Rolex watches; £10,000 for a diamond ring and another £10,000 to buy a share-holding in a construction company. He also had a bank account in the Republic of Ireland that had accumulated nearly 176,000 Irish punts over a 20-month period to December 1995. Additionally, £35,050 in cash was found in a safe at his home when it was searched as part of the investigation. His claim that he had saved the money over a period of time did not stand close scrutiny – the cash was in consecutively numbered £50 notes!

Examination of Falconer's finances showed that he also acquired assets beyond his income, though without the ostentation of Simmons. These included a bank account in Jersey with credit entries over a four-month period amounting to £11,500. A search of his home revealed almost £16,000 in sterling and US dollar banknotes.

The four convicted defendants were sentenced at Southwark Crown Court on 17 November 2000. Simmons, who was described by His Honour Judge Jackson as "being at the centre of a web of corruption ... who had reaped huge rewards", was sentenced to three years' imprisonment, Falconer six months, Thomas twelve months and Hutchinson four months.'

The above example highlights the value of a culture which encourages fraud reporting. Without the initial report from May Gurney the fraud may have remained undetected.

Supply frauds – underdelivery

4.9   On a busy building site or at a factory, large amounts of goods are delivered on a regular basis. It can be easy for a dishonest company (or their employees) to deliver less than has been ordered, but still bill for the full amount. Steps to prevent and detect this include the following:

Control	In place?
Check supplier credit references – they may contain information of previous reported problems.	
Always create a goods received note at the time of delivery, detailing items delivered and cross-referencing to the company's original order.	
Check all goods delivered are as stated on the delivery note as soon as possible to confirm contents are as listed (open cartons to check contents are as listed). Any delay will leave the suppliers with the argument that the stock was stolen at a later time.	
Always match invoice details to goods received note and order prior to payment – this should be part of the authorisation procedures used by the company.	
Rotate staff handling goods received to try and prevent collusion between those receiving and those delivering goods.	

Dummy invoices

4.10 Staff or external parties may try to get money from a company by using bogus invoices. The invoice will purport to be for certain goods or services that have not in fact been supplied. Set out on page 56 is an invoice with some suspicious characteristics. This could be used to alert staff to the type of things to look out for when considering if documentation is genuine. The suspicious characteristics are highlighted on the second version of the invoice on page 57.

Checking the VAT check digit

4.11 All VAT numbers include two 'check digits' at the end of the number that are related by a formula to the other numbers. You can use this to check if a number is valid. However, it will not tell you if a valid number is being fraudulently used by another business.

1st 8 digits of VAT no.		8 to 2		Product
5	×	8	=	40
6	×	7		42
7	×	6		42
4	×	5		20
5	×	4		20
1	×	3		3
2	×	2		4
				171

Sum from previous	171
Deduct constant until negative	–97
	74

Sum from previous	74
Deduct constant until sum is negative	–97
last 2 digits of VAT no.	–23

The check digit on the invoice on the following page should be 23 not 34

4.12 The Customs & Excise website gives a number of tips, set out below, for spotting those that may be committing VAT fraud. You may think it is not up to you to report if someone you are trading with appears not to be dealing properly with VAT, but remember, if they can cheat Customs they can cheat you too.

John James Trading

John James Trading Ltd
15 Hillside Road
Edinburgh

07966 111234

VAT registration 567 4512 34
Date 1.3.00
Invoice no 2

Invoice for:

Fees in relation to web services provided in March	£20,000
VAT	£3,500
Total due	£23,500

Please remit direct to our bank:

AC	0987 654322
Sort code	18 23 45
Barclays	Jersey

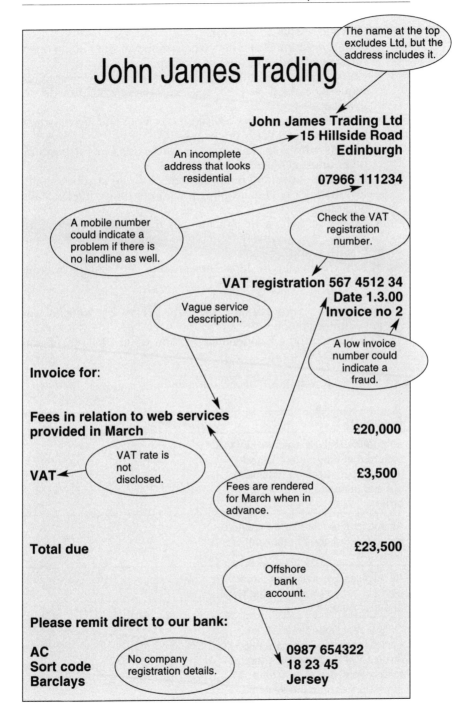

The name at the top excludes Ltd, but the address includes it.

John James Trading

John James Trading Ltd
15 Hillside Road
Edinburgh

An incomplete address that looks residential

07966 111234

A mobile number could indicate a problem if there is no landline as well.

Check the VAT registration number.

VAT registration 567 4512 34
Date 1.3.00
Invoice no 2

Vague service description.

A low invoice number could indicate a fraud.

Invoice for:

Fees in relation to web services provided in March

£20,000

VAT rate is not disclosed.

VAT

£3,500

Fees are rendered for March when in advance.

Total due

£23,500

Offshore bank account.

Please remit direct to our bank:

**AC
Sort code
Barclays**

No company registration details.

**0987 654322
18 23 45
Jersey**

'VAT fraud – what to look for

- Shops, restaurants and bars where money is put into an open till drawer, and sales are not rung up;
- Construction and building services where the suppliers request payment in cash and are reluctant to provide an invoice;
- Businesses which offer a discount for cash and are reluctant to accept credit cards or cheques;
- Traders who want to complete transactions in car parks or other unusual places;
- Electrical goods and mobile phones for sale at substantially less than normal retail selling price from shops, market stalls and pubs;
- Businesses which do not number their sales invoices and request that payment is made to someone other than the business; and
- Advertisements in local newspapers and shops offering goods or services VAT free.

For more information see the HMCE website at www.hmce.gov.uk
Call the Customs Confidential Hotline 0800 59 5000 if you suspect a VAT fraud.'

4.13 Controls to help prevent dummy invoice fraud:

Control	In place?
All goods received are checked to ensure that they were ordered and a goods received note filled out and attached to the copy order.	
All invoices received are matched to the related goods received note.	
All invoices are authorised after being checked to ensure that GRN and order match to invoice.	
Only a very limited number of senior managers, who are not involved with writing out cheques to suppliers, are able to enter a new supplier onto the system.	

Control	In place?
Certain details for a new supplier must be entered, including, for example, registration number for a company, address, telephone number, credit reference.	
Cheques for suppliers are only signed on sight of accompanying documentation.	

4.14 People can have many motivations for committing a fraud but the one in the example below is perhaps one of the more unusual. The fraudster was found to have been funding a lifestyle involving several wives, by submitting large volumes of invoices to lots of companies hoping that some of them would pay. As not all companies checked their invoices carefully, a number assumed the invoices were genuine and paid up. The fraud squad eventually caught up with him, realising that as well as the fraud he was a bigamist with several wives, none of whom knew about the others.

4.15 In addition to the risk of dummy invoices being paid by the company, there is the risk that genuine payments are intercepted and the details changed in order to steal the money. Good controls can, as always, help to prevent this type of fraud.

Control	In place?
Where possible all payments are made via Bankers' Automated Clearing Services (BACS) or Clearing House Automated Payment System (CHAPS).	
Does the Company follow procedures for protecting BACS payments recommended in the BACS user guide? (see http://www.apacs.org.uk for contact details of BACS).	
Where payments are not made via BACS are payable orders and cheques crossed non-transferable, ie account payee.	

Control	In place?
Are adequate controls in place to ensure changes to payee bank details are only made by restricted officers?	
Is written confirmation of a payee's bank account always supplied and is it authorised by either their bank or a senior officer within their organisation?	
Are postal cheques sent by post in ways that do not reveal that a payment is enclosed, eg avoiding using window envelopes?	·
Are there arrangements in place for very high payable orders to be collected by payees or for them to be sent by courier or special messenger?	
Are blank spaces on payable orders/cheques filled with significant characters and asterisks to help prevent names, addresses and amounts being extended?	
Are cashed/drawn payable orders/cheques returned to the company and checked to ensure the payee's name has not been amended?	
Are payable orders/cheques subject to physical controls. Is a register maintained?	
Are unused/void payable instruments kept in a safe place? Are there controls over their destruction?	

Control	In place?
Is it possible through a search of the payee's database to identify accounts for which bank details have been altered in anyway in the previous six to nine months? Check a sample with correspondence from the relevant payee.	
Do the procedures in place permit BACS payment instructions to be reversed in order to correct errors? Do they allow for adequate control?	
Investigate any anomalous BACS transactions.	
Is it possible to identify any payee accounts in foreign locations by their addresses or sort codes?	
Is it possible to identify all advance payments and investigate for subsequent invoice receipts?	
Is it possible to extract vendor VAT numbers and check them for mathematical consistency with Customs and Excise rules?	
Is it possible to interrogate for duplicate payments checking the bank account to which each payment was made?	
Are controls over the setting up of payees adequate, ie segregation of duties, supervisory checks to ensure only bona fide vendors are set up? Are staff duties regularly rotated?	
Does the creditors department receive 'fraud flashes' from relevant websites or any other information on fraudulent invoices? Is this information passed to creditors clerks?	

Stock theft and cover up

4.16   The construction industry can be particularly at risk of stock fraud as it is often easy for stock to be stolen from a building site. If staff are aware that this is the case, they may take advantage by stealing items themselves and writing it off as lost by external theft. Stock can also be written off as damaged by certain members of staff, who have in fact taken the items for their own use.

Prevention and detection

Control	In place?
Adequate physical security, including fences, locked areas, dog security patrols and surveillance should be put in place, commensurate with the value of stock at risk.	
All staff should have their CVs thoroughly checked and references taken up. Up to 25% of all Curriculum Vitae have been shown to contain major inaccuracies – if someone is willing to lie to get a job, they are probably willing to lie to get some stock or other asset.	
All write-offs of stock should be checked and authorised by a senior member of staff.	
Write-offs should, where possible, be compared from person to person and site to site. That way someone committing this fraud is likely to be found out, as the statistics of write-offs will be different from other sites or managers.	

Double invoice fraud

4.17 This is a fraud which generally involves collusion between two members of staff at different companies that trade with each other. The diagram below shows the key elements:

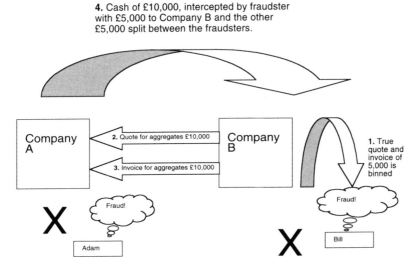

4. Cash of £10,000, intercepted by fraudster with £5,000 to Company B and the other £5,000 split between the fraudsters.

Company A — **2.** Quote for aggregates £10,000 → Company B

3. Invoice for aggregates £10,000

1. True quote and invoice of 5,000 is binned

Fraud! — Adam

Fraud! — Bill

The double invoice element is that there are essentially two versions of the invoice and indeed the other documents in respect of the purchase. Adam asks Bill to get a quote for some aggregates, on the understanding that he, Adam, will get it approved by the relevant manager at Company A. Bill quotes a figure, as far as Company B's records are concerned, of £5,000. However, he bins the actual document and replaces it with a quote for £10,000. Adam duly ensures that this is accepted – perhaps he is the one that approves quotes – and the goods are delivered. When the invoice for £10,000 arrives there is nothing to suggest a problem, as all the other documentation, which has already been authorised, has shown a figure of £10,000. The invoice is paid, but as two cheques – £5,000 to Company B and the rest to Adam and Bill. Alternatively one cheque may be issued, but Bill will be able bank it and write out a cheque to himself, for example, for £5,000.

4.18 Controls that will assist in the prevention of such a fraud are as follows:

Control	In place?
A preferred list of suppliers, where all suppliers on the list have been checked by senior management for quality, value for money, ability to meet deadlines and financial stability. This will not eliminate the fraud, but it will make it more difficult to use a supplier that has not been carefully considered by the company for general suitability.	
Obtain several quotes when goods are ordered, or check prices against other company prices. It is often possible to use the Internet to quickly check a variety of prices to make sure that the amount being quoted is reasonable.	
Separation of duties – individuals should not be able to handle payment/receipts if they are also handling other aspects of the transaction such as approval of the order. If Bill is not able to receive the inflated cheque from company A, or Adam is not able to write out two cheques to company B, the fraud will probably be discovered as the cheque for £10,000 will be queried.	
Staff vetting – it is essential to check staff credentials and references to help prevent a fraudster moving on from one organisation to another and repeating their crime.	

Control	In place?
Review of management figures – if gross profit ratios are checked against expected figures, and other expenses checked against budgeted figures, the company is much more likely to notice that some areas of expense are inflated. For this to happen, management must first of all put together realistic and informed budget figures.	
Internal audit – if an internal audit department exists and randomly checks a sample of transactions for aspects such as value for money accounting irregularities etc, this will act as a deterrent as well as a means of detection for fraud.	

Debtor fraud

5

5.1 There are a number of different types of debtor fraud that are possible. We will look at some of the more likely, together with steps to take to prevent or detect such frauds as follows:

- Teeming and lading;
- Bad debt fraud;
- Credit note fraud;
- Long firm fraud;
- Insolvency fraud;
- Invoice factoring fraud.

Teeming and lading

5.2 This fraud literally means taking and giving and was originally a coal fraud. The workers delivering coal to a large number of households realised that it would be very difficult to notice if they happened to leave a couple of extra bags at their own houses. This was because more coal was regularly being loaded on to the lorry and so the missing coal would not be noticed unless there was a detailed check of every bag of coal to the point in the delivery round that the lorry had got to. Even then, of course, it was easy for the workers to maintain that it had fallen off the back of the lorry! Clearly there is now not much demand for large quantities of coal to be delivered and so now the most common form of this fraud is with debtors. The principle of taking from one to give to another is still there.

How does it work?

5.3 Imagine a member of staff who works in the sales ledger department – we will call them Bigpockets for ease of identification. One day he or she is a bit short of money and when a cheque comes in from a customer (or better still cash) Bigpockets steals it, alters the payee name and banks it for their own use. If this is where it ended Bigpockets would soon be discovered because the debt would become overdue and get chased by another department or individual. As the debtor has paid they will quickly point out the fact that the cheque was sent and has now cleared their bank account. To prevent this discovery Bigpockets covers up the theft by adjusting the records of other receipts. This is done by allocating the next payments made, not to their proper accounts, but to the original account. If we had three debtors initially it might work like this:

- Debtor A owes £300 – this is stolen by Bigpockets.
- Debtor B owes £200 – this is banked in the company account but recorded as a part-payment of debtor A's account.
- Debtor C owes £100 – this is banked in the company account but again recorded as a part-payment of A's account, which is now cleared.

As you can see, unless the £300 is returned to the company there will always be a shortage funds and so Bigpockets will have to continually adjust where the receipts from other debtors are posted. The aim is to always ensure that any difference in payments by debtors and receipts to the company look like timing differences rather than an actual loss of money to the company. It is not possible for the fraudster to take a holiday or be off sick unless they can be confident that no-one else will do their job whilst they are away.

Control	In place?
Segregation of duties between those receiving cash or cheques from debtors and those able to record these items in the company's records.	

Control	In place?
Adequate checking of CVs to help ensure honesty of staff in these jobs.	
Regular review of accounts details (on a sample basis) to look for odd amounts that have been received from debtors – usually a whole invoice or statement balance is paid. If odd amounts are shown it may be a fraud.	
Rotation of staff in the debtor's department, particularly if holiday is not taken.	
Always use someone else to cover the tasks when the normal member of staff is off sick and be suspicious if that member of staff tries to make excuses for why their work should not be covered by someone else.	

Further controls that are relevant to debtors are included in the section on control of receipts, below.

Bad debt write-offs

5.4   Another debtor fraud occurs where someone within the company misappropriates the receipts from a debtor and then hides them by recording them as bad debts written off. This is a simple fraud, although it usually also needs cheque fraud, as debtors rarely pay in cash. The fraudster may alter the payee slightly on the cheque and open up an account in that similar name, in order to bank the proceeds.

Control	In place?
All write-offs are authorised by a senior member of staff who does not have any access to cheques received from customers.	
Write-offs over a certain level are authorised by two members of staff.	
Statements are issued to customers on a regular basis, showing amounts written off.	
A letter is written to a customer asking for payment of the amount involved before the debt is written off (if they have in fact paid they will query the letter and the fraud will be uncovered).	

Credit note fraud

5.5 On a similar basis to the above fraud using bad debt write-offs to hide theft of receipts, credit notes could be raised to hide theft of receipts. Tight controls over the receipt of income will help prevent teeming and lading and other thefts of receipts.

Control	In place?
Does the company provide clear and concise payment instructions on their invoice documentation?	
Does the Company provide payment details such as address and account number?	
Are cheques requested to be made crossed and account payee only?	
Are customers encouraged to pay by bank giro credit transfer?	

Control	In place?
Are all cheques stamped on receipt 'account payee' and with the Company's name?	
Are all cheques received entered either onto a check register or receipt book and where applicable authorised or signed by another officer?	
Is all income receipted into income (cash and deposit sheets)? Are receipts issued in respect of payments received by the cashier?	
Are cash and deposit sheets controlled as part of controlled stationery? Are records kept of all issues and are these used sheets checked for sequential numbering to ensure they are complete?	
Are cash takings relating to, for example, staff restaurants, car parks, vending machines, collected by two officers? Are takings agreed to till rolls or usage counters and differences investigated?	
Are takings agreed to a detailed breakdown by a supervisor and signed for on transfer?	
Is there separation of duties between the cashier, cash collectors and officers preparing bankings?	
Are reconciliations performed regularly between: • cash income recorded as banked; • the bank account; • income records?	

Control	In place?
Are income budgets, actual to budgeted, regularly reviewed and monitored against each income heading?	
Are write-offs, adjustments and credits to debtor accounts authorised by a senior officer?	
Select a sample of 10 write-offs/ adjustments/credit notes and investigate to determine whether their treatment is appropriate.	
Do the Company's standing order/ financial instructions specify that bank accounts in the name of the company must only be opened and maintained by the Director of Finance?	

Long-firm fraud – the disappearing act

5.6 This type of fraud targets businesses by gradually building up trust before finally committing the fraud.

How does it work?

5.7 The fraudsters, lets call them Crooked Co, approach a company (Goodies Ltd) asking to buy goods. As Crooked is a new company or unknown to Goodies, it is agreed that goods will only be sold cash-on-delivery. The goods are sent and the cash is paid; both parties are happy. These cash purchases continue for some time until Crooked asks if it can have some credit. Goody considers this and decides that a small amount of credit would be acceptable. Crooked continues to make regular purchases, paying all invoices promptly and without dispute. Goody believes it has an ideal new customer.

Then comes the crunch. Crooked ask for an extra large order; maybe it's Christmas or they have just signed a big contract. Goodies decides to accept the order – after all, Crooked have always paid promptly before. This time, however, Crooked does not pay up but vanishes. Goody has lost its goods and all hopes of payment. The fraudsters will, no doubt, move on to pastures new and repeat the exercise.

How to prevent it

5.8 Careful procedures before accepting new customers are the best prevention, although not foolproof. Controls should include the following:

Control	In place?
Check that the customer's address is valid (the postcode can be looked up at www.royalmail.co.uk. A search on the postcode will give the address and the names of the businesses operating from that address).	
Check company phone numbers – be wary if there is only a mobile number when goods are being traded. Use directory enquiries to find a phone number.	
Check the accounts filed at Companies House (where the supplier is a company).	
Consider taking a credit reference from an agency or another company.	
If a customer asks for a much larger order than normal, consider visiting them to check whether their operations seem permanent or temporary.	
Ensure that if staff are worried that a fraud may be intended or in progress there are procedures to contact your local police.	

Insolvent debtors

5.9 Sometimes debtors are unable to pay their debts – this is not in itself a fraud. But if the customer never intended to pay for the goods, then there is fraud. The example below is taken from the SFO's report for 2000/01. The controls to try and prevent this fraud are the same types of controls that are needed to prevent long-firm fraud.

'Street market traders defraud suppliers

(a) Defendants – R v Dennis Michael Cook, Paul Leslie Lester and Keith Martin Brace
(b) Crown Court where trial was heard – Birmingham Crown Court
(c) Date of acquittal/sentence passed – 5 July 2000
(d) Principal nature of charges – Conspiracy to defraud
(e) Police force that supported the investigation – West Mercia Police

Cook, who controlled a number of street market trading businesses, and his assistant, Lester, during 1995/96 deliberately set out to defraud more than fifty suppliers of goods. They operated through street markets and out of the back of goods vehicles. They retailed toys, fancy goods, household and electrical items. They also dealt in meat, cheese and other foodstuffs. Takings were invariably in cash. Suppliers were not paid or cheques were cancelled. Complaints about the condition of the supplied goods were used as a pretext to avoid payment. As an excuse, Cook also claimed that he had re-sold goods valued at some £600,000 to the Ukraine but had been let down on payment. Suppliers to Cook's crooked trading operation were defrauded of over £1 million. Cook was also charged with fraudulently reclaiming VAT.

The prosecution was brought jointly by the SFO and HM Customs & Excise. Brace was acquitted but Cook and Lester were found guilty and sentenced to five years and 21 months imprisonment respectively.

Subsequent to the trial Cook was made the subject of a confiscation order for approximately £1.3 million. Should he fail to pay this sum he will serve a further five years imprisonment.

(During the investigation the SFO interviewed Cornelius Joseph McCarthy, a solicitor engaged by Cook. McCarthy failed to provide all relevant documents concerning Cook's business affairs under investigation. They were subsequently discovered through the execution of a search warrant. McCarthy was convicted in April 1998 for contravening a Section 2 notice (Criminal Justice Act 1987), and fined £1,000 and ordered to pay costs of £750.)'

Forged credit rating

5.10 Even with controls in place your company can still end up being a victim of fraud. The case below involves the fraudulent altering of a credit rating in order to obtain credit that would otherwise not be forthcoming. It is always best to only accept information from a trusted third party (eg the agency itself) and not a copy passed on by the company wanting credit.

'Bodycare products

(a) R v Peter Clarence Foster
(b) St Albans Crown Court
(c) 28 September 2000
(d) Use of forged documents
(e) Hertfordshire Police

Peter Foster, a former senior executive of Foremost Bodycare Products Ltd, was sentenced to 33 months' imprisonment on three counts of using forged documents and was also disqualified from acting as a company director for five years.

He had pleaded guilty to using forged documents in an attempt to obtain credit from suppliers to his slimming products business. He had used "doctored" Dun & Bradstreet documentation to suggest that his company's credit risk rating was higher than it actually was.'

Invoice factoring fraud

5.11 Many companies make use of the services of invoice factors. Such companies will pay a percentage of the debtors figure in advance, then keep the receipts from the debtors as the means of paying off the advance and receiving their charge for the service. There is a risk, however, that the invoices put forward for factoring do not relate to genuine invoices. The case below taken from the SFO's annual report 2000/01 shows such a case.

'Invoice factoring

(a) Defendants – R v David Ross and Cameron Ross
(b) Crown Court where trial was heard – Winchester Crown Court
(c) Date of acquittal/sentence passed – 10 November 2000
(d) Principal nature of charges – Fraudulent trading
(e) Police force that supported the investigation – Gloucestershire Constabulary

Cameron Ross was sole director of Harley Marketing Ltd, a direct mail marketing and print broking business near Cirencester. His brother David (an undischarged bankrupt) was general manager. In 1995 they secured a factoring arrangement with International Factors Ltd, a subsidiary of Lloyds Bank, which enabled their business to obtain money from the factoring company against invoices issued by them to their customers. They were advanced £1.3 million against a total of £2.5 million of invoices and credit notes.

The arrangement was terminated in 1997 and the factoring company was left with over £600,000 of unpaid invoices, which they wrote off. Investigations later showed that many invoices issued by Harley Marketing were bogus; no goods or services had been ordered or provided. In some cases, where the fraudsters received orders, they factored the invoice but failed to deliver to their clients. There were also instances where Harley Marketing kept payments mistakenly sent to them by customers instead of being sent to the factoring company.

David Ross was found guilty and sentenced to three years' imprisonment and disqualified from acting as a company director for ten years. Cameron Ross, who admitted to assisting his brother to manage a company whilst he was disqualified through bankruptcy, received three months and was similarly disqualified for six years. He was acquitted of fraudulent trading.'

5.12 Factoring companies are clearly a specialised business, but whenever you are paying out money for an asset it pays to check that the asset is genuine. In the case of debtors, the following checks may help to ensure that the debts are real:

Control	In place?
Debt is backed up by invoice and goods despatched note, or other evidence that the service has been supplied.	
List of debts is checked for repeats of items.	
List of debts is checked to ensure that it casts (adds up) correctly.	
A sample of debtors is contacted to ensure that the debt is genuine (where an auditor does this they will refer to a debtors' circularisation).	
List of debts is agreed to the company's control account for debtors.	
Debtor's details are checked to ensure that the company really exists.	
Company credit references are checked.	
Credit references for individuals involved with the management of the company are checked.	

Payroll and expenses fraud   **6**

Payroll fraud

6.1   Salaries and other costs connected with the payroll are often the largest cost that a company has. It follows that it is a tempting area for any fraudster with potentially rich pickings. Adequate controls will help to prevent, or at least detect, many payroll frauds and it is almost always worth ensuring that such controls are in place and actually operating on a regular basis.

6.2   One major example of a payroll fraud was given earlier in the section on employee fraud (see 1.30). It involved both dummy employees and wage rates in excess of agreed rates. Discussed below are a number of other types of payroll fraud. By understanding the types of fraud that can take place you can be better prepared to ensure controls exist that will prevent them.

PAYE fraud

6.3   Within the construction industry many employees move from one job to another as self-employed bricklayers, etc. They present a certificate to show that they are genuinely self-employed and so the employer does not deduct any tax. A fraud could be committed by a worker who presents a false certificate or promises to bring the certificate in at later date. The company then pays the worker gross of tax and National Insurance when in fact they should be deducting both and accounting for employers' National Insurance. The result is that the company can end up with the liability for taxes, and fines, as they have not correctly deducted them. There is also the possibility that site managers may collude with staff to pay them gross, when this is not permitted, in order to keep the wage bill down or to take the extra funds themselves.

Control	In place?
All certificates should be carefully examined and a copy kept on the personnel file.	
In the absence of a certificate, tax should be deducted in the normal way.	
Internal audit departments should carry out random checks at different sites to ensure the appropriate documentation is held.	
Many firms of accountants will offer a 'PAYE' audit. Companies should consider the benefits of such a check on a periodic basis.	

Dummy employees

6.4 The presence of casual workers in hotels, restaurants and other such companies gives an opportunity to carry out a payroll fraud. Cash wages could be requested for temporary staff that do not in fact exist/work for the company. The cash will then be pocketed by the individual or perhaps paid to an accomplice to make the fraud appear more genuine, then split between the two fraudsters. This type of fraud can also be carried out for salaried employees, especially where there is a lack of segregation of duties, with individuals being able to add or amend employee details as well as run the monthly payroll.

6.5 Adequate controls will go a long way towards preventing or detecting this type of fraud. Typically, it is because a member staff is trusted too much that they are able to get away with payroll fraud. The list below sets out the controls that should be used in a payroll department over both payment and human resource functions. It is important that those responsible for the human resource aspects are kept separate from those responsible for the regular payroll cycle. The list below also includes the kinds of sample checks that internal audit might be expected to do. If there is no internal audit department there should be consideration of these checks being carried out be someone independent of payroll.

Controls over payments

Control	In place?
Are all employees paid by BACS?	
Where payments are not made via BACS, are payable orders and cheques crossed account payee?	
Where open cheques are made, is the employee required to collect the cheque and sign for it? Is evidence of the person's identity checked?	
Are there adequate controls in place to ensure changes to employees' bank details are only made by restricted officers and on receipt of adequate documentation?	
Are postal cheques sent by post in ways which do not reveal that a payment is enclosed, ie avoiding using window envelopes?	
Are blank spaces on payable orders/cheques filled with significant characters, ie asterisks to help prevent names and addresses being extended?	
Are unused/void salary/wages payments kept in a safe place? Are there controls over their destruction?	

Control	In place?
Do controls over CHAPS payments include the following requirements: • branch bank details typed on the form rather than pre-tendered or stamped; and • company staff always telephone the bank in advance and require bank staff to confirm receipt of the form?	
Are cheques subject to physical controls? Is a register of cheques maintained?	
Are any repayments of overpaid salary or allowances made to a department independent of the payroll function?	
Are returned cheques or unpresented cheques followed up independently of the payroll section?	
Do procedures in place permit BACS payment instructions to be recalled/reversed and corrected? Do they allow for adequate control? Investigate any anomalies	
Is it possible to identify accounts in foreign locations by their addresses or bank sort code?	
Are clear written procedure notes followed by all staff involved in the payroll function?	
Are agency payments made only on submission of timesheets which are independently certified by a specified manager for that department?	

Control	In place?
Is certification on returns/ timesheets agreed with copies of authorising signatures held in the payroll department?	
Select a sample of 20 employees from the most recent pay run and ensure each has a positive reporting record (evidence of attendance at work)?	
Select a sample of 10 payments in respect of agency staff and ensure each has an appropriately signed timesheet.	
Select a sample of 15 employees to whom overtime payments have been made and trace to appropriately authorised positive returns and documents held in the department.	
Are all new starters entered on the payroll/human resource system checked and agreed to supporting documentation by a senior officer for authority by either payroll or HR?	
Determine what procedures are in place for payment of arrears to leavers. Are arrears to leavers paid by cheque or BACS? What procedures are taken to validate the leavers' address/bank account, ie are leavers' addresses confirmed in writing?	
Select a sample of 20 payments made in respect of arrears to leavers and ensure bank accounts or address details can be traced to supporting documentation.	

Control	In place?
Are staff duties regularly rotated?	
Do all staff with payroll responsibilities take their annual leave entitlement and is this monitored? Are unusual leave patterns monitored?	
Is output from payroll regularly checked by other pay clerks and differences investigated?	
Are there controls in place to ensure all payroll costs are charged to a valid departmental code?	
Is access to the payroll system restricted by appropriate hierarchical computer or other controls? If passwords are used, are these individual and changed regularly?	
Are all amendments to the master file including leavers and changes in pay levels independently authorised?	
Are payroll preparation and payment duties strictly segregated?	
Are controls over normal payments applied to urgent or emergency payments?	

Controls over accounting

Control	In place?
Are payroll suspense accounts regularly reviewed and cleared?	
Where a payroll is processed by an agency, are output reports checked against expected output before payment is made?	
Where external processing takes place, are arrangements made with the other branches using the facility to check for staff appearing on more than one payroll?	
Are standard exception reports produced and investigated within a set time, ie for overtime, or allowance > than a fixed £sum or weekly/monthly net pay > a fixed £sum, emergency tax codes for more than 6 months, duplicate names or National Insurance numbers?	
Must claims for allowances and expenses be made within a specified time?	
Are reasonableness checks performed on staff expense claims over a specific value? Are these referred to the appropriate manager for second approval?	
Are claims checked to independent data, ie mileage chart, certified course attendance lists?	
Are receipts required to support claims for reimbursement?	

Human resource controls

Control	In place?
Are references for all new employees always obtained prior to confirming appointment?	
Staff recruitment procedures include standard verification of all qualifications claimed.	
Where applicable, are all staff required to provide details of any unspent convictions under the Rehabilitation of Offences Act?	
Does the staff induction pack make new employees aware of their duties and responsibilities as regards confidentiality and the Data Protection Act 1984?	
Are terms and conditions of employment clearly stated and do management ensure that all staff are aware of them? Do staff sign to confirm acknowledgement and acceptance of the consequences if they are broken?	
Does each department periodically confirm the accuracy of a schedule containing the names of all employees currently charged to their department, the post held, salary and grade of each post?	
Are payroll and human resource functions managed independently, even if within the same department?	

Control	In place?
Does the human resource function approve a tabulation recording salaries for relevant employees following company-wide salary settlements?	
Is the payroll master file periodically checked by the HR function to ensure that each post is authorised, the correct person is shown in post and that the basic salary and allowances are correct?	
Are clear written procedures and instructions for claiming allowances and expenses given to all staff?	

Expenses fraud

6.6 For many organisations employee expenses are often their biggest expense behind salaries. It is therefore a fertile ground for fraud. Some level of fraud within expenses may not be regarded as anything other than a normal perk of the job – for example if the firm is willing to pay a taxi fare, but the employee gets the bus or tube, they may feel justified in claiming for the taxi fare. The company of course may feel quite different as the purpose of paying the taxi fare may be to reduce the travelling time taken by the employee. A clear policy that claims must be based on actual expenses incurred and guidance as to the accepted level and type of expenses is vital if there is not be any confusion over expenses. It is also important for companies that they have accurate records of expenses paid to employees as the P11D requirements mean that most expenses need to be notified to the Revenue. The controls in the table below, together with those in the previous table, will help prevent expenses fraud.

Control	In place?
Expense policy is written out clearly and all employees are aware of the rules.	

Control	In place?
All expense claims need to be authorised. Above a certain limit, approval in advance of costs being incurred is needed.	
All expenses to be accompanied by receipts (where they exist) and receipts agreed to expense claim.	
Mileage claims to be checked for reasonableness prior to payment.	
Expenses should be analysed against expected costs and compared between different employees with a similar job, where possible.	
Internal audit to carry out random detailed checks on expenses and employees made aware of this policy.	
Expenses for hotels/travel to be linked in with work diary to check that trip was made for business purposes.	

6.7   It is often very difficult to make these sorts of checks on every single expense claim as it can cost a considerable amount of time and money to do so. There are, however, a number of computerised expense handling software systems that can improve control and reduce cost. An example of the impact of using computerised systems for expense claims can be seen in Ernst and Young Australia. It used to cost $28 for them to process a single claim and take 20 days from creation to payment of the claim. After introducing Captura's web-enabled expense solution, the firm saves half of its previous processing costs and frees staff for fee generating work. In addition to this the firm is able to keep a closer eye on its expenses and check that agreed rates are being paid. Although fraud was probably not a driver in making the decision to change to an automated system, the use of such a system will allow organisations to check automatically that:

- hotel and travel expenses consistent with diary information and each other;

- selected suppliers used (assuming the organisation has decided that they will use a particular supplier);
- standard rates from selected suppliers have been applied;
- calculations of mileage are correct.

Other systems include Necho's NavigatER package, Concur Expense, and Cevas Global Expense.

Agency staff fraud

6.8   In many sectors the use of agency staff is particularly important. This includes bodies such as NHS trusts and schools, where frequent use of agency staff is made. This gives the opportunity for staff or management at the agency to charge more than the agreed rate or more hours than actually worked by the staff.

Control	In place?
References for agencies are taken up prior to their use: • Details of who owns and runs the agency, including a credit check; • Details of how they vet staff supplied, particularly in high risk areas such as working with children or in the health sector; • Details of rates to be charged, including any additional charges for travel, unsocial hours etc.	
Timesheets are always kept for agency staff and signed off by their line manager as evidence that hours have been worked (line managers should be aware of the importance of checking the accuracy of such forms).	
Invoices received are always checked to timesheets for details of hours worked and to agreed contract rates.	

Control	In place?
Expenses are checked for supporting documentation or, where mileage is charged, evidence of the accuracy of distance travelled (if the distance is from home, check the home address of agency staff by asking them to provide the details and check that the mileage is reasonable).	
All invoices clearly marked as paid when paid.	
All documents relating to the invoice, such as timesheets, attached to invoice as a record that they have been paid.	
Reconciliation of total hours worked to amount paid carried out on a regular basis wherever possible. If records of total hours are not kept, then a check on reasonableness.	

6.9   The example below is taken from the BBC's website, www.bbc.co.uk. It shows the extent to which fraud can be perpetrated, due to a lack of adequate controls, by a single person.

'Allcare Locum Agency fraud

Dr Dimitri Padelis, of south London, who ran a locum agency, is believed to have made up to £4m, on top of the legitimate charges. He repaid just £348,000 to the NHS after being found guilty of two counts of fraudulent trading and three of false accounting between 1991 and 1995. He was jailed for four years.

Dr Padelis, 45, ran a locum agency called Allcare which provided freelance doctors to hospitals across the UK – including Northern Ireland.

Padelis claimed the overcharges resulted from errors by hospital administrators, doctors or his own staff.

He was ordered to pay £100,000 in costs and disqualified as a company director for five years, and faces being struck off by the General Medical Council.

The fraud was spotted by an auditor at Gwynedd Hospital in Bangor Wales.

How it was done:

- It was discovered that one in five of the invoices sent out by the agency were inflated with **additional hours.**
- **Duplicate bills** were also sent out.
- Padelis also repeated claims for hours worked, **travel expenses** and **National Insurance contributions.**
- He used headed notepaper and adverts in the British Medical Journal to paint an impressive picture of a well-established business, with offices in Birmingham, Manchester, Bristol and Glasgow. In reality all calls were diverted to London.'

Sector fraud 7

7.1   Some fraud is particularly associated with the sector in which an organisation operates. This section of the book looks at some of the more common areas for fraud in the following sectors:

- Hotels;
- Retail;
- Manufacturing;
- Charities;
- E-business;
- Public sector;
- Professional firms; and
- Insurance.

Of course, most of the other frauds mentioned in the book could also apply to these organisations as well as those dealt with specifically in this chapter.

Hotel sector

7.2   The hotel sector has a number of characteristics that can make it the target for fraud. In particular there is often a lot of cash around, from bar takings for example, as well as valuable and easily portable assets, like alcohol and hotel consumables. The risk of many of the frauds can be reduced by good recruitment procedures and good separation of duties between staff. If the staff that are recruited have no history of previous dishonesty there is a better chance that they will, in fact, be honest. To this end certain procedures should be undertaken to help ensure their honesty, particularly if they are going to have responsibility for or authority over the company's assets.

Misappropriating takings by not recording occupancy

7.3   Even today many people will pay cash for a hotel room. This gives an easy opportunity for staff on reception to pocket the cash, but fail to record the occupancy. If other controls do not exist the hotel will not realise it has lost some of its takings.

Control	In place?
Ensure records of occupancy are not kept by those responsible for taking cash. Records from housekeeping about rooms occupied overnight could be used to check expected income.	
Take up references when employing staff.	
Reconcile takings with expected takings based on occupancy each night.	
Count takings with at least two people present.	
Ensure authorisation at a high level where rooms are to be offered free or upgrades to more expensive rooms given.	
Use comparisons between budgeted and actual to identify possible fraud.	
Use comparisons of profit margins with other similar hotels – either other hotels in the same group, or make use of a benchmarking service that will give detailed analysis of key ratios for similar hotels.	

Watering down alcohol/replacing with cheaper brands

7.4 Most hotels have busy bars and this gives rise to a number of potential frauds. Staff may water down spirits with the effect that they charge the customer the full price for a partial measure. The excess takings could then be siphoned off, as often the customer will not require a receipt and so a lower level of takings can be rung up. Staff could replace expensive brand names with cheaper versions, selling the more expensive bottles – it is perhaps more likely that this fraud will not result in individual staff making a profit, but rather the hotel/bar itself making extra profits by misrepresenting what is being sold.

Control	In place?
Regular dipping of a sample of spirits/beers is possible. Brand holders will send staff out with a batch of special dipping sticks which change colour if the item tested is not the brand listed.	
Any complaints made by customers about watering down etc should be recorded and investigated. Those on duty at the time should be noted.	
Internal audit should make secret visits to check authenticity and quantity of measures.	
Alcohol should be kept locked up with only limited access by staff.	

Consumable stocks

7.5 Theft of consumables (tissues, toilet roll, shampoo etc) can be a problem in any hotel. A similar fraud can be carried out in any business that has consumables, such as pens, paper, print cartridges etc. Items are stolen but the theft is treated as proper usage of the item in question.

Control	In place?
Stock of consumables is kept securely (measures appropriate to value of stock).	
Issue of consumables is controlled – for example, by completion of a signed request form. In a hotel this could be a pre-printed form with a section for each room to be cleaned and the items being taken from stores to clean those rooms. Stock is then issued according to the form.	
Authorisation is needed for issue of high value consumables.	
Monitor use of consumables by checking the actual level of usage with expected usage (for example, from budget information) or carrying out a reasonableness check (how many toilet rolls could realistically have been used in month?).	
Any abnormal usage is investigated.	

Retail fraud

7.6   In 2001 retailers lost 1.76% of their turnover to 'shrinkage' by customers and staff, fraud by suppliers, and waste and administrative errors. This compares with a European average of 1.42%, an increase of 1.5% on 2000.

The problem cost British retailers £3.9bn, of which £2.9bn was directly attributable to crime. Across Europe the cost to the sector was almost Euros 30bn (£18.3bn). The survey showed that retailers believed the high rates were mainly due to customer theft (46%) with 28.5% put down to staff or supplier pilfering. A further 8% was attributed to supplier fraud.

7.7 A knowledge of potential techniques for fraud can help those responsible for running or auditing the company to recognise problem areas.

Replacing barcodes

7.8 As most retailers, even small ones, use barcodes passed over a sensor to ring an item up on the till, this fraud is always a risk. A customer will take a barcode from a cheaper item and stick it over a more expensive item's barcode. For example, the fraudster could take a barcode from an alarm clock and stick it over that for a television. They then take the television to the checkout and the false barcode is scanned. In some situations there will need to be collusion with the person on the checkout to ensure that the code is not questioned, as it will show up on the screen as an alarm clock. However, in many cases staff will not check the description of the item on the till and so will not notice the discrepancy. If they do notice the customer may explain it away as someone else's mistake.

Not scanning items

7.9 A variation on the theme is for an item not to be scanned at all. This requires the collusion of someone on the checkout and a customer (a friend or relative perhaps). The customer takes the items to the checkout and they appear to be passed over the scanner. However the checkout operator pulls the item out of range or covers a part of the bar code and ignores the ensuing bleep. The goods 'bought' are then split between the perpetrators.

Cash taken and explained as errors in giving change

7.10 There is clearly a large amount of cash being taken in many retail establishments, although the increased use of credit and debit cards has reduced this to some extent. It is still possible, however, for staff members to take cash when a customer pays money over. This may involve putting the money down while the change is counted out and then, when the customer is putting their change away, the checkout operator can take the money rather than put it into the till. If the loss of cash is noted the member of staff will explain it away as an error.

Controls to help prevent or detect retail fraud are given in the following table.

Control	In place?
Video monitoring of all checkouts with the readout on the till showing up on the monitoring unit so that false bar codes or non-scanning can be picked up.	
Review of the amount of takings at each till for each shift – large stores with a high turnover will normally find that they build up a pattern of normal takings for certain tills and times of day. Variations from this will highlight a problem.	
Strict rule that no member of staff is allowed any cash on the shop floor – that way, if any is found there is a presumption of wrong-doing and the staff member will need to explain non-compliance with the rules at the very least.	
Spot searches of staff lockers and person (permission needed as part of contract for example).	
Pre-employment screening – if you hire people where there is no indication of previous dishonesty they are more likely to be honest.	
Cash takings for each till checked against till records on a daily (or shift) basis.	
Staff required to sign on and off a till so that a trail exists of who was on a particular till for particular transactions.	
Strict rule that no till can be left unlocked for any period of time when it is not being used.	

Refunds fraud

7.11 Many retailers make it straightforward for customers to get refunds on goods in order to maintain good customer relations. However, this also means there may be a temptation to abuse the situation. The following types of refund fraud are possible:

- A customer brings back an item and asks for a refund, but the item was in fact shoplifted rather than bought.
- A customer colludes with a member of staff who will give refunds for a supposed item that is damaged or has perished. In fact the customer has not returned anything and the refund is a sham.
- A customer complains that goods are unsatisfactory, when in fact there is nothing wrong with them, because the company gives extra money to unsatisfied customers
- Customers bring back clothes, for example that have been worn, and attempts to get a refund saying they do not want the item.

Control	In place?
All refunds require customer name and address as well as signature.	
Sample of refunds checked on a regular basis to ensure address really exists and to check name where possible. Any regularly recurring names should be highlighted for possible further investigation.	
Refunds only to be dealt with at certain tills/by certain staff.	
Staff allowed to take refunds are more senior/have good references.	
All refunds over a certain level need to be authorised by more senior member of staff.	

Cheque fraud

7.12 The diminishing use of the cheque has been bolstered by a continuing rise in cheque fraud. The money lost through the counterfeiting of cheques intercepted in the post grew by almost 50% last year to £11.25m. Cheque fraud has become so much of a problem that the banking industry and the City of London Police have now got together to raise awareness of fraud.

Customers may try and use cheque books which are not theirs or use cheques when no funds are available.

Control	In place?
Cheques accepted only with a valid banker's card which covers the transaction amount.	
Staff trained in details that must be recorded and checked for guarantee to be effective. It is often easier to use a stamp or automatic printing of details by the till to ensure this is done.	
Staff aware that signature on bank card must be agreed to that on cheque.	
Cheque should be signed in presence of the cashier.	
List of stolen cheque books/cards to be available on all checkouts with reminder of rewards available for reporting when a stolen chequebook/card is used.	

Credit card fraud

7.13 This area is covered under Internet fraud as well, but is still a major problem for 'bricks and mortar' retailers.

Control	In place?
Credit cards ideally accepted using electronic system which checks that there is sufficient limit on the card and that it has not been reported stolen.	
If an electronic system is not in place, list of stolen cards kept up to date and at the checkout for all staff to check.	
All staff trained in fraud awareness and signs of a problem (training information is available on the APACS website, www.apacs.org.uk).	
Staff made aware of reward system for reporting stolen or suspicious cards.	
Signature checked with that on the card. If there are suspicions, customer card is retained whilst further checks are made.	
Card holder asked to confirm billing address for card – if the card has been stolen this will often not be known. (This is usually only practicable for high value items or items delivered to home address.)	

Manufacturing frauds

7.14   Manufacturing businesses are potential victims of long-firm fraud and any supplier fraud – these are discussed in the section on construction frauds (see **4.9**).

Stock fraud

7.15   Some stock is more desirable than other stock – electronics items sell well on the black market and high-value, easily transportable items will also often be popular targets. Almost any stock, however, is potentially at risk The most obvious means of stock fraud is perhaps to steal it but then miscount it at the stock take. If you know you have stolen ten items then you just make sure that ten extra items are listed on the stock take sheets compared to those actually present. This type of fraud can be prevented or made much more difficult by appropriate controls over the stocktake (see below).

Stock may be marked as having been scrapped when in fact it has been taken by a member of staff. Stock may be delivered to a 'customer' who is in collusion with someone within the organisation, even though the customer has not been approved for credit control purposes. The customer does not pay and the amount is written off as a bad debt. Stock may be delivered to a customer but the customer will deny ever having received it (even though they did). The company may then be unable to recover its debt or will have to re-send the goods.

Control	In place?
All stock should be kept physically secure.	
Use of video surveillance is considered as a deterrent.	
All items leaving the warehouse should do so only with an authorised despatch note.	
All items delivered must be acknowledged by a signed delivery note.	
Stock should be counted on a regular basis (or a proportion counted on a regular basis).	
Stock should be counted by staff other than those who work in the warehouse or have direct responsibility for stock.	

Control	In place?
Stock should be counted by staff working in pairs to reduce the chance of fraud or error.	
Stock counted should be reconciled with any continuous stock records maintained and differences investigated.	
Spot checks on stock should be made by internal audit where it exists.	
Analytical review of stock movements should be carried out on a regular basis, for example: • which stocks have a high level of purchase but low usage; • which stocks have not been used during the period; • compare actual stock use to budgeted use where figures available; • which stocks have been written down in value during the period.	

Charity frauds

7.16   It is often easy for charities to be either direct or indirect victims of fraud. Fraudsters may see charities as an easy target and send 'get rich quick' type schemes to them. Alternatively, they may use a charity's name to raise money, then keep the money for themselves. This results in a loss to the charity of donations they may have received and a potential tarnishing of the charity's reputation.

Examples

7.17   The example below was taken from *The Sunday Times,* 7 October 2001.

'New charity fraud

The Red Cross has given warning that fraudsters are using bogus Internet sites to solicit money which they claim will help victims of the September 11 attacks. The latest appeal purports to raise funds for the American Red Cross, the United Way of New York City and the New York Community Trust charities and asks donors to provide credit card details.'

The lesson here is that individuals and companies should always check that donations that they are making are to registered charities. The Charity Commission's website, www.charitycommission.gov.uk, allows you to check that a charity is registered.

7.18 The Charity Commission has responsibility for regulating all charities, with the aim of giving the public confidence in the sector. The article below highlights the type of action they will take where there is a problem. The helpline, for reporting concerns about charities, is also given. The article is taken from M2 Presswire, 3 October 2001:

'UK Government: Crackdown on charity fraud

Following a joint investigation by the Charity Commission and Southampton Police, a man was sentenced to six months in prison at Southampton Crown Court on 28 September 2001 *for theft and deception from the Solent Ambulance Service.* The Charity Commission, the government department responsible for regulating and supporting charities, began an investigation into the charity in June 1999 following information from the police concerning allegations of theft from the charity's funds by the accused, Geoffrey Smith. Further investigations by the Commission uncovered other incidents of abuse, all of which Smith pleaded guilty to.

Local Head of Investigations at the Charity Commission, Stephen Grenfell, said: "The Commission is pleased that our work with the police led to the successful prosecution and imprisonment of Geoffrey Smith. The Commission takes a firm stand on charity fraud and will continue to work with the police and prosecuting authorities to prevent wrongdoing." The Charity Commission's aim is to give the public confidence in the integrity of charities which includes identifying, where possible, suspected abuse and bad practice through regular monitoring of charities or the Commission's complaint procedure. The Commission will not tolerate dishonesty or theft against charities and will take the firmest action against the very small minority whose activities damage the public's confidence in charities.

If anyone is concerned about a charity or individuals involved in a charity they are advised to contact the Charity Commission helpline on 0870 333 0123.'

Frauds in charity shops

7.19 Most charity shops are run by volunteers and sometimes this makes the charity embarrassed about introducing proper controls. This should not be the case, though, if the charity wants to protect its assets and its reputation.

7.20 Fraud in charity shops will usually involve the takings being stolen by a volunteer working in the shop, although it might also be that the volunteers take all of the good items of stock donated to the charity and sell them for personal gain or keep them.

Control	*In place?*
All donated items should preferably be opened by two people and a list produced of goods received.	
All takings should be recorded on the till and the till roll reconciled with the cash takings each day.	
If no till is available a list of sales should be kept using prenumbered, carbon copy receipt pads.	
If more than one shop exists the takings and profitability can be checked against other similar shops for indications of a problem.	
A record should be kept of when particular volunteers are working in the shop.	
References for volunteers should be taken.	

Control	In place?
Customers in the shop can be encouraged to ask for a receipt, by notices in the shop. This helps to make sure that takings are run through the till.	
Video surveillance could be introduced if felt justified – the costs of such systems are becoming lower.	
A whistle-blowing policy should be in place and known by all volunteers so that if they suspect something is amiss, they know where they can go to give a confidential report.	

Theft from charity collection boxes/envelopes

7.21 This could be seen as an easy way to make money – offer to stand with a collection box for a charity or even to count the money from a collection programme. A fraudster could then keep the proceeds or some of the proceeds from the collection for themselves and record that a lower amount was collected.

Control	In place?
All boxes to have a seal which will clearly show if the box has been opened. All envelopes used to have an instruction that they should be sealed.	
Clear instructions to be issued to all collectors that boxes must not be opened, except by certain authorised volunteers.	
Boxes and envelopes should be opened in the presence of two people wherever possible.	

Control	In place?
Volunteers to have references checked if they are to be responsible for a large amount of money.	
All volunteers to be issued with identity cards to allow public to be confident that they really are epresenting the charity.	
Records to be kept of the results of collections – where many collections are run it should be possible to establish an expected outcome against which to check the actual outcome.	

Theft of donations sent to charity

7.22　It can be much easier to steal cheques received in the post for a charity than for other types of organisation. The charity usually has no knowledge of what has been sent to them in the post and therefore no way to check its completeness. In a trading organisation receipts of cheques are generally as a result of an invoice being raised, so although it is possible to steal such receipts more effort is needed to cover up the theft (teeming and lading for example – see 5.2). A good set of controls over post opening is therefore vital for all charities.

Control	In place?
Two people are always present when the post is opened.	
People opening the post are employees whose CVs have been checked especially thoroughly.	
All receipts are logged immediately in a manner where any missing items would be noticed (on numbered sheets, in a book where pages are numbered or where removing a page would be noticed).	

Control	In place?
The receipts log is checked to the bankings list on a daily basis.	
The post is kept in a secure area prior to and after opening (in a locked letter box, then a safe, for example).	
Charity literature discourages people from sending cash in the post and encourages them to use the full charity name and blank out any space left on the cheque.	
Any instance where a donor complains of not having a receipt or thank you letter for their donation is fully investigated to ensure the money was received by the charity.	
Where extra donations are expected, for example as a result of a campaign to encourage this, any extra staff asked to open post have had their CVs and employment history checked for any indication of dishonesty.	

Grant fraud

7.23   Organisations and some individuals award grants to charities or other entities to enable them to carry out certain work. Such grants will come with conditions pertaining to their use, but there is sometimes a situation where the grant is claimed when not meeting the criteria or where a change in circumstances subsequently results in the criteria being breached. It is important for organisations receiving grants to have in place controls to ensure that the criteria for receipt continue to be met. However it is also normal for the body awarding the grant to send in independent (or their own) auditors to check on compliance.

Control	In place?
All conditions pertaining to a grant are clearly understood by the recipient.	
Controls are implemented to check compliance with the criteria on a regular basis.	
Receipts of grant are correctly recorded as such.	
Expenditure relating to the grant is recorded as such and checked to ensure that it meets the conditions of the grant.	
Any potential breaches of the conditions are notified to the board (or equivalent) as soon as possible so that steps to rectify or deal with the situation can be taken.	
Any possible repayments are made known to the auditors and those preparing the accounts for possible inclusion as a liability.	

Manipulation of charity accounts

7.24 Whilst we have already looked at some of the general techniques that can be used in an effort to manipulate the accounts of companies, charities have additional requirements that can lead to misrepresentation. A charity is required to produce a Statement of Financial Activities (SOFA) and this requires a split between various categories of expense as follows:

- Cost of generating funds;
- Charitable expenditure:
  (i) costs of activities in the furtherance of the objects of the charity;
  (ii) grants payable in the furtherance of the objects of the charity;
  (iii) support costs for (i) and (ii);
  (iv) managing and administering the charity;
- The total resources expended.

7.25 Charities may wish to show more of their money being spent on activities in the furtherance of the objects of the charity, compared to the other categories. There may therefore be misdescription of certain costs in order to mislead the reader of the financial statements. If this happens deliberately it is most likely to be done by senior staff at the charity and will be difficult to guard against except by good corporate governance. The external auditor will also have an important role to play in checking that expenditure has been properly allocated. The list below sets out the types of checks that could be carried out to help confirm that expenditure has been properly allocated. Some can also be used as controls to help ensure that mistakes in allocation are not made.

Control	In place?
The nature of the different categories of expenditure (as listed by the Charity SORP 2000) is understood by those with a responsibility for classifying expenses.	
The importance of classifying correctly is understood. (The Charity Commission oversees charity accounts and is likely to take firm action even in the case of accidental misclassification.)	
Appropriate records are kept of the decisions as to what type of expenditure certain items constitute, where this is difficult to determine. (Some costs do not clearly fall in a particular category and the charity needs to carefully consider these items and be consistent with its treatment of subsequent similar items.)	
Controls are in place to ensure that all items of expenditure are classified prior to entry in the accounting records.	
The authorisation of invoices for payment should include a check as to the category of expenditure.	

E-business fraud

7.26   E-businesses are at risk of the same types of fraud as any other organisation. They employ staff, they buy supplies, they may have debtors and they accept credit card payments and maybe cheques. However, there are some frauds and areas of vulnerability that are more specific to this type of business. Some of the frauds also apply to any business connected to the Internet even if it does not trade on the Internet.

Internet and computer fraud

7.27   Many companies worry about the potential impact of external attacks on their systems. Indeed, the increasing incidence of malicious computer attacks over the Internet is a key driver for the booming IT security industry and has fuelled the uptake of technologies such as firewalls and intrusion detection systems. However, recent research, such as the CSI/FBI Computer Crime Survey 2001 (see www.gocsi.com), indicates that the threat lurking within organisations from an insider attack is by far the greatest security risk. Rather than a stranger breaking into your network, the insider attack is about colleagues breaking your trust. An insider attack is best defined as the intentional misuse of private systems or data to which the attacker has valid authorisation to access. However, it is especially important to be sure that the insider attack you are dealing with was a deliberate act and not an accident or a simple error. Many organisations have developed the 'tough-outside, soft-inside' security model, meaning the majority of effort and expense is spent securing the network perimeter from external attack using security technologies. Worst-case scenarios see organisations oblivious to attack, as the insider operates on parts of an organisation's network or on unmonitored specialised systems.

7.28   Difficult to prevent, an insider attack has a high impact on an organisation and can often lead to the direct loss or exposure of critical data. Similarly, systems that are key to the business process of an organisation are likely to be much more vulnerable to an insider attack than any outside threat. Consider, for example, a purchase ordering system. The purchase order business process may require final acceptance from a specific group, such as business managers. Other examples may include the company timesheet system, e-mails and confidential management reports (salary reviews, redundancy briefings). A failure to adequately control access to the system, for reasons such as a poor quality or shared password, may allow an insider to circumvent the access-based control and raise valid purchase orders without permission. In this case, a good security policy should identify that access to the system must be technically limited and probably technically audited. A regular analysis of the audit data, such as business managers confirming the purchase orders they accepted each month, should reveal any compromise of this technical security control.

7.29 The key issue is that internal security controls must be deployed within the context of an overall information security policy. Security policy can be defined as well-written and rigorously implemented information security guidelines, backed up with technical and procedural controls. A good policy should identify the business processes it is trying to protect and identify the value of the processes. Every business process is created with an unconscious and implicit risk management threshold – or the level of risk to which an organisation is willing to expose both itself and its customers. It is the measure of a successful security policy that it identifies this risk management threshold and outlines the necessary precautions to be taken.

7.30 The goal is to move beyond the creation of a policy to its implementation, monitoring and enforcement. While the implementation and enforcement differs according to the firm, there are a number of generic operational guidelines that can help reduce the risk of internal hacks. In short, security technology alone is not enough. The use of intrusion detection systems within a network is recommended, but is no panacea for identifying insider attacks. A regular analysis of logs from internal systems is required – a centralised logging infrastructure makes this a much more feasible goal.

7.31 The insider threat is not a risk that is going away. In fact, the current wave of redundancies hitting the hi-tech, banking and telecommunications sectors in particular could widen the digital threat. Today, ill-prepared organisations will increasingly find that, as well as physically clearing their desk of its contents, employees are emptying their former company's documents, databases, and spreadsheets of confidential data, long after they have left their office door keys behind.

Control	In place?
Do not allow employees who are leaving to send e-mail from the organisation (or at least monitor their e-mail and check whether it appears to contain any confidential details).	
Log all users of the system and review log regularly for indications of odd patterns of usage: • systems not needed by an employee being accessed, • odd times for access, • attempted access denied.	
Use an intrusion detection system that will provide a warning that access to the system is being attempted from outside of the system.	

Internet fraud

7.32   Many businesses are already trading over the Internet or have plans to do so within the medium-term future. This is not surprising when independent analysts estimate that by 2005 $30bn of transactions could be made over the Internet. Unfortunately there are a number of problems with trading on-line, not least of which is the level of fraud experienced by customers (putting them off using the web) or merchants (costing them money). What are the risks facing on-line merchants and what steps can be taken to reduce them?

Spoofing

7.33   This is where a fraudster copies a legitimate site and fools people into giving their credit card number. The fraudster then rapidly uses the card details to make purchases on-line or by phone before the theft of details has been noticed.

Unauthorised disclosure

7.34 If credit card numbers are submitted 'in the clear', ie without additional security, hackers can intercept the number and use the card details illegally.

Unauthorised action

7.35 A disgruntled employee or customer may maliciously change the website to prevent it accepting orders or otherwise providing the normal service.

Data alteration

7.36 The content of a website may be altered to make it offensive or put off customers in some other way. An example of this occurred not long ago, where a disgruntled website designer, who had helped a company set up their website on a contract basis, added pornographic and other offensive material to the company's site. The action hit the company very hard as large numbers of customers were put off using the site and the company itself. Another version of data alteration is where transaction details are intercepted by a hacker and the amounts, names or credit card numbers are changed.

7.37 Out of the above risks, it is the spoofing and interception of details that are most likely to result in fraud.

Reducing the risk

7.38 What controls can a business put in place to try to limit the impact of fraud? The first step will have to be a secure server. (This is a server with a mixture of special hardware and software, such as a firewall, that helps to keep the data on it secure.) No customer will wish to see their credit card number advertised to anyone using the web due to the lack of a secure server.

7.39 A number of systems are available that can be used to make trading on-line more secure. Veri-sign is one of the providers of digital certificates, also known as server IDs. Server IDs are issued by a trusted third party called a certification authority (CA). Veri-sign is one of the largest CAs, having issued more than 300,000 server IDs. The CA that issues a company's server ID is vouching for the company's right to use that company name and web address. Veri-sign or another certification authority will check the organisation's credentials and carry out a thorough background check to ensure that the organisation is what it claims to be. The CA then issues a Server ID which the organisation can use on its website to prove its identity. Other bodies that provide similar certification include Webtrust, set up by the ICAEW.

How do server IDs work?

7.40 Veri-signs server IDs work in conjunction with secure sockets layer (SSL) technology, which is the industry standard for web-based systems. This allows a secure communications channel with customers using popular browser and e-mail software. This gives a number of benefits to the company and its customers:

- authentication – customers can be sure that you are who you say you are.
- message privacy – SSL allows credit card details to be securely transmitted.
- message integrity – an alert is received if any details of the message have been changed en route.

Different levels of SSL technology are possible. For example, 40-bit SSL is strong enough for most intranets and lower volume websites. 128-bit technology is the world's most powerful and according to RSA labs would take trillions of years to break using today's technology.

7.41 By implementing a secure system of communication and identity verification your organisation will be reducing the risk of your customers becoming victims of fraud and also reduce the risk of people being fooled by a copy of your website. Web users need to know that they must look for the 'padlock' icon which indicates a secure site and for indicators of identity verification.

Credit card fraud

7.42 The increasing use of the Internet has led to many on-line frauds, the most frequent of which is probably credit card fraud. Surveys suggest that customer concerns about security of web transactions are a major barrier to companies' e-commerce plans. A May

1999 Gallup poll of UK consumers found that only 7% felt secure about submitting credit card details over the Internet, while Visa found, in a 1999 cross-EU survey, that only 5% of consumers trusted e-commerce. Credit card companies report that the Internet accounts for 50% of all complaints but only 2% of all transactions. As use of e-commerce grows, it seems inevitable that web fraud will become more widespread. While computer fraud may be harder to commit than mere credit card theft, the stakes could be much higher.

7.43 Figures from the Association for Payment Clearing Services (Apacs – www.apacs.org.uk) reveal that credit card fraud rose by 50% in the year to September 2002, and instances of fraudulent transactions cost the banking industry £373m.

7.44 Credit card fraud can occur in a number of ways. Perhaps the simplest is that the fraudster acquires the details of a credit card by picking up discarded credit card slips from dustbins or the like. The fraudster then quickly uses the card to make as many purchases as possible before a problem is noted. (This can of course be done on the High Street, but there is added anonymity in using the Internet.) The fraudster will buy things that can easily be sold on such as electronic equipment, CDs etc and will choose the quickest despatch method, to help ensure they receive the goods.

7.45 Another method of fraudulently using credit cards on the Internet is to make use of a number of websites that offer generated credit card numbers. These sites will provide a credit card number that will meet the check digit criteria used by the banks. Although it will not have a name or address to go with it, the fraudster will often still manage to make purchases based on a generated number. In some cases the card number will be genuine and an unsuspecting victim will find they have a charge on their card from an unknown source. However it is the company who sold the goods that will lose the money (most of the time), as the credit card companies will require refunds for transactions found to be fraudulent.

7.46 Many companies are now turning to automated software to help them pick up on the transactions that are more likely to be fraudulent. Such software checks a whole range of factors, usually using the firm's past experience of transactions that are fraudulent. It then checks the transaction characteristics against the characteristics of a fraudulent transaction to give a warning not to accept it or to carry out further checks. Using software to help in fighting fraud is dealt with in more detail in Chapter 11.

Identity theft

7.47 A growing method of committing fraud is for the fraudster to 'steal' someone else's identity in order to make purchases, borrow money etc. A particularly successful occurrence of this was a famous case where a fraudster had been using the identities of an Oregon couple to make more than $250,000 (£172,000) in purchases over eight years, cheekily sending his victims an annual Christmas card. To steal their financial personas, all he had required was a pre-completed credit card application sent out as part of a marketing push, which his dupes had discarded without destroying.

7.48 Companies are at risk of losses if they are found to have accepted fraudulent details, but individuals may also find themselves suffering losses. In order to limit the ability of the fraudster to commit this type of crime, individuals need to take care with their personal information. Credit card slips should be carefully kept and destroyed, and bank and lender statements should be carefully scrutinised for suspicious activity. Companies can advise customers of steps to take to protect their identity, as this will in turn help to limit the amount of fraud that the company suffers.

Security breaches

7.49 Sometimes it is the damage to a company's reputation or exposure of private data held by an organisation that is the problem. An example of the problems created by security breaches is given in the article below, taken from the *Western Mail*, 26 December 2001.

> 'The adult website Playboy.com recently became the victim of a serious security breach caused by hackers.

> Customers of the organisation began to receive e-mails from a group operating under the name "Ingrelock 1524". The e-mails contained details of the customers' credit card numbers and expiry dates, as well as a number of warnings to the recipients, including "not to trust companies with your details online".

> It was also claimed that the group had had full access to the Playboy. com network since 1998.

> In response, Playboy hired a computer security firm to audit the systems.

Of particular concern was the hacker's threat to use "100,000s of customer details" to purchase products "resulting in $10m worth of fraud claims being made to credit card and, in turn, insurance companies globally".

The president of Playboy.com has warned all its customers to contact their credit card companies and check for unauthorised charges.

According to Mark Rhys-Jones, head of the IT Dispute Management team at Cardiff solicitors Eversheds, recent surveys have confirmed the increase in security breaches caused by hackers.

"A CBI survey of 148 companies from varying industry sectors has revealed that two thirds had experienced a serious incident in the past year."

"Of these, 45% were perpetrated by hackers. A survey by the Interactive Advertising Bureau has shown that online credit card fraud is up from pounds 5m to pounds 8m since last year."

"Furthermore, a report by PwC in September 2001 has revealed that global companies lost US$1.4trillion in revenue from security lapses last year," said Mr Rhys-Jones.

The main damage caused by hacking is the loss of confidence by Internet customers, particularly in relation to sensitive information, such as credit card details.'

Security measures

Firewalls

7.50 A firewall is a set of related programs, located at a network gateway server, that protects the resources of a private network from users from other networks. (The term also implies the security policy that is used with the programs.) An enterprise with an intranet that allows its workers access to the wider Internet installs a firewall to prevent outsiders from accessing its own private data resources and for controlling what outside resources its own users have access to. Basically, a firewall, working closely with a router program, examines each network packet of data to determine whether to forward it toward its destination. A firewall also includes or works with a proxy server that makes network requests on behalf of workstation users. A firewall is often installed in a specially designated computer separate from the rest of the network so that no incoming request can get directly at private network resources.

Virus scanners

7.51   Even home computers should have a virus scanner and intrusion detection system installed, as otherwise there is the potential for loss of some or all of the data on the system. This might mean the loss of confidential information which could be used to defraud individuals or companies whose data has been found or corrupted. A virus can cause huge disruption to the organisation's normal operating capacity. One of the best known providers of virus scanning software is Symantec, who also provide firewall and other security solutions. Their website (www.symantec.com) contains explanations of how the products work and include items suitable for large and small enterprises. Other companies that provide such products include Sophos and McAfee.

Public sector fraud

7.52   The heading public sector fraud covers a whole range of activities and organisation types as the public sector is, of course, vast. There is already a good deal of guidance as to how to deal with the threat and reality of public sector fraud, one particularly good document being 'Managing the Risk of Fraud – a guide for managers', produced by HM Treasury in 1997. The guide begins with, among other things, the seven principles of public life, as set out by the Nolan committee on standards in public life, which are worth repeating here in order to introduce the issue.

1. Selflessness – holders of public office should take decisions solely in terms of the public interest. They should not do so in order to gain financial or other material benefit for themselves, their family or friends.
2. Integrity – holders of public office should not place themselves under any financial or other obligation to outside individuals or organisations that might influence them in their performance of their official duties.
3. Objectivity – in carrying out public business, including making public appointments, awarding contracts, or recommending individuals for rewards and benefits, holders of public office should make choices on merit.

4. Accountability – holders of public office are accountable for their decisions and actions to the public and must submit themselves to whatever scrutiny is appropriate to their office.
5. Openness – holders of public office should be as open as possible about all the decisions and actions they take. They should give reasons for their decisions and restrict information only where the wider public interest clearly demands.
6. Honesty – holders of public office have a duty to declare any private interests relating to their public duties and to take steps to resolve any conflicts arising in a way that protects the public interest.
7. Leadership – holders of public office should promote and support these principles by leadership and example.

Whilst these principles clearly cover issues much wider than fraud and corruption, they are nonetheless key in understanding the type of attitudes and policies required in public sector organsiations, particularly from their office holders. It goes without saying that all those holding such office should be fully aware of these principles and that staff working within the organisations should also understand the importance of these rules.

7.53   There are many types of corruption and fraud that are possible in public sector organisations. A fair number of these will, of course, be similar to the types of fraud for a commercial organisation. Because of this it is important for managers within the public sector to consider their risk areas, just a commercial entity should do. Set out below are some examples of particular frauds found in the public sector or directed at public sector funding.

Optician frauds

7.54   An optician is able to claim certain amounts from the NHS in respect of items such as children's glasses and eye tests. Children are permitted two sets of glasses paid for or subsidised by the NHS. A fraud can be perpetrated whereby the optician claims for two pairs of glasses for the children on their lists, even though the child only takes one pair. If the child then happens to need a second pair the optician will issue a pair and not claim any extra from the NHS. In reality though only a relatively small number of children are likely to need a second pair and so the optician makes a healthy profit on extra sets claimed.

7.55   A variation on this fraud is where the optician claims for expensive lens types but only fits cheaper lenses. Again a healthy profit is made.

Dentists and opticians

7.56 Both opticians and dentists are able to claim for eye tests/check-ups for children and certain other groups of patients. There is a possibility that the proprietor claims for eye tests and check ups not actually given. Although a form needs to be signed to indicate that a test has been received, it is relatively easy to either forge details on the forms or to get patients to sign two forms at once. Many patients will not check carefully what they are signing, particularly if the dentist or optician creates the impression of being in a hurry.

7.57 In addition to the fraud with check-ups it is possible, especially with dental work, that the dentist actually does expensive but unnecessary work on a patient in order to claim the money. This is a particularly nasty fraud as it often results in pain, permanent damage to the teeth and considerable distress as it is usually children for whom claims for work can be met by the NHS.

GP frauds

7.58 Along a similar line, GPs are able to claim a vast range of items from public funds as most of their services are free at the point of provision. This gives an opportunity to claim for extra supplies, extra fees for staff support, practice running costs and so on. These types of frauds are most likely to be at the management level, and so when funds are received they are probably recorded as genuine income of the practice, obviously increasing the profit available to the proprietor or partners. Sometimes though, they could be perpetrated as employee frauds if an individual is able to skim off the excess takings created by submitting false claims.

Indications that such frauds may be happening

7.59

• Profits are much greater than other similar practices.
• Analytical review reveals unlikely relationships:
  – A test can be carried out to check how many eye tests could be carried out in a week with the available staff. The amount allowed as a claim for each test can then be used to calculate the maximum income expected from eye tests. If this is exceeded by the actual income there is an indication of fraud.

- A check of the number of children on an opticians register can be compared with the number of glasses issued over a period of time. If this indicates that a lot of second pairs of glasses are issued this may indicate a fraud.
- A review of claim forms may indicate that signatures appear to be of a very similar style, or that whan addresses are checked they don't exist or the people listed on the form don't live there.
- If an individual within the practice is committing the fraud alone, it might be apparent that they appear much wealthier than other members of the practice.
- An individual may always fill out the claim forms themselves and be reluctant for anyone else to take over. Perhaps if they go on holiday they will tell other members of staff to leave all the claim forms until they return.
- A practice may seem to carry out a large amount of specialist work – this may be because they have a particular specialism, but it could be an indication of fraud as they are claiming for expensive procedures not actually carried out.
- Dental work may be carried out on children when it is inappropriate for their age – certain procedures are only suitable for adults or older children and so a review of claim forms by a dental expert should identify this.

The following controls will help to limit the incidence of false claims.

Control	In place?
Budgets of income prepared and compared to actual on a regular basis with differences investigated – including where income is greater than expected.	
Claim forms are checked to ensure details are of genuine patients and match up to appointments made (if necessary this could be done on a sample basis).	
Claim forms reviewed by someone other than the person preparing them before being submitted.	
Claim forms are numbered and the sequence checked to ensure that forms cannot be submitted then suppressed while the income from them is stolen.	

Control	In place?
A regular check is made to ensure that all claims made have been received and banked.	
Staff vetting procedures are used to help ensure honesty of partners and employees, including temporary staff.	
Fraud policy statement exists and training is given to staff in ethics and fraud awareness.	
Staff are made aware of whistle blowing procedures.	

Solicitors frauds

7.60 Many solicitors do a certain amount of legal aid work where they claim for work done from public funds. A fraud is possible whereby the green forms used to claim the aid are falsely completed. This may be by:

- adding extra hours for the work done;
- adding disbursements not actually incurred;
- double claiming for the same case;
- opening up several 'cases' when actually the matter would be properly dealt with as one case;
- miscasting the form so that more is claimed than the actual total of items listed;
- creating entirely false claims for non-existent cases.

This type of fraud, like the health providers above, could be perpetrated by management or by staff. If management are involved only outside scrutiny will reveal the fraud, unless a member of staff blows the whistle. An important aspect will be that claim forms are checked carefully before payment. Below is a list of possible controls that could be exercised by the practice to help prevent employee fraud or by those approving and paying the claim.

Control	In place?
All claim forms are cast (added up) to ensure there are no addition errors.	
Disbursements are checked against invoices or other evidence that the cost has actually been incurred.	
A database of claims is kept and new claims are checked against existing ones to see if there is a repeat of details – either as an entire duplicate claim or as a new case incorrectly opened.	
Claim forms are pre-numbered and regular checks made to ensure that there are no missing forms (these forms could be used for fraudulent claims with the money being collected by a partner or member of staff).	
All claim forms are reviewed and authorised before submission to check for reasonableness.	
Where work is claimed on an hourly basis, hours claimed are reconciled to time sheet records.	
Details on claim forms are checked to diaries to ensure consistency – if a claim has been made for appearance in court was this shown in the diary.	
Periodic checks are made to ensure that diary entries are accurate by checking the lists of court cases heard on particular days.	
Money received is checked against claim forms to ensure that all claims are paid (and money has not been syphoned off by an employee or partner).	

Control	In place?
Staff vetting procedures are used to help ensure honesty of all staff, particularly those with authority to make claims and handle cash.	

7.61   The following is an example from the SFO's website.

'Legal Aid Board defrauded

(a) **Defendants – R v Alan Pritchard, Peter Lane and Brian Anthony O'Connor**
(b) **Crown Court where trial was heard – Birmingham Crown Court**
(c) **Date of acquittal/sentence passed – 7 and 8 June 2000**
(d) **Principal nature of charges – Conspiracy to defraud**
(e) **Police force that supported the investigation – West Midlands Police**

The defendants were found guilty of defrauding the Legal Aid Board of around £2 million. Pritchard, the only solicitor in the Birmingham practice of Walton & Co., and the other two defendants, engaged by him, hoodwinked members of the public into signing Green Form applications for legal aid. They were sentenced at Birmingham Crown Court on 7 and 8 June to prison terms of five years, four years and three years respectively.'

Professional firms fraud

7.62   Where professional firms handle client money there is often a very large amount held that provides a temptation to the potential fraudster. Someone with authority over these accounts may find themselves short of cash and initially borrow some money from the client accounts. In a similar way, if the practice is short of money there may be a temptation to use clients funds to tide them over a difficult patch. All organisations that handle client money will be covered by regulations concerning its handling and it is expressly forbidden for client money to be used for other purposes, even on a temporary basis. Solicitors accounts rules cover this issue, as do the FSA regulations.

7.63   The following is an example of a professional firms fraud from the SFO annual report 2000/01.

'Solicitor plundered clients' accounts

(a) Defendants – R v Alan Scott Whittingham
(b) Crown Court where trial was heard – Winchester Crown Court
(c) Date of acquittal/sentence passed – 6 June 2000
(d) Principal nature of charges – False accounting
(e) Police force that supported the investigation – Dorset Police

Alan Whittingham was a partner in Oscar H Whittingham & Sons, a Bournemouth solicitors' practice. He pleaded guilty to a number of counts of false accounting relating to the misuse of clients' funds over a ten-year period. Some of the money taken by Whittingham was used to offset defaulted payments on loans made by clients of the practice, often without their knowledge, to small local building contractors which became insolvent. He had failed to take suitable security for the loans. His fraud was uncovered during a routine inspection by the Law Society and the SFO inquiry opened in June 1997. He was sentenced to two years imprisonment and ordered to pay £150,000 costs. His criminal actions resulted in the Solicitors Compensation Fund paying almost £2 million to his victims.'

7.64 A variation on the theme of using client's funds is seen in the example below, where an insolvency practitioner uses the funds collected for the benefit of creditors of insolvent companies to prop up his own business. Where the perpetrator of such a fraud is the person who owns and runs the business it is impossible to put in place internal controls that will prevent it. In this type of case, the fraud is most likely to be discovered by the regulating authority (or auditor where there is one) carrying out routine checks or responding to concerns raised by third parties or staff.

'Insolvency practitioner stole liquidated assets

(a) Defendants – R v Robert John Orme
(b) Crown Court where trial was heard – Birmingham Crown Court
(c) Date of acquittal/sentence passed – 14 July 2000
(d) Principal nature of charges – False accounting and theft
(e) Police force that supported the investigation – West Midlands Police

Robert Orme was a Birmingham insolvency practitioner and partner in the firm of Knights Chartered Accountants. He became aware that the firm was bankrupt and attempted to cover up the real situation by using funds realised from the assets of insolvent companies and individuals in order to prop up the business. This involved him making false entries in client accounts and false returns to Companies House. Around £300,000 was misappropriated in this way.

Orme, who pleaded guilty, was sentenced to 21 months' imprisonment.

(Though the sum involved was below the notional threshold for SFO cases the matter was prosecuted by the SFO because the bank accounts used by Orme to channel funds were amongst a number of accounts examined by SFO investigators in 1997 in an unrelated case).'

Investment businesses

7.65   Investment businesses are a very specialised area, as they are covered by a large number of regulations as set out by in the Financial Services and Markets Act (FSMA) regulations. Among those requirements are specific ones covering the systems and controls that an investment business is required to have in place and audit requirements with regard to these. This means that an investment business effectively has certain statutory responsibilities to have in place controls to prevent fraud and error.

7.66   The Financial Services and Markets Act 2000 (known as N2) came into force on 1 December 2001. Under the FSMA, responsibility for the regulation and supervision of the financial services sector passes to the Financial Services Authority (FSA). As a result the FSA has assumed the regulatory functions previously undertaken by the SROs. There is a huge amount of legislation which needs to be complied with and the box below contains a summary of the key areas of the rules.

Block	Sourcebook or manual	Handbook Reference Code
Block 1 High Level Standards	Principles for businesses	PRIN
	Senior management arrangements, systems and controls	SYSC
	Threshold conditions	COND
	Statements of principle and code of practice for approved persons	APER
	The fit and proper test for approved persons	FIT

Block	Sourcebook or manual	Handbook Reference Code
	General provisions	GEN
Block 2 Business Standards	Five interim prudential sourcebooks (one of which applies to investment businesses)	IPRU (INV)
	Conduct of business	COB
	Market conduct: • Code of market conduct • Price stabilising rules • Inter-professional conduct • Endorsement of Takeover Code	MAR
	Training and competence	TC
	Money laundering	ML
Block 3 Regulatory Processes	Authorisation	AUTH
	Supervision	SUP
	Enforcement	ENF
	Decision making	DEC
Block 4 Redress	Dispute resolution: complaints	DISP
	Compensation	COMP
	Complaints against the FSA	COAF
Block 5 Specialist source-books	Collective investment schemes	CIS
	Credit unions	CRED
	Professional firms	PROF
	Lloyd's	LLD
	Mortgages	MORT
	Recognised investment exchanges and clearing houses	REC
	United Kingdom Listing Authority	UKLA
Special Guides	Service companies	SERV
	Small friendly societies	FREN
	Oil market participants	OMPS
	Energy market participants	EMPS
	Glossary of definitions and index	–

Further details can be found on the FSA website (www.fsa.gov.uk) and the regulations can be obtained from the FSA.

Objective of rules

7.67 The primary objective of the rules is investor protection. This includes protecting the investor against fraud, and so meeting the requirements of the Act is vital for fraud prevention as well as for legal reasons. The rules include the following:

(a) Financial rules, which are designed to ensure that an investment business is financially sound, has appropriate internal controls and is able to meet its commitments;
(b) Client assets rules, which require segregation of money and investments held for clients and also include rules covering the arrangements for custody;
(c) Conduct of business rules, designed to ensure that an investment business deals fairly, honestly and with due skill, care and diligence with its clients.

7.68 Compliance with these rules is monitored in four principal ways:

(a) internal monitoring;
(b) submission of regular returns from the investment business to the regulator;
(c) monitoring and inspection of the investment business by the regulator;
(d) annual reports to the regulator by the investment business's auditors.

7.69 Annual reports from auditors constitute an important part of the regulator's system of supervision and, where relevant, cover the following:

(a) an opinion as to whether the reporting entity's financial statements give a true and fair view;
(b) an opinion as to whether the entity meets the regulator's requirements for the calculation of financial resources;
(c) an opinion as to whether the entity's accounting records and systems of internal controls meet with the regulator's requirements; and
(d) an opinion as to whether the entity has complied with the regulator's rules concerning the handling of client assets.

7.70 One of the key areas from the viewpoint of fraud prevention are the rules on control systems. A summary of the main points is given below.

Control systems

7.71   Underlying any control systems adopted by an investment business is the control environment. Such an environment is created by management having and showing a positive attitude towards the operation of controls and by an organisational framework which enables proper segregation and delegation of control functions and which encourages failings to be reported and corrected. Thus, where a lapse in the operation of a control is treated as a matter of concern, rather than being largely overlooked, the control environment will be stronger and will contribute to effective control systems. A weak control environment will undermine detailed controls, however well designed.

7.72   Within this control environment, the control procedures needed to ensure that the business is conducted to protect investors' interests should be commensurate with the investment business's needs and particular circumstances, and also with the inherent risks of the business undertaken. The size of the investment business will have an important bearing on the design and formality of the systems and controls. The operating procedures and methods of recording and processing transactions used by small investment businesses often differ significantly from those of large investment businesses. Internal controls which would be relevant to a large investment business may not be practical or appropriate in a small one. Management of a small investment business has less need to depend on formal controls for the reliability of the records and other information, because of personal contact with, or involvement in, the operation of the business itself. Nevertheless, the need for a positive attitude to the control environment is equally relevant in both small and large investment businesses.

7.73   Management should consider these factors in the design and maintenance of a control system. It should also recognise where appropriate the cost of a particular control, as against its purpose and expected benefit.

Control objectives

7.74   For the foregoing reasons, different systems and controls may be deemed adequate in different investment businesses, if they provide reasonable assurance that certain control objectives have been achieved. In designing the systems and controls, management should address inter alia the following general control objectives:

(a) the business is planned and conducted in an orderly, prudent and cost-effective manner in adherence to established and documented policies;
(b) transactions and commitments are entered into only in accordance with management's general or specific authority;
(c) client assets are safeguarded and are completely and accurately recorded;
(d) the assets of the business are safeguarded and the liabilities controlled;
(e) the risk of loss from fraud, other irregularities and error is minimised, and any such losses are promptly and readily identified;
(f) management is able to monitor on a regular and timely basis the investment business's position relative to its risk exposure;
(g) management is able to prepare complete and accurate returns for the regulator on a timely basis in accordance with the rules; and
(h) issues relating to compliance with the rules are resolved in a timely manner to the satisfaction of the regulator.

Items (c)–(e) above represent those parts of the control objectives particularly relevant to fraud. Management of an investment business must design controls in order to meet the above control objectives.

Computerised systems

7.75 Investment businesses frequently have a high degree of computerisation. While the control objectives described above apply in both a manual and a computerised environment, there are nevertheless certain requirements of an internal control system peculiar to a computerised environment. In designing a control system, management needs to understand the interaction between manual and computer controls and how they contribute in aggregate to the achievement of the control objectives.

7.76 Clearly, the emphasis between the two forms of control will be dependent not only on the degree of computerisation but also on the circumstances and particular risks of the investment business. The greater the degree of computerisation, the greater the emphasis that will need to be placed on the general and application controls of the computerised function, as part of the overall systems of internal control. However, the routine processing of a computerised system is generally more reliable than that of a manual system.

Documentation of systems and controls

7.77   Systems and controls, including the assignment of responsibilities, should be clearly documented if they are to be understood, communicated and operated effectively and consistently. Although only some regulators have explicit requirements to this effect, investment businesses and their auditors consider appropriate documentation a prerequisite of an adequate system. Failure to maintain such documentation could be a reportable matter.

Internal audit and compliance departments

7.78   The effective operation of a control system may be enhanced by an internal audit department or by specific monitoring performed by a compliance department. The existence of such departments and their scope and objectives are matters for management. In assessing the effectiveness of such departments, the auditors will consider the terms of reference of the departments, their independence from operational personnel and management, the quality of staffing and to whom they report in the investment business.

Risk of fraud and error

7.79   In addition to the conditions or events mentioned earlier as increasing the risk of fraud or error, the following factors may be especially relevant for an investment business (this list is not exhaustive):

(a) backlogs in key reconciliations, particularly those with brokers and exchanges and for bank accounts and safe custody accounts – both the investments business's own and those relating to its clients;

(b) inadequate segregation of duties between the front, middle and back office staff;

(c) complex products inadequately understood by management;

(d) inadequate definition of management responsibilities and supervision of staff;

(e) elements of the remuneration package (particularly bonuses) for certain staff which are directly linked to reported profits.

Example of bank fraud – recent experiences

7.80 Ricardo Garotte was sentenced to seven years' imprisonment for stealing more than £4m from two banks while working as a temporary member of staff. It is believed the police are still trying to trace more than £2m. Garotte used false references to get temporary work and was just about to land a staff job with a third bank when the police caught up with him. This case shows the seriousness of the fraud risk and highlights the need to thoroughly screen staff, including temporary staff, prior to employment. The warning signs of potential fraud are usually evident although many employers fail to spot them (eg gaps in CVs, unexplained changes in living standards, staff not taking holidays, working unsociable hours, turning down promotions and resigning unexpectedly among others).

Insurance fraud

7.81 Motor insurance fraud is a major problem area. It is estimated that whiplash fraud alone costs £200m per annum. Total insurance fraud is estimated at £645m (1999 figure) per annum. Many people see this as an easy way to make money – they submit a false claim, get the money and don't care about the impact that the level of fraud has on the premiums for all other motorists. Similar frauds take place with household and holiday insurance creating many more claims than is genuinely the case or exaggerating the level of the claim.

7.82 Various industry initiatives have been set up to combat the trend of increasing fraud. These include:

- the Motor Insurers' Information Centre, a database of all privately insured drivers and their vehicles;
- the Motor Insurance Anti-Fraud and Theft Register, which is limited to total losses;
- the Claims Underwriting Exchange, which records motor and non-motor claim details; and
- the recently launched Association of British Insurers' anti-fraud strategy, which includes a section on the website, www.fraud.org.uk.

7.83 Steps that help to pick up on a fraudulent claim include the following:

Control	In place?
Involve legal advisers early on and check details on claims whilst there is still evidence, such as the supposed damage to a vehicle. Some claims take a long time to process and by the time they are investigated a story has been carefully established together with 'witnesses' to back it up.	
Make use of the Waddell criteria for picking up inconsistencies on claims. (Dr Gordon Waddell and his colleagues developed the criteria in order to try and establish whether further psychological assessment of a patient with lower back pain was required. The criteria can also be used to help identify if an injury is genuine or not. The criteria can be found on a number of websites, including www.gelmans.com.)	
Train staff to recognise indications of fraud including: • liability being conceded too readily; • parties involved being of the same age, location and background; • injury claims that are intimated but the police/ambulance services were not called to the scene of the accident.	
Share information with other industries, other insurers and even other departments within the insurer's business.	

Control	In place?
Consider geographical profiling. Fraudulent activity is one aspect crying out for pooling of data. It is well known that hotspots exist wherever there are close communities or links with the Continent.	
Gaining early access to claimants' medical records is important.	
Watch for a delay in reporting symptoms, or a change in symptoms (such as the 'bad leg' changing from one side to the other).	
Consider making use of secret surveillance. (The defendant's expert should not be told surveillance is being undertaken, otherwise the prosecution will trip him up. The timing of service of video evidence is crucial. It should be served after substantive medical reports have been finalised on both sides, but before joint discussion between them.)	

7.84   Other problem areas for motor insurers include:

- Exaggerated claims – for example, saying that symptoms have lasted much longer than is actually the case.
- Claims for psychiatric disorders – these can be difficult to disprove.
- Body shops seeking to overcharge insurers for work done. However this can usually be controlled by the insurer having a network of approved garages to carry out work at agreed rates. This sometimes leads to concerns by the repairers that they are being paid an unfairly low rate. Unfortunately, this can then back-fire on the insurer, as the repairer has a motive to defraud them.

Case studies

7.85   A retired police officer aged 35 claimed he was unable to work in any occupation and could not walk. He then disappeared, but was traced to a farm in France. A video was obtained of him lifting bales of hay and other heavy manual work, following which the claim was quickly finalised.

7.86   A claimant was filmed outside his brother's house just before going for a medical examination. He had to run back to the house to get his walking stick and also filled up his car with petrol on the way. Video evidence of this agile behaviour contrasted starkly with his shuffling gait on leaving his car and attending the examination.

Source of case studies: Kennedys, a US loss adjuster.
See further www.kennedyclaims.com

Frequent motor fraud scenarios

7.87

- One vehicle suddenly cuts in front of another. The second vehicle stops abruptly, deliberately causing a third motorist to run into the back of it.
- An unsuspecting motorist tries to merge into traffic. Another driver gives way and waves him on. As soon as the first driver makes his move, the second driver accelerates into him and subsequently denies that any signals were given.
- A vehicle reverses into the path of an innocent motorist or deliberately reverses into a stationary vehicle. The fraudster alleges the other driver ran into his back.
- The owner of a damaged vehicle claims he has been the victim of a hit-and-run incident. He also claims for personal injury and damaged clothing.
- The owner submits a fraudulent accidental damage report for a vehicle with pre-existing damage. The vehicle has been acquired cheaply and insured comprehensively with the intention of claiming.

Other insurance frauds

7.88   As well as motor insurance, claims on holiday and household insurance are also a problem. Again, sharing of data is helpful to

build up a profile of suspect cases. Accurate record keeping, to identify retrospective factors in a claim that might indicate fraud can be
very helpful. It is then possible to build or tailor a computer model to
pick up on factors that may indicate a problem early on in the
process. More information about using technology to beat fraud is
given in Chapter 11 on fighting fraud with technology.

7.89 In addition to detecting fraudulent claims, the insurance
industry funds campaigns to try and get the message across that
insurance fraud is a crime like any other. Below is an example of an
insurance industry poster, used in a campaign in 1999–2000.

Investment frauds 8

8.1   Investment frauds can be targeted at individuals or companies. However, because of the availability of contract details, many of these scam offers to invest are aimed at company directors. An awareness of common frauds in this area will help to protect management staff and the company itself from becoming victims.

Investment scams online

8.2   One example of a major investment scam took place a few years ago in the US. An individual set up a site on the Internet with the banner 'The Next Microsoft?' at the top. The site went on to explain that the director of the company had invented a keyboard to be used with the thumbs in order to avoid RSI of the fingers. The fraudster asked for investors to send him money for a stake in the company implying that there would be fantastic returns for them. He also managed to secure advertisements for his site on other, respectable sites, by promising to issue shares as payment or part-payment for the adverts. A number of investors sent in their cash, sending sums of $5,000–$10,000 or thereabouts. However, there was never any effort to produce the keyboard (a picture on the website was just a mock-up) and he spent the money on a lavish seaside apartment, wine, women and entertainment! He was however caught, found guilty and sentenced to 10 years' imprisonment.

Prime Bank frauds

8.3   The use of the words Prime Bank in any offer to invest or request to borrow is likely to lead to the suspicion that fraud is involved. The term is used to try and make investment schemes, etc look authentic, by causing the reader to think of the major banks with which they are familiar. However the major banks do not use the phrase Prime Bank when describing themselves and neither do the majority of legitimate financial advisers or companies.

8.4   The example below was taken from the Internet – note the use of the words Prime Bank in capitals to try to emphasise its impor-tance. Although no-one was found in connection with this offer document, it gives away a key piece of information that suggests it is fraudulent. The document clams that you can get a rate higher than that offered by the prime bank and yet there will be no more risk to your money than if it was deposited at the so-called prime bank. There is, of course, always a risk/return trade off. If an investment is to offer high returns there will be a high level of risk. This may be a legitimate risk that the investor is willing to take, but in this example there is supposed to be no risk. The scheme could be a pyramid investment scam (see **8.5** below).

'Inve$tit Opportunities
Serious Investing

SECURING YOUR INVESTMENT

The money that you invest is not spent. It is not used to purchase stocks, bonds or property or to finance construction projects. It will not be used to finance or manage projects. The corporation with whom you will work will help you deposit your entire principal into a WORLD PRIME BANK account with full repayment to you backed by a PRIME BANK GUARANTEE, the most secure repayment option any bank can provide. The corporation does not spend your money; in fact, at no time will your money be controlled or accessed by the corporation.

The entire sum you invest will be placed directly into an account in a WORLD PRIME BANK (eg Barclay Bank) that will earn interest for you. The corporation with whom you will be dealing will not be taking your money but will make arrange-ments with you to transfer the principal amount into a PRIME BANK account. The PRIME BANK will sign a contract directly with you guaranteeing repayment of the entire principal with interest at the end of one year. In essence, the amount you invest is put into a protected, restricted account that will be under the total control of the PRIME BANK during the duration of the investment period. Because the full principal and a large part of the interest is paid directly by the PRIME BANK and directly to you at the end of one year, you are not dependent on the corporation for repayment of any principal or PRIME BANK interest.

The WORLD PRIME BANKS that are involved in this program are willing to handle the transactions and set up the account and repayment terms outlined here.

Depending on the particular investment option, a return of 8% or higher will include the interest on the money transferred into the PRIME BANK. The remaining return, which is negotiable, will be arranged and guaranteed by the target corporation via a separate agreement as part of the documents at closing. This agreement will require the dispersal of funds directly to you by the PRIME BANK in a manner and time identical to that of a Title Company dispersing funds as part of the closing on the sale of property. Again, the corporation will not handle this money or be in control of it at any time. The PRIMEBANK, which must be acceptable to you, will be responsible for direct payment to you in amounts and at times negotiated by you and the corporation president.

In some instances, all or part of the interest (or return) exclusive of the PRIME BANK interest, may be paid to you within one to six months of the closing date, meaning that you do not have to wait for the end of the year to begin receiving a return on the investment.

In all cases the term of the investment/loan period is one year from the date of closing. Investors may re-invest the principal under negotiable conditions for one or more years. In each instance, the investor will be helped in the steps to 'roll-over' the original principal while receiving the interest/return at the end of that year.

Sound too good to be true? Well, we checked it out. We believe the options provided are sound, secure and worth every million dollars you can spare. We are absolutely sure that you will not be disappointed in the return on your investment, especially because the entire principal and all interest is guaranteed in one short year.

We are so excited by these opportunities that we want to make everyone aware of them.'

Pyramid investment schemes

8.5   These schemes have, on occasion, become huge and one almost brought down the entire economy of Albania. They work like this – individuals, corporations or government bodies are asked to invest in a scheme promising very high rates of return. If they agree they will find that they do in fact get the returns promised, paid as discussed, on a regular basis. The investors are clearly very pleased and so suggest to their friends, colleagues etc that they too invest. Personal recommendation and proof that the returns are actually earned quickly encourages other investors. These too get their high return and the scheme expands. However, the returns are being paid out of the capital of the earlier investors. The result is that as the pyramid gets bigger it is more and more difficult to pay the new investors and eventually the scheme collapses with the loss of capital to all or most involved.

Advance fee fraud

8.6   This type of fraud, which involves fraudulent fee requests, often in connection with loan applications, is still a major problem, despite the large amount of publicity given to it in the hope of fore-warning victims. Some schemes are simplistic, others sophisticated but they all work in essentially the same way. Many have originated in Nigeria, but there are plenty of copycats elsewhere.

How does it work?

8.7   A letter, fax or e-mail is received asking for or offering a parti-cular service. Examples include an offer to arrange a loan for a busi-ness proposition and a request from a widow for the proceeds of her husband's estate to be passed through a UK bank account. Initially no money may be requested, as this helps to entice the victim into the deal. However, once the commitment of the potential victim is established a request will be made for funds. This may take the form of a request for expenses, an advance required until money is deposited outside its country of origin, a deposit or a straightforward fee in advance. Often there will be assurance that the sums paid will be refunded, again encouraging the victim to have confidence in the scheme. Of course, the end result is that the fraudster keeps the fees, and the service is never provided.

What to look for?

8.8   It can be difficult to know how to tell a potential fraud from a genuine business deal, but there are some pointers that can help. The following are features which have often be seen on advance fee fraud letters and which should put you on guard that all may not be as it seems:

- Off-shore jurisdictions being used (often several different ones).
- Letters from countries known to have a high level of fraud, eg Nigeria, Russia and former Eastern Bloc countries.
- Several parties may be involved (apparently without any real need).
- Complex deals may not seem to make business sense (where are *they* making money?).
- Quality of documentation may be poor, although sometimes it is genuine (but stolen) government headed paper.
- The deal looks too good to be true (trust your instincts, it probably is).

8.9   Letters containing fraudulent requests typically are complex in form, and usually display the following characteristics:

- multiplicity of parties;
- illusion of market/profitable trading;
- front organisations;
- lawyers acting for fraudster;
- temporary accommodation;
- advertising;
- syndicates of investors;
- faxed documents;
- poor quality document;
- non-circumvention/confidentiality clauses;
- exceptional rates of return;
- huge values;
- risk-free investment;
- fraudster's patience;
- delay and stalling victim;
- geography; and
- exotic instruments.

Terminology

8.10   Usually the terminology of the letter contains 'meaningless' or 'complex' references such as the following;

- Prime bank or instrument (major banks have indicated that Prime bank is not a term they would use);
- Stand by letters of credit (SLCs);
- Prime bank guarantees (PBGs);
- Prime bank notes (PBNs);
- Promissory notes;
- Medium term notes;
- Collateral commitments;
- Confirmation of fund letters;
- Federal Reserve Notes;
- Sovereign debt;
- Blocked funds;
- Conditional Swift/KTT transfers;
- Good clean funds of non-criminal origin;
- Trading/issuing/confirming bank;
- Ready, willing and able;
- Cusip numbers;
- Self-liquidating loan;
- Off balance sheet business;
- A year and a day;
- Top 100 prime/world banks;
- Forms 3030, 3032, 3034 and 3039;
- London Short Form;
- Escrow holder/fiduciary;
- Program managers;
- Collateral provider;
- Tranches;
- Roll/trading program.

8.11   Examples of advance fee fraud letters are shown below. They often arrive by e-mail, frequently as a result of a mail merge, where the name of the individual requesting the help as well as the addressee is changed in each letter.

Example 1: Advance fee fraud

'Dear Mr Smith,

In brief introduction, I'm Mrs Rosemary Osai from Sierra- Leone. My husband Mr Patrick Osai was the former operations manager of the Sierra Leone Gold and Diamond co-operation during the tenure of the democratically elected head of state president Ahmed Tijan Kabbah who was forced out of office by the rebels led by Major Paul Koromah. As a result of the otherthrow, top government officials and top civil servants who the rebel soldiers captured at the mining town of Bangashi district where he was in charge, may his gentle soul rest in peace. After the assassination of my late husband Mr Patrick Osai of Blessed Memory. I was busy ransacking his book shelves, incidentially, I found a key to his underground safe in his family villa. Upon my opening to his underground safe, I was surprised to notice among other things 2 big trunk boxes which contained the sum of US$18.5million (Eighteen Million Five hundred thousand united state dollars). I contacted my late husband friend who operated a fishing trawlers vessels through noble assistance, I and my family were smuggled out to Abidjan through costal river with the sealed trunk boxes containing the money. On our arrival, I decided to deposit these boxes in a private security company here in Abidjan for safe custody. Right now, your cooperation is highly needed to assist me lift these fund out of the security company to abroad for onward transfer. This is strictly on your advice in areas like real estate and stock markets or any other business you deem viable. Your compensation for this noble assistance is quite negotiable, for now 10% of this money stand as your commission for immediate transfer of this fund.

Please your assistance is highly needed and your urgent reply indicating your interest through the above contacts. Furthermore my evidence of the deposit of this sealed trunk boxes in the security company will be furnished to you as soon as I receive your reply. Please treat this transaction as confidential for this is the hope of my family's survivals, now that the bread winner is no more every correspondences should be directed to my son Mr Jerry Osai on his phone 225-003-06-75-35 for more information and clarification.

Thanks and God bless,

Best regards,

Mrs Rosemary Osai.'

Example 2: Advance fee fraud – e-mail version

'Subject: TREAT AS URGENT AND CONFIDENTIAL

CLEMENT NKONO,
AUDITING AND ACCOUNTING UNIT.
FOREIGN REMITTANCE DEPT.
UNION TOGOLAISE DE BANQUE,
LOME-TOGO.

Dear sir,

I am CLEMENT NKONO, the director incharge of auditing and accounting section of Union Togolaise De Banque Lome-Togo in West Africa with due respect and regard.

I have decided to contact you on a business transaction that will be very beneficial to both of us at the end of the transaction.

During our investigation and auditing in this bank, my department came across a very huge sum of money belonging to a deceased person who died on november 1997 in a plane crash and the fund has been dormant in his account with this bank without any claim of the fund in our custody either from his family or relation before our discovery to this development.

Although personally, I keep this information secret within myself and partners to enable the whole plans and idea to be profitable and successful during the time of execution. The said amount was the sum of u.s $25.5 million United State Dollars.

As it may interest you to know, I got your impressive information through my good friends who works with chamber of commerce on foreign business relations here in Lome-Togo. It is him who recommended your person to me to be viable and capable to champion a business of such magnitude without any problem.

Meanwhile, all the whole arrangements to put claim over this fund as the bonafide NEXT OF KIN to the deceased, get the required approvals and transfer this money to a foreign account has been put in place and directives and all needed informations will be relayed to you as soon as you indicate your interest and willingness to assist us and also benefit yourself to this great business opportunity.

Infact, I could have done this deal alone but because of my position in this country as a civil servant, I am not allowed to operate a foreign bank account.They would eventually raise an eye brow on my side during the time of transfer because I work in this bank. This is the actual reason why it will require a second party or fellow who will forward claims as the NEXT OF KIN with affidavit of trust of oath to the bank and also present a foreign bank account number where he will need the money to be re-transferred into on his request as it may be after due verification and clarification by the correspondent branch of the bank where the whole money will be remitted from to your own designation bank account.

I will not fail to inform you that this transaction is 100% risk free.

On smooth conclusion of this transaction, you will be entitled to 30% of the total sum as gratification, while 10% will be set aside to take care of expenses that may arise during the time of transfer and also telephone/fax bills, and 60% will be for me and my partners.

Please you have been adviced to keep top secret as we are still in service and intend to retire from service after we conclude this deal with you.

I will be monitoring the whole situation here in this bank until you confirm the money in your account and ask me to come down to your country for subsequent sharing of the fund according to percentages previously indicated.

All other necessary informations will be sent to you when I hear from you.

I suggest you get back to me as soon as possible stating your wish to this deal.

Yours faithfully,

CLEMENT NKONO.'

Insolvency fraud   9

9.1 There are certain types of fraud associated with companies that go into some sort of insolvency procedure. The most well known of these is probably the phoenix company. In addition to this, there may be those that strip the assets out of a company when they see it is in difficulty, and those that set up a company with no intention that it should ever pay for the bills it runs up. There are a number of offences under the Insolvency Act 1996 and these are summarised in Appendix G.

Phoenix companies

9.2 Here a company is run for a period of time, building up debts as it goes. There may or may not have originally been an intention to pay the debts, but the end result is that the company is unable to continue. At this point the remaining assets may be diverted out of the company and attempts made to hide them. Once the company is in insolvency proceedings there are little or no funds left – this typically results in the insolvency practitioner being unable to investigate the whereabouts of the assets as creditors will be reluctant to fund this. The directors of the company still want to make money and so they continue to trade, perhaps using a slightly altered name for the company. In many cases, the director might be disqualified from acting as a director, and so makes use of a friend or relation to act as a 'front' for the company. Of course, none of this is legal, but it can be difficult to track down and stop the fraudster's activities before they cause their company to become insolvent.

9.3   An example of insolvency fraud is as follows:

'R v Robert Pollock and others
Case: Alpine Double Glazing

Two persons were found guilty and received prison sentences at the Central Criminal Court, Old Bailey on 2 July 1999 – Robert Pollock received four years, the other person three years – for offences relating to asset stripping and fraudulent trading in a 'phoenix' company. A third person was acquitted. Certain reporting restrictions apply.

Investigation conducted with the Metropolitan Police.'

9.4   Another example of an insolvency fraud, this time where several companies were set up with the specific objective of duping customers and not paying suppliers.

'Luxury car hire fraud

(a) Defendants – R v Gary Robert Massingham, Anthony John
Massingham and Mark John Roe
(b) Crown Court where trial was heard – Luton Crown Court
(c) Date of acquittal/sentence passed – 30 November 2000
(d) Principal nature of charges – Fraudulent trading
(e) Police force that supported the investigation –
Hertfordshire Police

The defendants operated luxury car rental businesses in Hertfordshire that grossed almost £1 million during the period under investigation. However, they set about trading fraudulently. They used four different trading names – Marque One Rentals Ltd, Marque One UK Franchising plc, Elite Rentals Ltd and Performance Car Share Ltd – and adopted other confusing and delaying practices in order to obscure their actions. Creditors were unpaid and customers were duped out of their deposits by false claims, eg that they had caused damage to the cars. In addition to the four trading names they used numerous accommodation addresses and mail and telephone redirections, and the use of false names to frustrate clients with complaints. An example of this was exposed by the BBC 'Watchdog' programme in 1996.

The defendants admitted their guilt and were sentenced to prison terms of two and a quarter years, one and three quarter years and two and a quarter years respectively. All three were also disqualified from acting as a director until 2007. Additionally, Roe was given a sentence of six months for an unconnected fraud prosecuted by the Crown Prosecution Service in 1997. He was absent at sentencing and a warrant was issued for his arrest.

Proceedings were still underway against another defendant at the year-end.'

Recent developments in dealing with insolvency fraud

9.5   Recently a government pilot scheme – The Insolvency Service Civil Recovery Scheme – has been running to provide a way for insolvency practitioners to investigate the whereabouts of funds and try to recover them. The scheme involves situations where the insolvency practitioner suspects that the directors have diverted funds out of the company. Under the scheme, insolvency practitioners and lawyers work on a 'no win no fee' basis to take legal proceedings against fraudulent directors whose companies have gone into compulsory liquidation. At present, the scheme only runs in the South-east and East Anglia, but it is hoped that it will expand nation-wide. So far the scheme has been successful, with some cases resulting in the return of 100% of money owing to creditors.

Steps to prevent becoming a victim

9.6   Companies trying to avoid losing money to a phoenix company or similar enterprise will find that the controls set out in Chapter 4 on procurement fraud and Chapter 5 on debtor fraud are particularly useful. If your organisation always checks new customers and suppliers carefully you are more likely to notice the companies which appear risky and may be involved in fraud.

Money laundering   10

10.1   This is a huge problem on a global basis. Money laundering is the practice of cleaning up illegally obtained money and laying a complex trail to lose investigators. The aim is to transfer funds which have been stolen or obtained as the proceeds of criminal activity in order to make the funds difficult to trace. It is often linked to drugs, vice and large-scale crime. In some countries there are no legal prohibitions on laundering or banking system controls to prevent or detect it and therefore these countries are more at risk of money laundering and other fraudulent activities. General indicators of greater risk are:

• weak/no money laundering legislation;
• high degree of organised crime.

The Financial Action Task Force (FATF), set up by the G7 countries in 1989, maintains a list of countries whose money laundering regulations are weak or non-existent. This has resulted in a number of countries improving their legislation in order to be removed from the list, including such countries as the Bahamas, Cayman Islands, Liechtenstein and Panama. The current list of Non-Cooperative Countries or Territories (NCCT) is available on the Internet at interdev.oecd.org/fatf.

As an example of how big the problem is, American investigators estimate that money laundering in Russia amounts to up to $100bn per annum (the official Russian Gross Domestic Product is only $167bn), while in the UK in 1996, drugs accounted for 2.1% of consumer expenditure – consumers spent £9.9bn on drugs, £1.2bn on prostitution, and £0.8bn on illegal gambling.

10.2   The UK has some of the strongest laws and highest standards of enforcement of illegal acts and money laundering. Legislation in the UK is provided in three forms:

* primary;
* secondary;
* explanatory guidance published by trade associations and professional bodies.

Primary legislation

10.3   This is of general application and covers the following offences:

* acquiring, possessing or using the proceeds of criminal conduct;
* concealing or transferring the proceeds of criminal conduct;
* assisting another to retain the proceeds of criminal conduct;
* tipping off suspects or others about a money laundering investigation;
* failing to report knowledge or suspicion of money laundering relating to drug trafficking or terrorism.

Secondary legislation

10.4   The secondary legislation applies to those who carry on a relevant financial business. The regulations cover:

* internal controls and communication of policies;
* identification procedures;
* record keeping;
* recognition of suspicious transactions and reporting procedures;
* education and training of partners and staff.

10.5   A relevant financial business is defined in detail in the Regulations, but in summary is likely to be an organisation which does any of the following:

* provides services relating to the issue of securities;
* provides services or advice on capital structure, industrial strategy, mergers or the purchase of undertakings;
* provides portfolio management or advice services;
* provides safe custody services;
* conducts any investment business within the meaning of the Financial Services Act 1986.

How does it work?

10.6   Money laundering can occur in many ways. The basic objective is to make money from criminal activities look as if it is legitimate. This may happen, for example, by dispersing the money through many different bank accounts to try and hide its origins, or using an unwitting company or professional as a 'trading partner'. This latter situation will not necessarily involve monetary loss for the business but it is clearly undesirable to be used for a money laundering operation. Often, suspicion of money laundering activities will be cast upon the unwitting company, with potentially disastrous consequences.

We normally think of money laundering as involving three stages:

* placing;
* layering;
* integrating.

Placing

10.7   This is getting the money into the banking system and can be made very difficult by the money laundering regulations that most countries have. Because of this many criminals will set up businesses that look legitimate as a way of explaining how they have so much cash.

Layering

10.8   Once the money is in the system the launderer will often wish to try and hide its origins by moving it around as much as possible. This is known as layering. Money may be moved through several different accounts and a number of different countries, often concentrating on those allowing investors more privacy.

Integrating

10.9   In order to use the money from criminal origins, the launderer needs to integrate it into the mainstream economy. This may be done in a variety of ways, but often it is linked with the first stage of placing the money by using a business as a way of getting cash into the banking system and of explaining where it has been generated.

What to watch for?

10.10 Anyone wanting to deal in large amounts of cash should be suspected. After all, cash is what the drug runners and many other criminals have to clean up.

10.11 Your business could be used by money launderers wanting to integrate their money into the legitimate economy. If you are aware of some of the methods used you will be better able to avoid finding yourself being questioned by police officers about dubious transactions in your business. The following sections give examples of some of the methods used to launder money. Training staff to recognise such transactions will help to prevent laundering and for businesses covered by the regulations is compulsory.

Methods of laundering

10.12 New customers purchasing large quantities and then returning them for a refund, without a good reason, may be looking for a cheque from a legitimate business.

10.13 Professionals such as accountants and solicitors can get caught if a client asks them to hold some monies pending a deal. The deal is then called off and a request made for the return of funds. This all seems perfectly in order, until you realise there never was a deal and the launderer now has a squeaky-clean looking cheque from a trusted professional.

10.14 Financial services companies have special responsibilities under the Money Laundering Regulations 1993. This is because, together with banks and other similar organisations, they sell financial products. The money launderer may buy an investment, but then cancel it during the cooling off period allowed. They now have a cheque from a major insurance company, which is easy to explain to the bank as, for example, a maturity of a policy.

10.15 Casinos can be used by the launderer. A large amount of cash is taken to the casino and exchanged for chips – some of these are gambled but a significant amount are retained. The gambler then returns the chips to the cashier and is given a cheque. The cheque can then be placed into the banking system and explained as winnings from the casino. It is worth bearing in mind, however, that such establishments have very tight security, including video surveillance, which may deter the potential launderer.

10.16 Bookmakers can be used to launder money if the launderer is willing to accept that a proportion of the money will be lost in the process. Regular visits to a number of bookmakers are made, and with bets placed on a variety of races or events a certain amount of winnings will be recovered. This income then has an explanation – it is from legitimate gambling – and so it can now be spent or banked with less chance of suspicion being raised.

10.17 In one particular case this method of laundering backfired on the launderer. A bookmaker became suspicious of a regular gambler, thinking that he was perhaps part of a gambling ring that was somehow rigging the races or events. The bookmaker therefore kept very detailed records of all the bets placed, including copies of the videos taken whilst the man was on the premises. When the police started to investigate the man in connection with other laundering offences they noticed that he went regularly to the bookmakers. They were then able to take possession of all the information that had been kept regarding bets placed by the individual they were investigating and use them as evidence against him.

10.18 Antiques may be popular purchases for launderers, perhaps intending to take them out of the country before selling them on. Cash purchases used to be common in the antiques business, but with the money laundering laws now in place large cash purchases should raise the suspicion of the staff in the shop and require a report to the National Criminal Intelligence Service (NCIS).

10.19 Car dealers can sometimes be at risk of being used to launder money, as individuals often bring large amounts of cash to buy a car. There may of course be a legitimate reason for the cash, such as the person has just sold their last car for cash as they did not wish to become a victim of a bounced cheque. Merely paying cash will not be enough to raise the suspicion of laundering in this type of situation. However, if some other factors exist such as regular purchases of cars, then there may well be a suspicion. This will need to be reported to NCIS.

10.20 Auction houses can be used by the launderer. A sale of an asset through an auction house is agreed, with the asset probably being on loan from someone rather than one owned by the criminal. An accomplice bids for the asset at the auction until they are the final bidder. They buy the asset with cash (this would require a certain amount of collusion with someone at the auction house, otherwise the cash purchase would be reported as a suspicious transaction). The auction house then writes a cheque to the 'owner' of the auctioned property. The result is that the launderer now has a cheque from an auction house, which looks legitimate and can be explained relatively easily as the proceeds from auctioning a family heirloom, for example.

10.21 Another technique for laundering money is to place small amounts of cash into a large number of bank and building society accounts that are all held under different names. Transferring these funds between accounts then becomes a straightforward financial exercise.

10.22 Any business which handles large amounts of cash is potentially suspect. These suspicions could then be confirmed by evidence such as the presence of a dominant owner/manager, poor record keeping and large transfers between bank accounts. Suspicions should also be raised about businesses which trade actively with countries which have weak legislation on money laundering and/or limited or no banking supervision legislation.

10.23 If a business has been set up specifically to launder then suspicions could be aroused where:

- The reported turnover of an organisation does not equate with its apparent size;
- Managment appear to have little knowledge of the business which the company purports to operate;
- The company offers unusual trading terms; or
- The business seems to be doing very little trade, but is making lots of profit.

Cyberlaundering

10.24 With the increased use of the Internet for transactions, an additional way of laundering money is presented. E-cash can be used to buy things over the Internet, and some forms of this are anonymous, so the person receiving the money would not know who paid it. Digicash (www.digicash.com) is a form of e-cash: an account can be opened with a bank that offers this service and the cash is loaded into an e-cash account. This can then be sent via secure e-mail to the supplier of goods or services over the Internet. The system uses blind signatures, which means that it is virtually impossible to trace the e-cash. From a launderer's point of view this is very desirable. As it becomes easier to buy valuable goods on the Internet, the use of e-cash to hide the laundering trail could be very useful. At present the hard cash received from crime will still need to placed into bank accounts, but it is foreseeable that in the future e-cash may become the proceeds of crime in the first place.

Legal responsibilities for accountants and other professionals with regard to money laundering.

10.25   The Money Laundering Regulations require all those to whom they apply (generally all those authorised under the Financial Services Act 1986, including accountants) to establish and maintain procedures:

- for the identification of clients;
- for record keeping;
- for internal reporting;
- as may be reasonably necessary for the purposes of forestalling and preventing money laundering.

10.26   The regulations require that employees engaged in relevant financial business are provided with training in recognition and handling of transactions carried out by a money launderer and are made aware of the firm's procedures and the legal requirements in relation to money laundering. If there is a suspicion of money laundering this must be reported to NCIS without tipping off the client/prospective client. It is a criminal offence not to report suspicions to NCIS or via the relevant internal procedures for staff.

Steps required

10.27   If your organisation is to avoid being used unwittingly for laundering purposes and you and your staff are to avoid being accused of crimes, such as failure to report a suspicion of money laundering, it is essential that you consider the following points:

Control	In place?
Ensure that you know what aspects of the legislation apply to your company/organisation.	

Control	In place?
Ensure your staff have an understanding of the principles of money laundering so that they would recognise a dubious transaction.	
Ensure you have in place an appropriate reporting structure so that staff know to whom suspicions should be reported.	
Consider using rules-based software to highlight transactions that may involve money laundering.	
Ensure staff understand the consequences (prison, for example) of not reporting their suspicions.	

Future Developments

10.28 The money laundering rules and regulations may soon be extended as a result of new legislation. Make sure that you keep up to date with changes in legislation by reading information on money laundering sent to your organisation, consulting with your legal advisors and using resources on the Internet. The FSA website (www.fsa.gov.uk) contains the relevant rule book for FSA regulated organisations. Further information can be found by using the websites listed in Appendix M.

Technology for fighting fraud **11**

Biometrics

11.1 Although computers can be used to perpetrate frauds that were not previously possible, technology can also be used in the fight against fraud. One of the key developments that we are seeing at present is the use of biometrics as a security measure. Rather than rely on a signature that can be easily forged (or cannot practically be given because items are dealt with on the computer) or a password that can be guessed or cracked, companies are increasingly relying on identity checks using biometrics. For example, facial recognition can be used to speed up the process of checking identity with an identity card. Biometrics also has the potential for reducing fraud in government applications, such as a low cost way to check the identity of individuals claiming unemployment benefit. Other methods of checking identity include iris and fingerprint recognition.

11.2 Many of these systems are starting to appear in our everyday life. Fingerprint recognition systems for laptop computers are available for under £200. More and more companies are likely to rely on this type of identification system, rather than risk the corruption or theft of corporate assets because an unauthorised person has gained access to their system.

11.3 Some banks and building societies are already using face recognition technology to help ensure that ATM operations are being carried out by the correct person. Iris technology can provide a system to check identity for the most secure areas of an organisation's operations. Lower cost versions where fewer parameters are checked are also available.

Signatures

11.4   An individual's signature has long been used as a method of identification. However, it has drawbacks in that it requires someone to check the signature against a sample, which can be slow and costly. Using a signature written on a digital pad, previously stored information about that signature can be used to verify it. Such a system can be used to gain access to a PDA (personal digital assistant – Palm, for example) by storing the signature and later re-entering it to provide evidence that the person logging on is the legitimate user. On a much larger scale, it can be used by banks or other organisations to help verify the identity of customers, wherever they are and without manual input being required. An example of how such a system can work is given on the Bio4 website (www.bio4.co.uk) and is reproduced below.

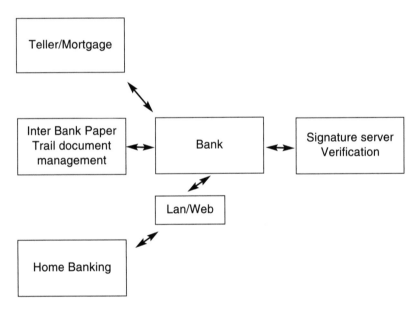

11.5   The term digital signature often causes confusion, as there are two versions. The first is a code, a PIN or similar replacement for a signature which is used as evidence of identity. The potential problem with this, the same as for any other password, is that it is possible for the password to be stolen if the computer on which it is held can be accessed. The second version is a normal signature given on a touchpad, which then has its various attributes, such as speed, pressure etc, tested against a previously stored signature.

Checking identity for access to computer systems

11.6 It is more secure if more than one method of identity is checked. Many organisations use a two-tier system of identity check:

- something the individual knows – a password or PIN;
- something the individual has – a 'key' that constantly generates new numbers.

The person trying to gain access to a system needs to enter both the PIN and the number generated by the authenticator key. The computer that they are trying to connect to will recognise both pieces of data and allow access to be made. The biometrics discussed above could be added to this two-tier system, or be used to replace one or both of the aspects above.

Data mining

11.7 This expression is used to describe the process of finding valuable information from the vast amounts of data that many companies now store. Data mining is often considered in connection with terms such as data warehousing or data marts. A data warehouse is essentially an enterprise wide database, storing all of the data that an organisation needs. A data mart is a smaller scale set-up designed to satisfy the decision-support needs of a particular division, rather than the whole organisation.

11.8 Many organisations may have a number of databases rather than one data warehouse. However, it may be able to create a virtual data warehouse for use with data mining techniques with appropriate software.

How can data mining assist in finding fraud or money laundering?

11.9 If you can build up experience or knowledge of what factors are likely to indicate a fraudulent or money laundering transaction, a system can be written (or tailored) to highlight those problem transactions for further analysis. Such systems may be used by banks to detect potential money laundering, and by any type of company to detect possible fraud. Internet companies that work on the basis of large volumes of potentially risky credit card transactions may be particularly keen to use such systems. The system can highlight the transactions that are more likely to be fraudulent, based on past experience, and allow these to be rejected or checked further before they are accepted. Data mining is an extremely powerful tool and often used by companies, not for fraud detection, but to gain a better understanding of the company's customers. Where such a system is already in place it may be relatively easy to add an extra module that helps to fight fraud.

11.10 Another system uses the data submitted on credit card Internet transactions to try and prevent the acceptance of fraudulent transactions. Similar systems can be used to pick up transactions that raise the suspicion of money laundering, for example because the amounts involved are much larger than usual, beacause deposits and withdrawals are very close to each other in terms of dates and amounts or other features that have been seen on previous suspicious transactions. The example below is a case study from Cybersource (see also www.cybersource.com).

'Nike's Internet shop

Key business and technical challenges:

When nike.com went live in January 1999, they were utilizing CyberSource Credit Card Payment Services. Fraud screening was performed manually. However, within only three months, the incidence of credit card fraud on the site had reached an unacceptable level.

Nike learned that simply validating the credit card numbers doesn't assure a valid transaction. If the card turns out to have been stolen, the transaction is going to be voided later. And the merchant is ultimately responsible when the transaction is fraudulent. Creating a secure shopping environment that would protect Nike customers and the company was top priority. However, Nike realised that the manual process to screen for online credit card fraud was a drain on valuable resources so they quickly set out to find a solution.

Solution:

Nike implemented the CyberSource Internet Fraud Screen enhanced by Visa on its nike.com Internet storefront. On the nike.com site, the CyberSource Internet Fraud Screen Service is used in conjunction with the CyberSource Credit Card Processing service to provide a scalable, fast, convenient, fully automated and secure payment process.

Each time a customer places an order, the CyberSource system obtains credit card authorization and performs a fraud screen in real-time. The CyberSource fraud screen application examines 150 different factors to calculate the risk of fraud in a requested purchase – all in a few seconds. Each transaction receives a rating or "score" that assesses the likelihood of fraud. At that point, an informed decision to accept or reject the transaction can be made.

Results:

In addition to processing fast, efficient credit card authorizations, the CyberSource solution has helped Nike dramatically reduce incidences of credit card fraud on its Internet storefront. Because of the scalability and reliability of CyberSource data centers, where the Internet Fraud Screen service is operated, Nike also benefits from the ability to handle surges in demand for services. Further, with the help of CyberSource technical support, Nike benefited from a tight integration with creative content, commerce software and logistics.'

Surveillance technology

11.11 Closed circuit television is getting cheaper all the time, with very basic systems available for around £100. Such technology can act as a powerful deterrent to the fraudster if they know that their actions are being watched. Covert surveillance is covered by a number of laws and so you should consult your legal advisors before putting such a system in place. In addition to video surveillance, identity cards with appropriate chips or magnetic information can be used to track employee or visitor progress around a site. This type of technology is much more complex and expensive but may be worthwhile in certain situations.

Developments in fighting fraud

Webcards

11.12 Recently some banks have started to offer virtual credit cards for use over the Internet. One of the first of these providers is Cahoot. The questions and answers below are taken from their website (www.cahoot.co.uk) and show how the risk of your details being stolen and abused is reduced.

'Q. What is the Cahoot webcard and how does it work? The Cahoot webcard is a virtual card that allows you to use either your Cahoot debit or credit card online without ever having to expose your real card numbers over the web. The Cahoot webcard works by generating one-off transaction numbers as a substitute for your real card details. It means that you can pay for things quickly, securely and conveniently online and it can be used at any website.

Q. How secure is it really? With the Cahoot webcard you never have to give out your real card details over the web. The transaction numbers it generates can only be used once and have a maximum purchase value limit set by you. Nobody can access your real details when you shop with the Cahoot webcard – you can even buy things from non-secure sites without putting your financial details at risk. You're also still covered by purchase protection, just as you would be if you were paying with your real card. And in addition, to be totally secure, the Cahoot webcard service will close automatically if left inactive on your desktop for five minutes or more.

Q. Can I use my Cahoot webcard for all my online transactions? The Cahoot webcard can be used at all websites that accept Cahoot credit and debit cards and it could be used for telephone ordering too. However, there are a few occasions when you should **not** use webcard for purchases such as purchases that require you to present your actual plastic Cahoot credit or debit card as proof of identity. For example when collecting cinema tickets and some airline tickets bought online. Always check the merchant's policy before purchasing.'

PIN numbers

11.13 The APACS website (www.apacs.org.uk) contains some details of the initiatives being introduced to combat fraud.

'The most revolutionary change ever for fighting fraud will be the use of secure chip cards in conjunction with PINs. Banks and retailers share a vision for using this system by the end of 2004.

Using a better method of identifying the cardholder combined with the chip's ability to verify that a card is authentic will drastically improve security and significantly reduce most types of fraud.

PFPF (APACS' Plastic Fraud Prevention Forum) continues its significant investment into a range of initiatives to combat fraud in the medium-term. These include using intelligent computer systems to detect fraud at an early stage; a cardholder address checking system for card-not-present retailers; retailer education; hot card files carrying details of lost and stolen cards; and maintaining a close partnership between banks, retailers and police.

Fraud on plastic cards is an unwanted by-product of their popularity. Although absolute crime prevention is inconceivable, close liaison and sharing of information between the banks, police and retailers, along with a common commitment to fraud prevention, are key to successfully fighting plastic card crime.'

E-money services

11.14 With more and more transactions taking place over the Internet it is not surprising that a new form of payment is being sought by customers who do not have credit cards. The advent of e-money fills the gap that is created by those who do not have a credit card, either through choice or because they are ineligible, due to their age or other factors. An example of such a service is NOCHEX. The following is a quote from their CEO Philip Sheldrake.

'With the growth of the Internet, society has changed rapidly and so have the needs of consumers and businesses alike. Both are demanding faster and more secure services. E-mail money services such as NOCHEX offer a natural alternative to the traditional cheque and offer added convenience, as the continual increase in subscription to these services demonstrates.

E-mail money services such as NOCHEX offer a convenient, secure and instant means of transferring money, helping to reduce the annoying clearing delay and the worry of cheque fraud. It is now possible to send money to any individual online and millions of people and businesses are already using e-mail money across the world.'

Organisations such as CIFAS further improve fraud prevention and detection by facilitating the sharing of data about potential fraudsters. Appendix H gives further information on their work.

11.15 Whether such services will actually make it more difficult for fraud to be perpetrated or will just shift the emphasis from cheque fraud to other versions of fraud remains to be seen. Potentially though, the use of technology could make it more difficult to succeed in diverting payments from their intended destination.

11.16 A number of the issues connected with e-money have been addressed by the government and the FSA. The article below, taken from an M2 Presswire in 2001, summarises some of the key points:

'Key issues for consumers

- E-money can offer consumers a flexible, secure and conven-ient way of making low value transactions, for example on public transport or in carparks.
- E-money may complement credit card use, for example by providing an attractive alternative means of conducting small scale transactions over the Internet.
- It could also be an attractive payments alternative for consumers who do not possess credit cards or bank accounts.

HM Government has indicated that the Financial Services Compensation Scheme will not apply to e-money issuers. Consequently, customers will have no access to compensation should an e-money issuer become insolvent.

The proposed regime includes a number of features to help protect consumers, consistent with the FSA's objective of appropriate protection for consumers:

- E-money issuers must set a limit on the amounts of money that may be held in individual e-money "purses". The purpose of this limit is to protect holders of e-money by restricting their individual loss should they lose their purses or should the issuer fail.
- Customers must have access to relevant and comprehensible information and guidance on information about redemption rights including any fees payable on redemption.
- Full disclosure of the risks associated with the product must also be made including the liability of holders for any loss arising from misuse, loss, malfunction, theft of, or damage to, their e-money purses or any electronic device on which e-money may be held.
- E-money issuers will be included within the scope of the Financial Ombudsman Service and must also have their own procedures for dealing with customer complaints.'

11.17   New technology is constantly being developed, so it can pay to consider what products might be suitable for fighting fraud in your organisation. Appendix M contains details of a number of websites for companies that provide technological solutions to fighting fraud. These sites often contain detailed material explaining how the products work. In addition, you may find that a general search of the web using a search engine such as vivisimo.com will give more material that will explain any new developments or changes in prices, making the technology more affordable.

The external auditor's role　12

12.1　What can you expect from your auditor, in terms of prevention and detection of fraud? Or maybe you are the auditor and you are planning how to meet your responsibilities and client expectations. In this chapter we will look at what the auditor should be doing and the limitations to their work. This is perhaps particularly relevant at a time when the name Enron is on every auditor's and finance director's lips.

12.2　The auditor's responsibility is set out in Statement of Auditing Standard 110 (SAS 110):

> 'Auditors should plan and perform their audit procedures and evaluate and report the results thereof, recognising that fraud or error may materially affect the financial statements.'

The key point to note is that the auditor has a responsibility to look for 'material' misstatements, however they have arisen.

12.3　SAS 220 Materialty and the audit states that:

> '...an item is material if its omission or misstatement would reasonably influence the decisions of an addressee of the auditor's report.
>
> Materiality may be considered in the context of the primary statements (P&L, statement of total recognised gains and losses, balance sheet, cash flow statement) or of individual items within them. Materiality is not capable of general mathematical definition as it has both qualitative and quantitative aspects.'

In reality the auditor will need to start off with a mathematical definition of materiality in order to be able to plan the amount of testing needed.

12.4 As a rough guide an item may be regarded as material if it constitutes at least a certain percentage of a key figure as given below:

Turnover (depending on size)	1–3%
Net asset /liabilities	4%
Profit	5–10%

However, as mentioned above, there is also a qualitative aspect to materiality. A fraud or error that is only 3% of profit may be regarded as material if, for example, it changes a profit into a loss. This is because a change of that nature is likely to influence the addressee of the report, even though the adjustment itself is quite small. In addition, the fact that the item is a fraud rather than any other type of expense may make it more likely to be material.

12.5 The importance of the concept of materiality from the viewpoint of detecting fraud is easy to see if we think about the amounts involved in some companies' accounts. Large companies may produce their accounts in units of £millions – a fraud of £100,000 will represent just a one point change in a decimal place. For example, profits could be stated at £3.5m or £3.6m and this is unlikely to affect the view of users. Indeed, a much larger fraud may still be immaterial from the auditor's point of view and so no work will be directed specifically at finding such an item. However, a £100,000 fraud may well be regarded as significant by the company's management and something that warrants an effort to prevent or detect it. It is therefore vital to recognise this limitation on the work of the external auditor with respect to fraud.

The auditor's work on fraud

Stage 1 – Risk assessment

12.6 The first stage is to assess the risk of material fraud or error being present in the financial statements. SAS 110 has an appendix with a list of conditions that increase the risk of fraud or error being present. Today's audits take a risk based approach, which means that more effort will be directed to those areas of the financial statements which are more likely to be wrong. This means that the auditor will use the examples listed in SAS 110, or often a pre-printed question-naire, to help assess the risk of fraud or error. (An example of such a questionnaire is reproduced in Appendix D. The items listed on it that are particularly relevant to fraud detection are highlighted in bold.)

12.7   The SAS lists the types of items that may be regarded as fraud and contrasts them to the types of items that are regarded as errors. Fraud may involve:

• Falsification or alteration of accounting records;
• Misappropriation of assets or theft;
• Suppression or omission of transactions, documents or records;
• Recording of transactions without substance (ie recording sham transactions);
• Intentional misapplication of accounting policies;
• Wilful misrepresentation of the entity's state of affairs.

Whereas errors are:

• Mathematical or clerical mistakes in underlying records;
• Oversight or misinterpretation of the facts;
• Unintentional misapplication of accounting policies.

In reality it may be difficult, in some cases, to determine whether a misstatement is due to a fraud or error. The auditor must therefore keep an open mind. The Standard points out that there is a greater risk of failing to detect fraud, compared to error, for a number of reasons including the fact that there has been a deliberate effort to hide fraud.

Professional scepticism

12.8   Auditors are often criticised for failing to detect fraud. The latest example of this is the Enron case – although it is not known for certain at time of writing whether fraud took place, it seems highly likely. The auditor must be wary of this and exercise professional scepticism if they are to have the best chance of detecting fraud. In practice the reason for the auditor failing to detect fraud is often a lack of such scepticism. If the auditor is too ready to believe what management or other members of staff have told them, then they will miss the clues that fraud has taken place.

12.9   Take the following example of a response given when an auditor was trying to perform a purchases test:

'Phillips and Co do not give us invoices as they ask for cash on delivery.'

An enquiring mind would have asked why it was relevant that they delivered only for cash; an invoice should still exist for VAT, tax and accounting purposes. In fact what was happening was that Phillips and Co were a dummy supplier and the member of staff questioned was taking all of the payments for himself. He had not been very thorough, however, and never bothered to create false invoices to back up the payments.

The SAS gives a number of examples of the types of conditions that will increase the risk of fraud and error. These are set out in the appendix to the SAS (see Appendix C).

Stage 2 – general procedures required

12.10   Once the risk has been assessed, the auditor will design tests to ensure that they have a reasonable expectation of detecting material misstatements. This will usually involve the normal tests required to detect any error, plus an awareness of the possibility of fraud so that further enquires can be made if something unusual is found. Where controls are weak and/or the risk of fraud is particularly high, extra tests will be done to check for material frauds.

12.11   The SAS suggests a number of steps, as summarised below, to help ensure that material errors and fraud are found:

Step	Comment
Ensure staff are competent for the audit in question.	Where an audit has a high risk, it is necessary to use more experienced staff who will be better able to notice that something is amiss and to question management in a forthright manner when required. More involvement of both partner and manager may be necessary and a second partner review may be appropriate.

Step	Comment
Assess control environment and risk of fraud.	Even if controls are not to be relied upon as part of the testing process, a preliminary assessment of them must still take place. This will help identify whether the system is capable of producing true and fair financial statements and whether there are any particular areas that have a high risk of fraud and error due to weak controls.
Understand the business and the transactions, including substance rather than legal form.	Without a good understanding of the business it will be impossible for the auditor to check that transactions and balances are correctly stated. If an area is not understood by a member of the audit team they should know that they must pass it on to a more senior member of the team until it can be dealt with properly. If no one can understand the transaction or balance then it may be that the item is a fraud or error. A verbal briefing of the audit team can help everyone under-stand the key issues and risks of the client. Otherwise planning notes and permanent file information must be carefully read by all of the audit team.
Test any controls to be relied on to reduce other testing and pay special attention to areas of weakness.	As always, high risk areas are audited more thoroughly.

Step	Comment
Understand any instances of possible fraud, dishonest conduct, or breakdown in the accounting system of which management are aware (the auditor should obtain written representation regarding this where relevant).	The auditor must ask management about any instances of fraud or dishonesty (even if only suspected rather than proved) as this has an impact on the level of risk. The auditor should request this at the planning stage and ask for written confirmation at the final stage of the audit (as part of the letter of representation).
The auditor should be alert to: • control overrides; • unusual transactions; • insubstantial, vague or delayed replies to audit queries; and • unusual accounting judgements.	Every member of the audit team must understand the potential significance of these factors. There may be a tendency for vague or delayed responses to questions not to be documented, but passed over. This is clearly very dangerous as these are just the types of issues which may alert the auditor to fraud. Training of staff will be vital if they are to understand that even at the most junior level they must keep their eyes open for odd transactions or suspicious responses.
The importance of obtaining external evidence created by the auditor should be remembered.	The rules of audit evidence make it clear that evidence has a different level of quality according to its nature: • Documentary evidence is by far superior to oral evidence and in fact any oral evidence that the auditor is to rely on must be turned into documentary evidence. • Auditor generated evidence is the best type of evidence.

Step	Comment
	• Third party evidence can be very persuasive, but the auditor will need to consider the independence of the third party and their ability to give accurate evidence. • Evidence from within the entity is not very persuasive at all. Auditors cannot rely just on management representations for any material area of the audit – there must be corroborative evidence to back it up.

Analytical review

12.12   Although this is just one procedure that the auditor can use to find fraud, it is worth mentioning separately because it can be so powerful. As mentioned at **3.46**, where management fraud is an issue it can be difficult to pick up on evidence of the fraud. Certain members of the management team or individual staff are often able to create false documents that look entirely genuine, including relevant authorisations. Analytical review can however, pick up problems.

Example of a small scale fraud

12.13   An auditor was carrying out analytical review procedures at a funeral directors. One of the items in the profit and loss account was for fresh flowers. The cost had dropped considerably compared to last year and so the auditor asked the owner/manager why. The answer was that there should have been no cost for flowers at all, for this or the previous year, as a decision had been made to use silk flowers when the local florist closed down. It transpired that the woman who prepared the accounts was the sister of the florist that had closed down. She had been given all the old stationery and had used it to create further bills for the funeral home. She had then raised petty cash slips and taken the money herself. Because the usage of petty cash had been similar to before and because nobody had looked carefully enough at the expenses, she was able to keep the fraud up for some time. She only stopped because she ran out of stationery. It was this that the auditor had noticed, even though it was not in fact material. If the item had been material a more in depth consideration of expectations may have revealed (rather earlier) the fact that there should be no expense for flowers.

12.14 On a larger scale, analytical review might reveal the impracticality of the figures in a company's accounts. Perhaps sales are so large that the company would have to have two factories (rather than the one in existence) to provide sufficient goods. Maybe the gross profit margin is far in excess of what the auditor might expect from their knowledge of the industry. Maybe the average salary of staff is much higher than common sense would imply. Perhaps weekly cleaning costs are excessive, and so on. SAS 410 on analytical review gives more details as to how this technique forms an essential part of the audit.

12.15 The auditor should always consider analytical review in terms of the following stages if they want to make best use of the available information:

Stage of analytical review	Comment
Expectations	What should the ratios be showing given the business environment and the auditor's knowledge of the business?
Actual ratios/figures	Key ratios for the business should be calculated. Ideally a five or ten year history of ratios should be kept to assist in picking up peculiar patterns.
Variations	Where the ratios are not as expected they should be investigated. This might lead to discovery of an error or fraud.
Enquiry	Staff and management are usually asked for their explanation of a ratio that varies from expectation. However, the auditor should watch out for an invalid, vague or delayed response – it may indicate that the person being questioned is involved in a fraud.
Corroboration	The auditor can never just believe management representations on material areas of the accounts and so they must corroborate the answers to their queries. If this is not possible it may mean that the audit report needs to be qualified.

Stage 3 – an indication of fraud

12.16   Where the auditor finds an indication of fraud or error they should obtain an understanding of the event and carry out further tests if the item may be material. If it is clear that a fraud is minor, for example a small petty cash fraud, then the auditor may not think it necessary to carry out extra work. However, careful consideration needs to be given to the possibility that the fraud is in fact material or part of a wider instance of fraud within the organisation. Finding even a small fraud may also cast doubt on the representations given by a particular member of staff, requiring extra work to be done on other areas of the audit. When judging materiality of a fraud or error the auditor will need to consider all the financial consequences of the fraud. There may be fines or other penalties, including loss of a licence to operate for some entities as well as the magnitude of the fraud itself. The auditors may need to seek legal advice regarding the potential consequence of certain breaches in laws and regulations.

12.17   As always the auditor must document their findings and normally discuss them with management. However, this will depend on the circumstances.

Situation	Report to/discuss with internally	Report externally	Include in audit report
Member of staff is thought to be involved	Management	If required by regulator or in the public interest	If material and not prop- erly disclosed or creates a fundamental inherent, uncertainty or if there is a limitation in scope (see below).
Individual director is thought to be involved	Rest of board of directors	A report in the public interest is needed – this casts doubt on the integrity of a director	
Executive board involved	Audit committee, if exists	A report in the public interest is needed – this casts doubt on the integrity of a director	
External fraud suspected	Management	If required by regulator or in the public interest	

Stage 4 – Reporting fraud

Reporting to third parties

12.18   The auditor must consider whether a matter should be reported to the authorities as one of public interest. If management are involved in a fraud (or suspected fraud) the auditor will make any external report without consulting with management. In other instances the auditor will inform management that they are making such a report.

12.19   The auditor may wish to take legal advice before doing this as they could be sued for breach of confidence or defamation if they are proved wrong. However, they will be protected from such actions if they can show the following.

Breach of confidence:

• Disclosure is in the public interest;
• Disclosure made to the appropriate body;
• There is no malice in the disclosure.

Defamation:

• The disclosure was made in their capacity as auditors of the entity;
• There is no malice in the disclosure.

Auditors should include records regarding their disclosure, as it may be reviewed later. The records will be considered in light of:

• what they knew at the time;
• what they ought to have known;
• what they ought to have concluded;
• what they ought to have done.

Clearly the auditor could find their actions questioned if they do not report a fraud, just as if they do report a fraud. Each case must therefore be carefully considered.

Reporting in the audit report

12.20   Almost every type of audit report may be applicable when fraud has affected the financial statements, from an unamended clean report (the accounts are true and fair) through to an adverse one (these accounts are not true and fair).

Unqualified audit report

12.21 If a fraud has affected the accounts in a material way and it is properly disclosed (generally as an exceptional item in accordance with the requirements of FRS 3) the auditor may be able to issue an unamended 'clean' audit report. Such a report will also be appropriate when a fraud is immaterial.

Unqualified with inherent uncertainty

12.22 However, if the fraud is of sufficient magnitude it may cast doubts on the entity's ability to continue as a going concern, or give rise to other uncertainties about the future of the company which are fundamental to an understanding of the accounts. If this is the case then an additional paragraph regarding this fundamental inherent uncertainty is required. This paragraph draws the reader's attention to the section of the accounts which fully explain the nature of the uncertainty and and any actions the directors have taken to try and mitigate the effects of the uncertainty. Both FRS 18 'Accounting Policies' and SAS 130 'Going Concern' give guidance as to the appropriate disclosures that the auditor should check are included in the accounts wherever there is a significant uncertainty about the ability of the entity to continue as a going concern.

Qualified audit report – disagreement

12.23 If there is a fraud which has a material affect on the accounts and the auditor does not agree with the way that it has been dealt with or shown in the accounts, then a disagreement qualification will be given. This may happen if there has been insufficient or no disclosure of the fraud or of potential going concern issues arising from it. It may also arise if the auditor disagrees over the figures included in the accounts.

12.24 An 'except for' qualification is given for material items which do not affect the entire picture given by the accounts. The qualification explains the item(s) that the auditor is not happy with, including any figures which are available, but states that:

> 'except for ... (those items explained) the financial statements give a true and fair view of the state of the company's affairs at (insert date) and of the profit/loss for the year then ended and have been properly prepared in accordance with the Companies Act.'

If the effect of the fraud on the accounts is so material and pervasive as to render them misleading the auditor will issue an adverse report:

'... the accounts are not true and fair...'.

This is clearly a very major occurrence and is rare in practice.

Qualified opinion – limitation in scope

12.25   On finding an indication of a fraud or error the auditor will normally attempt to get further evidence regarding the magnitude and nature of the fraud. However, the fraudster may have ensured that there is insufficient documentation to properly determine what has happened in the time available (or ever). In this case the auditor and the management may not know the true impact of the fraud, but nonetheless know that it has taken place. The auditor needs to let the reader know that they have not been able to check certain of the figures or disclosures in the accounts due to a lack of information. The type of report given where the matter is just material is:

'except for any adjustments that might have been necessary had we been able to obtain sufficient evidence of...'.

If the matter is so material or pervasive that the financial statements are misleading then a disclaimer is issued:

'we cannot form an opinion'.

SAS 600 and the amendments in the APB bulletin 2001/2 contain further information on audit reports.

Non-audit companies

12.26   For many companies there is now no statutory audit requirement. Most companies defined as small by the Companies Act and with turnover of less than £1million per annum are exempt from the statutory audit requirement. The government has also put forward proposals to increase this audit threshold to a turnover of £4.8m per annum. This change could happen as early as 2002. These companies may decide that they wish to have an audit to give extra reassurance that their accounts are true and fair, or they may wish to ask an auditor to do specific work on fraud detection. Where the latter happens the terms of the agreement must be carefully set out to ensure there is no misunderstanding on the nature of the work to be done. For the former, it must be remembered that an audit is only aimed at finding material errors or frauds.

The internal auditor's role   **13**

13.1 An internal audit department is a particularly important part of the controls that an organisation can put in place to limit its exposure to fraud, error and wider risks. The approach that an internal audit department might take when planning their work is set out below. Remember that even if your organisation would find a permanent internal audit department too costly, it is an area that can successfully be outsourced. This allows the benefit of experienced auditors without the full costs of keeping them employed on a full-time basis.

The diagram on page 184 shows the key stages of the internal audit process.

Risk review output

13.2 The main output from the risk review is a report summarising the results of the fieldwork and analysis. The key sections of such a report are likely to include:

- a high level internal audit 'Critical Risk Register' which will document the 'critical' risks in your organisation. This should include:
  - operational risks,
  - financial risks,
  - the risk of non-compliance with legal requirements, and
  - risks relating to damage to the organisation's reputation;
- identification of the high level controls and procedures which exist to mitigate the impact or the frequency of the potential risks;

Key stages of the internal audit process

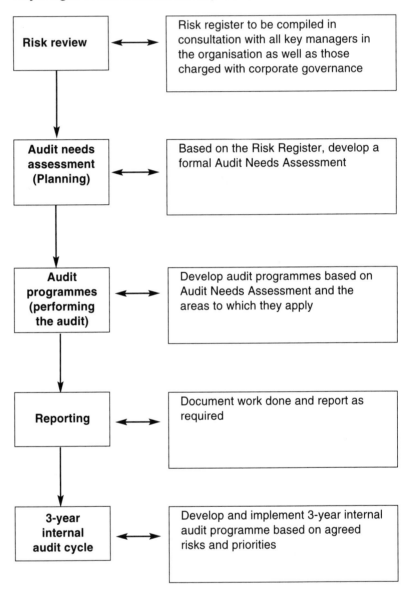

| Risk review | ← → | Risk register to be compiled in consultation with all key managers in the organisation as well as those charged with corporate governance |

| Audit needs assessment (Planning) | ← → | Based on the Risk Register, develop a formal Audit Needs Assessment |

| Audit programmes (performing the audit) | ← → | Develop audit programmes based on Audit Needs Assessment and the areas to which they apply |

| Reporting | ← → | Document work done and report as required |

| 3-year internal audit cycle | ← → | Develop and implement 3-year internal audit programme based on agreed risks and priorities |

- recommendations for further action where new risks have been identified;
- highlighting areas where unnecessary controls exist or where procedures could be streamlined;
- plans for an effective risk monitoring and control process.

The audit process itself should cover the following areas.

Planning

13.3 Each year an individual audit plan should be established in consultation with the top level of management. This plan should include:

- a list of the audit jobs to be completed;
- the reports to be produced;
- the resources available and their planned allocation;
- an audit timetable.

The internal auditor should collate appropriate background information – in the form of circulars, previous audit reports, etc – to obtain a thorough understanding of the area to be audited. Where areas of fraud risk have previously been identified, it is important that appropriate tests are planned to have a good expectation of finding such frauds.

Performing the audit

13.4 An audit programme should be drawn up that takes account of the expected key controls in relation to the risks identified. Emphasis should be given to those controls that are important for the organisation taking into account the views of external audit. The work should be performed using appropriate methods, for example walk through tests (see below) to confirm how key systems operate. Substantive testing (see below) will be used in situations where a conclusion is needed on the completeness, accuracy and validity of information or records.

Definitions

13.5 *A walk through test* is where the auditor takes a small sample, perhaps just one item, and follows it all the way through the system

185

from start to finish (or vice versa) to ensure that the system operates as expected.

A *substantive test* is a test of transactions or balances designed to substantiate the amount recorded. For example, checking the completeness or the valuation of a population is a type of substantive test.

Documentation

13.6   An example of an internal audit schedule is shown in Appendix E. All work should be clearly recorded to enable the key points raised to be understood and acted upon. Reporting might typically cover the following aspects for each test carried out:

• objective;
• method (including basis on which sample has been selected);
• results
• conclusions.

Reporting

13.7   A report should complete the internal audit process. It should include the following:

• an opinion on the adequacy of the internal control system;
• significant audit findings and conclusions; and
• practical recommendations.

Any serious weaknesses identified should immediately be reported to the board in order that prompt action can be taken to rectify the situation.

13.8   Many of the points raised in the section on external auditors will also be relevant to the internal auditor. For example, using staff with a sufficient knowledge of the business is just as important whether the audit work is internal or external. It is similarly important to ensure that staff carrying out internal audit work are fully aware of the risk of fraud and the steps required by their company's fraud response plan (if it has one).

13.9   In terms of fighting fraud, there are two advantages that an internal audit department has over the external auditors.

(a) Internal audit can carry out tests throughout the year, whereas the external auditor will often visit only once or twice. This means that random spot checks on assets or transactions can take place at any time without warning.

(b) Internal audit can concentrate on fraud to the degree required by management, rather than just look for material fraud as defined by reference to the financial statements. Management may want the search for fraud to be far more wide-ranging than that done by the external auditors. With an internal audit department the work needed can be specified by management.

13.10 The internal audit function has a vital role to play as part of an organisation's corporate governance procedures. Internal audit should report to the audit committee (where there is one) or the board of directors. Their reports should be taken seriously and acted upon where required. If your organisation does not have an internal audit department they should regularly reconsider whether one is needed. More about the requirements on corporate governance is given in the chapter on the role of directors.

13.11 Further information on the role of internal auditors can be found on the websites of UK based professional accounting bodies (see Appendix M) and on sites such as www.theiia.org.

What to do on discovering a fraud   **14**

Contingency plans

14.1   When an organisation discovers a fraud, or suspected fraud, it is very helpful if they are clear on what to do next. Saving the company's assets may depend upon quick action, and trying to decide what action may be appropriate will delay the whole process. For this reason it is a good idea for an orgnisation to have a fraud response plan. This document will set out what should happen on discovery of a fraud or suspected fraud, so that management can proceed quickly giving the maximum chance of apprehending the fraudster and/or recovering the proceeds. It is also important to limit the effect of any bad publicity arising as a result of the fraud; another aspect that the plan should deal with.

14.2   Putting together such a plan can take time, but a full example fraud policy and response plan is included in Appendix J. This could be tailored to your organisation, or you could use the key points below to develop your own fraud policy and response plan.

14.3   Key areas that should be covered in a plan are as follows:

- who leads the investigation;
- dealing with publicity;
- reports to be made;
- gathering evidence;
- identifying an offender;
- recovering funds.

Who leads the investigation

14.4 When there is an initial suspicion of fraud the person/post named in the fraud response plan should be called upon to carry out an initial investigation. It may not be clear, at first, whether an irregularity is fraud or simply error. The investigator needs to have a good understanding of the business/organisation and needs to be able to find the time to deal with the investigation instantly – a delay could be very costly.

Dealing with publicity

14.5 Some organisations will wish to keep publicity to the minimum in order to avoid damage to their reputation. However, there are potential problems with this approach – it may send the wrong message to staff (or external fraudsters) that there will be no big fuss even if they are caught. In addition to this, if news of the fraud does leak it could cast the organisation in a negative light if it was clear that they were trying to keep the fraud secret. If the police are involved they may want or need to make a statement to the press about an actual or suspected fraud. They will normally consult with the victim before issuing any statement. In addition it is clearly helpful if the victim organisation consult with the police prior to issuing any statement of their own. There may be a possibility of information being revealed that will later prejudice the investigation or subsequent court case.

14.6 It is helpful for one person to be responsible for all dealings with the press and for all others with knowledge of the fraud to know that they should not make any statements to the press. Knowledge of the fraud generally should be kept to an absolute minimum number of people.

Reports to be made

14.7 A number of people, both internally and externally, may need to be contacted in event of fraud. The following provides a list of some of these and the reason for contacting them.

Person	Reason
Solicitors	Recovery of losses is of key importance. The swift appointment of a solicitor who specialises in recovery of assets will help to ensure that all necessary steps are taken.
Accountants (with forensic expertise)	In-house expertise to investigate a fraud may not be available. Most medium-sized and all large firms of accountant will have staff or partners that specialise in forensic accounting.
Police	It is good practice to report all suspected frauds to the police promptly. The police may be able to assist/carry out the investigation and help to prevent further loss of assets. A list of contact details for fraud squads around the country is given in Appendix F.
Insurers	The loss may be covered by insurance and so it is important to involve the insurers at an early stage to help ensure that a claim is dealt with properly.
Regulators	If the business is regulated, such as a bank or investment business, there will almost certainly be specific rules requiring details of frauds to be reported to the regulator. The business should ensure that their fraud response plan includes details of any reports required to be made to the regulator.

Gathering evidence

14.8   If evidence is to be used in a criminal prosecution it is important that it is gathered by police or personnel trained in the requirements of the relevant legislation. However, there will also be occasions when it is necessary for other members of staff to deal with items that may constitute evidence. In this case some simple procedures can help to preserve the integrity of documents or other records.

14.9   Paper documents are often present in a fraud case, perhaps giving an indication of how or by whom the fraud was perpetrated. Such documents should be placed carefully into an individual see-through plastic cover. This way it can be examined by those investigating the case, without them needing to touch it. There is, of course, the possibility that the documents will have fingerprint evidence on them, so it is helpful if a list of names of those who are known to have handled the document is kept. That way their finger prints can be taken for elimination purposes. No marks, even in pencil, should be made on documents that may form evidence in a case, as it reduces the value of that evidence. The police will usually want to take the original documents to help ensure their integrity. The organisation should include in their fraud response plan whether they are happy for this to happen in the early stages of an investigation.

14.10   Computer-based systems will commonly be involved in a case of fraud. They may have been used internally to perpetrate the fraud or they may have been attacked from outside the organisation. The fraud response plan must include someone with in-house expertise of the system (wherever possible). However, as it is possible that in some cases this person may be a suspect, details should be kept of an expert at the manufacturer of the equipment and/or of an external expert that could be called upon in an emergency.

14.11   The computer expert will need to be aware of the risk of data being lost from the system if it is turned off, but also of the risk that a 'time-bomb' has been left on the system that might cause even greater damage to the organisation if left to activate.

Identifying an offender

14.12   There is no offence of fraud and so prosecutions need to be for some other specific offence. Examples of offences that may be appropriate are listed in Appendix G.

14.13 Preliminary investigations will almost always be carried out by someone from within the organisation. At this stage it may not be clear if there has been a fraud at all and so someone who understands how the organisation works is needed. Where this happens, comprehensive notes or a tape recording of the interview should be kept. The interviewee should be accompanied by a responsible colleague. However, where more detailed questioning is needed it is better for the police to be involved. The organisation's fraud response plan should make it clear at what point matters should be handed to the police. This is because if all the steps required by the law are not taken, any information gained in an interview may be invalid for the purposes of a criminal prosecution.

14.14 Once a suspect has been identified it is clearly vital that they are not allowed to do anything that may damage the organisation, remove or conceal any evidence of their crime or communicate with others who may be involved in a crime. In these days of mobile phones and personal digital assistants, extra care must be taken that an individual is not sending a text message or e-mail even though they are under supervision. It should be remembered, however, that the suspect may be innocent and steps must be taken to ensure that their human rights are not prejudiced. This is another important reason for the involvement of a solicitor, although one with experience of employee law and human rights will be needed. It may be desirable that an employee is suspended whilst an investigation takes place, but again legal advice should be taken on the appropriateness of this in the particular case.

Recovering funds

14.15 Every victim of fraud will want to recover the funds that have been lost. Although the criminal justice system and the police can attempt to recover funds, it is often the civil system that is best suited to this aspect. The fraud response plan should have details of relevant legal advisers and accounting specialists. There are three stages to the recovery of funds:

- Tracing – ie finding where the assets have gone;
- Freezing – ie preventing them from moving further;
- Recovery – returning them to the victim.

These tasks are complex and require specialist knowledge and swift action if they are to be effective. Set out below is a summary of some of the key stages and legal points that are relevant.

Investigate the 'modus operandi'

14.16 In order to conduct an asset-tracing enquiry effectively, evidence must be obtained relating to all of the transactions which the target may have been involved in. The more complete this information is, the more reliable the evidence will be. It is clearly important to establish, where possible, which funds are which – ie do the funds traced correspond to those which are actually involved with the corruption or defective transaction?

14.17 The task of the investigator is to:

- examine the person's expenditure:
  - how much spent?
  - spent on what?
- determine how funds were accumulated;
- determine how much is remaining;
- discover how the funds were hidden.

Information available

14.18 Ideally there will be records such as:

- accounting records;
- journal entries;
- invoices;
- cheque requisitions;
- auditors' or accountants' working papers.

Note that it is often possible to restore deleted computer files, and thus to outsmart a perpetrator who thinks that by pressing the delete button evidence has been destroyed. There is a national hi-tech crime unit in the UK that can provide assistance to forces investigating crime involving computers or similar technology.

14.19 Other sources of evidence include:

- bank statements;
- credit card statements;
- paid cheques or cheque stubs;
- duplicate paying-in slips;
- bank debit and credit memos;
- regulatory reports re unusual transactions;
- credit applications;

- other deposits;
- stockbroker records;
- insurance policies;
- credit bureau records;
- personal tax returns;
- any other personal financial records;
- cash payments to local merchants;
- travel records;
- telephone call records (including mobile phone records).

All of these should be obtainable from an individual's or a company's bank (subject to obtaining the requisite authority) but equally there are a number of publicly held record registries which may give an investigator a clue as to the whereabouts of assets:

- HM Land Registry;
- Vehicle registries.

The former is open to public inspection whilst the latter is open to inspection with the appropriate authority.

One should not overlook such obvious sources of information as:

- newspapers;
- the Internet;
- discreet enquiries;
- direct interviews.

Legal proceedings

14.20   There are three stages of legal proceedings that may need to be considered:

- Interim Orders – to obtain information and\or freeze assets;
- Judgment or Final Order;
- Enforcement and recovery of assets.

Interim Orders

14.21   An interim order is one made before the substantive hearing of an action. In this context the gaining of information or freezing of assets may be necessary to enable the recovery procedure to go ahead. The courts have wide powers to make interim orders, examples of which are given below.

Search (and Seizure) orders (formerly *Anton Piller* orders)

14.22 In *Anton Piller KG v Manufacturing Processes Ltd* a German manufacturer sued its UK agent for giving confidential information to a competitor. To avoid the risk of the defendants destroying evidence when faced with a court order, the claimant's solicitors obtained a court order, without any notice to the other side, requiring the defendants to allow them to enter their premises in order to search for and seize the relevant documents. An *Anton Piller* order is very draconian, and efforts are normally made first to get the information by less drastic means, such as a simple injunction to deliver up the material. It is also time-consuming and expensive, and could even lead to a defendant bringing a counter suit for damage to their reputation.

Mareva-type injunctions – freezing of assets

14.23 In *Mareva SA v International Bulk Carriers SA* the defendants hired ships from the plaintiffs and failed to pay the hire charges. They had however received money from sub-hirers which was lodged in a London bank. Mareva gained an injunction to stop IBC from removing the money from this bank. These are now officially, and less memorably, called 'freezing orders'. In order to succeed, the claimant must prove that:

- there is a 'good and arguable' claim; and
- there is a serious risk that assets might be dissipated.

It is worth considering taking out similar orders in other countries to avoid the defendant moving assets abroad to escape the court's jurisdiction. There have been rare cases where a court has made a *Mareva* order affecting assets both in the UK and abroad. The effect of this order is to prevent the defendant or indeed third parties from dealing with the assets concerned until true ownership has been established. The order will be served on the defendant's bank, for example, who will then have to freeze relevant accounts. A *Mareva* order is often followed by ancillary orders, such as orders requiring affidavits as to ownership of assets, seizures of passports, letters of authority and orders requiring the cross-examination of individuals.

Order for delivery up of goods

14.24   If ownership can be established at the interim stage it is possible to obtain an order for delivery up of goods which are the subject matter of the action.

Order to provide information about property or assets

14.25   The court can order a party to provide information about the location of relevant property or assets and about ownership of those assets.

Court orders in relation to third parties

14.26   Orders which can be made by the courts to obtain information from third parties include:

- *Norwich Pharmacal* orders – requiring someone other than a defendant to give information, usually about the identity of alleged wrongdoers, even if their involvement has been unwitting (from a leading case of that name).
- Orders under the Bankers' Books Evidence Act 1879 – to bring bank documentation to court, not necessarily requiring bank officials to give evidence.
- Bankers' Trust Orders – requiring a bank to disclose the identity of an account holder.
- Subpoenas – requiring a person to appear as a witness in court, under threat of a penalty (*sub poena*) if he fails to do so. This can include a requirement for the person to produce specified documents.

Judgment or Final Order

14.27   Hopefully steps taken at the interim stage will allow the claimant to establish his case and can lead to matters being resolved. However, if matters are not resolved then the claimant may need to seek judgment against the defendant and\or some final order, for example the recovery of goods or taking of accounts. Where a defendant has acquired property of the claimant, for example unlawfully or for no consideration, in circumstances where he has been unjustly enriched, the claimant is entitled to claim back the property or an equivalent sum in cash from the defendant. The court has powers to allow a claimant to 'trace' the wrongfully acquired money or assets.

Enforcement and recovery of assets

14.28   Once a judgment has been obtained it is possible to take steps to enforce that judgement. Many defendants or judgment debtors will voluntarily hand over assets when faced with any of the procedures described above. Where compliance has to be enforced the following procedures are available:

- warrant of execution;
- charging orders and stop orders;
- third party debt orders (formerly garnishee order);
- attachment of earnings;
- bankruptcy;
- corporate insolvency procedures.

Warrant of execution

14.29   This is the most straightforward type of order – to gain entry to a defendant's premises and seize assets to the value of the outstanding debt. The County Court bailiff or the High Court Sheriff's Officer have power to enter premises (not forcibly) and seize assets other than those essential to the basic needs of the debtor, including the tools of his trade. These assets must be legally owned by the debtor. The goods are taken away and sold through a broker or at public auction, and the proceeds paid to the creditor.

Charging orders and stop orders

14.30   A charging order allows the court to impose a charge on specified property (normally land, buildings or investments) of a judgment debtor, enabling the creditor to be paid in priority to other unsecured creditors. This is particularly useful if the debtor becomes insolvent. This can lead to a separate enforcement order for the sale of the charged property. A stop order prevents securities being dealt with or dividends paid out to the debtor.

Third party debt order (formerly garnishee order)

14.31   If a creditor (A) is owed money by a debtor (B) who is himself owed money by a third party (C – known as the 'garnishee') an order can be made requiring C to pay the debt not to B but directly to A. C may well be a bank or trader who has ample funds and will readily honour the order.

Attachment of earnings

14.32   If the judgment debtor is in employment and has no assets other than his salary, an order can be made requiring the employer to make deductions from the debtor's salary and pay them over to the court for the benefit of the creditor. The debtor must have failed to make at least one payment due under the judgment, and the court will ensure that enough is left for the debtor's basic needs.

Bankruptcy and corporate insolvency procedures

14.33   Where an individual is unable to pay he can be declared bankrupt. A trustee in bankruptcy will then be appointed who has powers to take over all of the bankrupt's assets and realise these in the interests of creditors. One downside of this procedure is that the bankruptcy is conducted on behalf of all creditors and not just the claimant.

14.34   Where a judgment has been obtained against a corporation then there are a variety of insolvency procedures which can be used. Winding up a company may often be the most effective procedure, particularly if the directors have been guilty of any wrongdoing which has contributed to the insolvency.

Conclusion

14.35   The above is only a rough guide to the steps required to try and recover funds lost through fraud. You will need to work closely with your legal advisers in order to deal with this area effectively. Most firms of solicitors will have a website with information about their services. This can be useful if you do not already have legal advisors to whom you can turn in the event of fraud. An example is www.blandy.co.uk.

Appendices

Appendix A   The Turnbull Report – a summary
Appendix B   Charity Commission – strategic risk management
              framework
Appendix C   SAS 110: Fraud and Error
Appendix D   Example of an external auditor's inherent risk assess-
              ment
Appendix E   Example of an internal audit testing schedule
Appendix F   What to do if you suspect a fraud
Appendix G   Criminal offences that may be appropriate for cases
              of fraud
Appendix H   Organisations that help with the pooling of data
Appendix I   Fraud healthcheck
Appendix J   Example fraud policy and response plan
Appendix K   Model Fraud Policy Statement: Short Version
Appendix L   Model Fraud Policy Statement: Long Version
Appendix M   Useful websites and bibliography

The Turnbull Report – a summary

The Turnbull Report – the internal control requirements of the Combined Code – was issued in the autumn of 1999. It provides guidance to listed companies on how to apply the requirements in the Combined Code on Corporate Governance which relate to internal control. Companies should comply fully with the guidance for accounting periods which end on or after 23 December 2000.

Principle D.2 of the Code states that 'The board should maintain a sound system of internal control to safeguard shareholders' investment and the company's assets'. This Principle is elaborated by two Provisions:

- D.2.1 – The directors should, at least annually, conduct a review of the effectiveness of the group's system of internal control and should report to shareholders that they have done so. The review should cover all controls, including financial, operational and compliance controls and risk management.
- D.2.2 – Companies which do not have an internal audit function should from time to time review the need to have one.

The Turnbull Report provides guidance in respect of the following areas;

- maintaining a sound system of internal control;
- reviewing the effectiveness of internal control;
- board statements on internal control;
- internal audit.

This guidance is outlined below.

Maintaining a sound system of internal control

The board of directors is responsible for the company's system of internal control. It should set appropriate policies on internal control and seek regular assurance that it will enable it to satisfy itself that the system is functioning effectively. The board must further ensure that the system of internal control is effective in managing risk in the manner approved by the board. This system of control should be embedded in the operations of the company and form part of its culture.

Reviewing the effectiveness of internal control

Boards, or relevant board committees, should regularly receive and review reports on control issues from management and/or others qualified to prepare them. Issues to be considered as part of the regular review process should include the identification, evaluation and management of key risks, the effectiveness of the related system of internal control, and the actions taken to remedy any weaknesses found. An approach in which all key risks are covered each year is encouraged.

In addition to the regular review, Turnbull proposes that directors undertake a specific annual review for the purposes of making the internal control disclosures required by the Listing Rules. This should include, for example, changes in the nature and extent of significant risks, the company's ability to respond effectively to change and the quality of the regular review process.

Board statements on internal control

Boards are required to disclose, among other things, that there is an on-going process for identifying, evaluating and managing the company's key risks, that this process is regularly reviewed by the board in accordance with the guidance, and how the board has reviewed the effectiveness of the process. Furthermore, weaknesses in control that have resulted in material losses or contingencies requiring disclosure in the annual report should be reported. Boards should ensure that their disclosures do not give a misleading impression. The disclosures essentially amount to assurances that everything is under control, rather than a description of how the controls actually work.

Internal audit

Turnbull proposes that companies without an internal audit function should review the need for one annually. Similarly, where such a function does exist, the board should annually review its remit, authority, resources and scope of work.

Implications

Companies need to take action to implement the requirements of Turnbull. The report places emphasis upon the role of internal audit. In smaller companies, it may not be practicable to have an internal audit function. Turnbull says that in the absence of an internal audit function, the board will need to assess whether other monitoring processes provide sufficient and objective assurance. A briefing published by the ICAEW suggests that smaller companies may wish to consider the following issues.

Question	Answer
Can the quality of information about internal control which is regularly passed to the board be improved?	
Can the external auditors be asked to perform particular work on the higher risk areas?	
Can the individuals in charge of key departments or operating units be invited to attend part of a board meeting on a more regular basis, to account for, and answer questions on, the running of their part of the business and the managing of its risks?	
Can the regular agenda of the board be changed, so that there is more focus on risk and control on an ongoing basis?	

Question	Answer
Can more use be made of confirmations from key employees of compliance with the company's policies and codes of conduct?	
Can more be done to make sure that Turnbull is not treated as a 'one off' initiative? For example, by the directors consulting more with the workforce about whether the control strategies are succeeding and whether risks to the business objectives are being dealt with adequately.	
Can the directors take more of a role in monitoring on a 'peer review' basis?	

These suggestions will not be appropriate to every company. However, they provide a basis for discussion about how to implement Turnbull.

Charity Commission – strategic risk management framework

(Note – this document will be further developed in consultation with our stakeholders and will take account of the development of our regulatory and support activity)

High level risk/incident	Examples of possible impact/ consequence	Examples of Charity Commission response
A. Risks within the charitable sector		
(1) Poor governance/ mismanagement of charities	(a) inefficient/ineffective use of charitable resources. (b) loss of resources for beneficiaries and potential failure of a charity. (c) failure of services or suffering caused to beneficiaries. (d) disputes or legal action against charities (e) potential for fraud to occur. (f) loss of confidence in the charity or its trustees/employees.	(a) monitoring charity returns and accounts using a series of 'triggers' to alert us to possible areas of concern across a wide range of issues, eg: • whether charitable funds may be at risk • whether funds are being correctly used • whether trustees' expenses appear reasonable

High level risk/incident	Examples of possible impact/ consequence	Examples of Charity Commission response
		• whether the charity appears to be operating legally • whether there are any areas where we can provide support and guidance. (b) evaluating and responding appropriately to complaints about mismanagement and abuse, through use of our monitoring triggers (c) concentrating support activity (via visits, guidance etc) on those charities which deal with significant sums of money and/or assets or are dealing with areas where beneficiaries are most at risk (eg children, cancer patients, community care, animals etc). (d) improving our intelligence on what is happening within the sector. (e) internal systems (eg at registration) to spot problems in charities early on.

High level risk/incident	Examples of possible impact/ consequence	Examples of Charity Commission response
		(f) improvement of transparency and accountability of charities through public access to information on char-ities, publicity on action taken to put charities back on track etc. (g) programme of advice and guid-ance for charities to support them in managing their own risks in a proactive fashion to reduce the likelihood of a major breakdown in control arising (eg through advice by way of: telephone helplines; training events and semi-nars; guidance leaflets covering areas of common difficulty or concern etc). (h) working with other bodies such as umbrella bodies and support organisations etc. (i) use of our powers where appropriate to facilitate better use of charitable resources (eg via schemes and orders).

High level risk/incident	Examples of possible impact/ consequence	Examples of Charity Commission response
(2) Inappropriate action by a charity or its trustees/ employees (including abuse such as fraud and other illegal activity)	(a) trustees/employees obtaining illegal financial or other inappropriate gain from a charity. (b) inappropriate treatment of bene- ficiaries (c) inappropriate use of funds for non- charitable purposes or otherwise outside the charities remit (eg in support of a political, ideological or other cause) (d) other consequences covered in (1) above.	(a) monitoring programme (eg on trustee benefits) to detect issues of concern. (b) evaluation and investigation of complaints from the public, identified through monitoring or intelligence or other sources. (c) using our powers where appropriate, eg to open inquiries, appoint receiver/ managers etc. (d) liaison and working with other enforce- ment agencies and prosecuting authorities. (e) publicity on action taken to rectify abuse. (f) providing opportu- nity for whistleblow- ers to contact the Commission. (g) other responses set out in (1) above as appropriate.
(3) Inappropriate actions in the name of charity by unregistered organisations (eg 'scam charities')	(a) fraudulent or inappropriate fundraising eg through street collections, rose- selling etc (b) misrepresentation through people and organisations carrying	(a) increasing public awareness on giving safely through leaflets and other guidance. (b) increasing public awareness of the role of the Com- mission and

High level risk/incident	*Examples of possible impact/ consequence*	*Examples of Charity Commission response*
	out activities while claiming to be a charity. (c) loss of resources and/or reputation to bona fide charities	opportunities for providing us with information (eg through fundraising hotline). (c) liaison with other statutory bodies to allow then to take appropriate action. (d) other action under (1) And (2) above.
(4) Registration of an inappropriate organisation	(a) registration of a charity with inappropriate trustees (eg paedophiles, bankrupts) who put a charity and/or its beneficiaries at risk. (b) registration of a charity with non-charitable objects.	(a) use of risk assessment to identify those applications which require a higher degree of scrutiny before registration. (b) for all applications, checks on the proposed Trustees including checks for bankruptcy, disqualification as a Director, checks on address/telephone number, and checks to ensure that proposed Trustees have not previously been disqualified form acting as Trustees under Section 72(e) of the Charities Act. (c) for charities intending to operate with vulnerable groups of people or animals, checks against a range of

High level risk/incident	Examples of possible impact/ consequence	Examples of Charity Commission response
		external data sources to confirm the bona fides of the proposed Trustees.
		(d) review of a charity's proposed objects and governing document to ensure compliance with the law and with best practice.
		(e) where appropriate, review of the applicant's proposed business plan.
		(f) in cases where the charity will involve children, a review of the applicant's child protection policy.
		(g) in cases deemed to be complex or higher risk, meeting with the applicants to discuss their application.
		(h) in cases considered to be high risk, referring the charity for monitoring, support, or investigation action following registration, as appropriate.
(5) Failure or scandal at a 'major' house-hold name charity	(a) loss of public confidence in the financial management capability of charities leading to financial difficulties and under-	(a) targeting of Commission resources on high-value and high-profile charities. (b) working closely

High level risk/incident	Examples of possible impact/ consequence	Examples of Charity Commission response
	mining confidence in the sector. (b) loss of public confidence in the moral/ ethical integrity of charities. (c) weak control resulting in significant and highly-publicised fraud. (d) inappropriate governance leading to abuse of position/ power (financial or social).	with national charities (including inter change where appropriate) to facilitate good governance. (c) other action in (1) and (2) above

B. Risks relating to the Charity Commission itself

High level risk/incident	Examples of possible impact/ consequence	Examples of Charity Commission response
(6) Public mis-understanding of the role and powers of the Charity Commission which could lead to a loss of public confidence in its role and competence	(a) public misconception that Commission is able to control the day-to-day actions of charities (eg on use of resources, fundraising etc). (b) public misconception that, by receiving charitable status, an organisation has been 'Kitemarked' or accredited by the Commission in terms of the way it is run. (c) public misconception that the Commission monitors exempt and excepted charities and is responsible for any failings in this area.	(a) increasing public awareness of the role of the Commission via its website. (b) increasing public awareness of the role of the Commission via publications and the media outlining the role and powers of the Commission. (c) increasing public awareness via outreach – seminars, conferences, roadshows, stands at sector events etc. (d) progressing action with other Government Departments to improve the powers available to the Commission as appropriate.

High level risk/incident	Examples of possible impact/ consequence	Examples of Charity Commission response
(7) Commission not responding quickly, correctly or appropriately (eg to requests for advice, complaints about mismanagement or abuse etc)	(a) dissatisfaction with service. (b) lack of success in high profile litigation. (c) public loss of faith in Commission's ability to police the sector.	(a) internal management control systems which monitor performance against targets and identify cases requiring urgent action. (b) fast tracking of cases where the risk is perceived to be highest. (c) Quality Control reviews to ensure compliance with laid down procedures and processes. (d) internal systems which ensure proper advice taken where needed before action taken (eg Operational Guidance, legal and accounting advice). (e) customer service initiatives aimed at making service more effective (eg helplines) and complaint managers to deal with when things go wrong. (f) reasons given for decisions made. (g) system for reviewing decisions and complaints.

High level risk/incident	Examples of possible impact/ consequence	Examples of Charity Commission response
(8) Failure to keep register up to date and accurate.	(a) loss of confidence in the register as a reliable record of charities and their objects. (b) loss of transparency and accountability of the sector and of the Commission's effectiveness as its regulator. (c) poor service to the public	(a) requirements for submission of annual returns, accounts and data-base update forms, and enforcement action where these are not received. (b) monitoring of information and checks made eg on high risk activities, changes to charity trustees etc. (c) Independent quality control checks on the accuracy of the charity register and database, including comparisons to source data (eg database update forms, annual returns etc). (d) regular reviewing of the register, on either a thematic or sample basis to cleanse incorrect data and/or take appropriate action in respect of inac-tive charities.
(9) Inadequate resources are available to the Commission and/ or failure of its IT and other systems.	(a) inability to develop and improve services. (b) targets and objectives not met. (c) insufficient num-bers of staff with the right skills and experience available	(a) targets set for operational areas and progress monitored against them. (b) robust business planning systems in place to identify

High level risk/incident	Examples of possible impact/ consequence	Examples of Charity Commission response
	to enable the Commission to properly discharge its statutory duties. (d) inability of the public to access operational and information services required leading to customer dissatisfaction. (e) potential for security failures.	and make case for financial, people and other resources required. (c) HR systems for recruitment and selection, appraisal, raining and development etc. (d) development and regular testing of disaster recovery plan and business continuity plan. (e) maintenance of adequate security controls and standards.
(10) Inappropriate allocation of Commission resources in the light of the risks in the sector that need to be addressed and/ or considered.	(a) failure to protect charitable assets and beneficiaries most at risk. (b) failure to tackle most urgent and important issues affecting the sector. (c) imbalance of effort between functions carried out by the Commission according to their riskiness. (d) loss of public confidence in the Commission's ability to supervise sector appropriately.	(a) regular (at least annual) assessment of the risks to the achievement of Commission strategic objectives and allocation of resources accordingly. (b) development of risk indices, performance indicators and trend analysis to inform the allocation of resources. (c) effective review of resource allocation during annual business planning round.

High level risk/incident	Examples of possible impact/ consequence	Examples of Charity Commission response
		(d) operational management monitoring of resource allocation against in-year performance.

SAS 110: Fraud and Error   **C**

Statements of Auditing Standards ('SASs') are to be read in the light of 'The scope and authority of APB pronouncements'. In particular, they contain basic principles and essential procedures ('Auditing Standards'), indicated by paragraphs in bold type, with which auditors are required to comply in the conduct of any audit. SASs also include explanatory and other material which is designed to assist auditors in interpreting and applying Auditing Standards. The definitions in the Glossary of terms are to be applied in the interpretation of SASs.

Introduction

1   The purpose of this SAS is to establish standards and provide guidance on the auditors' responsibility to consider fraud and error in an audit of financial statements. This SAS refers to error as well as fraud because, having identified a matter which could cause a misstatement in the financial statements, auditors will be concerned to establish the circumstances giving rise to that matter and whether such misstatement was an error or occasioned by fraudulent conduct.

2   **Auditors should plan and perform their audit procedures and evaluate and report the results thereof, recognising that fraud or error may materially affect the financial statements. (SAS 110.1)**

3   No precise legal definition of fraud exists. It is for the court to determine in a particular instance whether fraud has occurred.

Auditors need to be alert to conduct which may be dishonest before considering whether it may be fraudulent. In particular circumstances, conduct may be dishonest in some respect but not fraudulent: for example, conduct which breaches an undertaking to follow a specified course of conduct required by a regulator. Where specific breaches of laws or regulations are concerned, auditors follow the principles and essential procedures set out in SAS 120 'Consideration of laws and regulations'.

4   For the purpose of this SAS 'fraud' comprises both the use of deception to obtain an unjust or illegal financial advantage and intentional misrepresentations affecting the financial statements by one or more individuals among management, employees, or third parties. Fraud may involve

- falsification or alteration of accounting records or other documents,
- misappropriation of assets or theft,
- suppression or omission of the effects or transactions from records or documents,
- recording of transactions without substance,
- intentional misapplication of accounting policies, or
- wilful misrepresentations of transactions or of the entity's state of affairs.

The implications of such matters and the extent to which it is reasonable to expect auditors to detect fraudulent conduct are considered in paragraphs 18 to 22 below. Appendix 2 contains commentary on the interpretation of relevant aspects of the Theft Act 1968, which is one of the most common statutes to which reference may be appropriate.

5   Auditors may encounter circumstances in which it is unclear whether possible misstatement arises from intent to mislead, from accidental oversight, from aggressive business practices or from unethical conduct. Where this is the case, they need to consider the nature of the circumstances in which the misstatement arose and any explanation received in order to determine whether error or fraud is involved. Auditors carry out this assessment in the context of assessing whether the financial statements give a true and fair view.

6   For the purpose of this SAS, 'error' refers to unintentional mistakes in financial statements, such as

- mathematical or clerical mistakes in the underlying records and accounting data

- oversight or misinterpretation of facts, or
- unintentional misapplication of accounting policies.

7 'Directors' means the directors (or shadow directors) of a company or other entity, the partners, proprietors, committee of management or trustees of other forms of entity, or equivalent persons responsible for the reporting entity's affairs, including the preparation of its financial statements.

8 In the context of this SAS, 'management' means those persons, who may include directors, who have executive responsibility for the conduct of the entity's operations and the preparation of its financial statements.

9 Guidance on the auditors' responsibility for the detection and reporting of material misstatements resulting from non-compliance with law or regulations when carrying out an audit of financial statements is provided in SAS 120 'Consideration of law and regulations'. Guidance on the auditors' responsibility to report direct to regulators in the financial sector is provided in SAS 620 'The auditors' right and duty to report to regulators in the financial sector'.

Responsibilities of the directors

10 It is the responsibility of the directors to take such steps as are reasonably open to them to prevent and detect fraud. This includes

- taking steps to provide reasonable assurance that the activities of the entity are conducted honestly and that its assets are safe-guarded;
- establishing arrangements designed to deter fraudulent or other dishonest conduct and to detect any that occurs; and
- ensuring that, to the best of their knowledge and belief, financial information, whether used in the entity or for financial reporting, is reliable.

They are also responsible for preparing financial statements that give a true and fair view of the state of affairs of a company or group and of its profit or loss for the financial year. Neither the assignment of particular responsibilities to management nor the audit process relieves the directors of these fundamental responsibilities.

11 In addition, directors and officers of companies have responsibility to provide information required by the auditors, to which they have a legal right of access under section 389A of the Companies Act 1985. That section also provides that is is a criminal offence to give to the auditors information or explanations which are misleading, false or deceptive.

12 The following steps, among others, may assist the directors in discharging their responsibilities for the prevention and detection of fraud and error:

- the practices contemplated in the document 'Internal control and financial reporting' giving guidance for directors of listed companies developed in response to the recommendation of the Cadbury Committee;
- the steps taken to develop within the entity an appropriate control environment, which is itself dependent upon the attitude, awareness and actions of directors;
- the development of a Code of Conduct, ensuring employees are properly trained in and understand its provisions, monitoring compliance and taking appropriate disciplinary action in cases of non-compliance;
- the institution and operation of appropriate systems of internal control including monitoring their effectiveness and taking corrective action where necessary.

13 In order to assist them in achieving the objectives in paragraph 10, directors of larger entities will often assign particular responsibilities to

- an internal audit function
- a legal department
- a compliance function, and/or
- an audit committee.

14 In planning and conducting their work, auditors seek to obtain reasonable assurance that financial statements are free from material misstatement, whether caused by error or by fraud. Doing so involves the auditors considering whether they may place reliance upon aspects of the internal control system (such as where there is an effective independent internal audit department) and, specifically, assessing the risk of material misstatement arising from fraud or error. However, an audit conducted in order to express an opinion on the view given by financial statements cannot be regarded as providing any further assurance on the adequacy of an entity's systems or on the actual incidence of fraud. Directors may therefore wish to commission more detailed investigations in particular instances of concern.

15 In certain sectors or activities (for example financial services), there are detailed laws and regulations that specifically require directors to have systems of safeguard the entity's assets and to ensure the reliability of its financial reporting.

16 Given the responsibility of directors to prepare financial statements that give a true and fair view of the state of affairs of a company and of its profit or loss for the financial year, it is necessary, where material error of fraud has occurred, for them to correct the accounting records and ensure that the matter is appropriately reflected and/or disclosed in the financial statements.

Responsibility of the auditors

Prevention

17 It is not the auditors' function to prevent fraud and error. The fact that an audit is carried out may, however, act as a deterrent.

The extent to which the detection of fraud or error may reasonably be expected

18 Auditors plan, perform and evaluate their audit work in order to have a reasonable expectation of detecting material misstatements in the financial statements arising from error or fraud. However, an audit cannot be expected to detect all errors or instances of fraudulent or dishonest conduct. The likelihood of detecting errors is higher than that of detecting fraud, since fraud is usually accompanied by acts specifically designed to conceal its existence, such as management introducing transactions without substance, collusion between employees or falsification of records. Consequently, 'reasonable expectation' in the context of fraud must be construed having regard to the nature of the fraud and, in particular, the degree of collusion, the seniority of those involved and the level of deception concerned.

19 An audit is subject to the unavoidable risk that some material misstatements of the financial statements will not be detected, even though the audit is properly planned and performed in accordance with Auditing Standards. This risk is higher with regard to misstatements resulting from dishonest or fraudulent conduct. The reasons for this include the following:

- the effectiveness of audit procedures is affected by the inherent limitations of the accounting and internal control systems and by the use of selective testing rather than the examination of all transactions;
- much of the evidence obtained by the auditors is persuasive rather than conclusive in nature;
- dishonest or fraudulent conduct may take place over a number of years but may only be discovered in a later year (for example because a fictitious asset becomes material to the financial statements); and
- dishonest or fraudulent conduct may involve conduct designed to conceal it, such as collusion, forgery, override of controls or intentional misrepresentations being made to the auditors.

20   The subsequent discovery of material misstatement of the financial statements resulting from fraud or error existing during the period covered by the auditors' report does not, in itself, indicate that the auditors have failed to adhere to the basic principles and essential procedures of an audit or have been otherwise at fault.

21   While the existence of effective accounting and internal control systems may reduce the probability of misstatement of financial statements resulting from fraud and error, there is always some risk of internal controls failing to operate as designed. Furthermore, any accounting and internal control systems may be ineffective against fraud committed by management, particularly if it involves collusion, internally or with third parties.

22   The detection of fraud committed by management poses particular difficulties for the auditor because management can be in a strong position to commit a fraud and conceal it from others within the entity and from the auditors. Actions that management may take to commit and conceal fraud include:

- introducing complexity into the corporate structure, commercial arrangements with third parties, transactions or internal systems;
- collusive acts with employees or third parties, whether related parties or otherwise;
- the override of internal controls set up to prevent or detect fraud;
- influencing accounting policies, financial statement presentation and accounting estimates affecting financial information used within the business or for external reporting;
- manipulating evidence available to, or responses to evidence requested by, the auditors, delaying the provision of evidence or making representations and responses to audit enquiries that lack integrity or are deliberately untruthful.

Auditors in the public sector

23   The responsibility of auditors of entities in the public sector as regards fraud and error are similar to those of auditors of limited companies and other entities in the private sector. The basic principles and essential procedures set out in this SAS therefore apply equally to auditors in both the private and public sector. However, in some ways the responsibilities of auditors of entities in the public sector go beyond those in the private sector by virtue of statutory or other prescribed duties and obligations.

The approach to be adopted by auditors

24   When planning the audit the auditors should assess the risk that fraud or error may cause the financial statements to contain material misstatements. (SAS 110.2)

Conditions or events which increase the risk of fraud and error include:

- previous experience or incidents which call into question the integrity or competence of management or other staff;
- particular financial or reporting pressures within an entity;
- weakness in the design and operation of the accounting and internal control systems;
- unusual transactions;
- problems in obtaining sufficient appropriate audit evidence, and
- inadequate control over data in an information systems environment.

Examples of these conditions or events are set out in Appendix 1.

25   Based on their risk assessment, the auditors should design audit procedures so as to have a reasonable expectation of detecting misstatements arising from fraud or error which are material to the financial statements. (SAS 110.3)

26   In order to have a reasonable expectation of detecting error or fraud, auditors

(a) include in the engagement team personnel competent to plan and conduct the audit having regard to the size and complexity of the entity concerned and to the industry in which the entity operates;
(b) make a preliminary assessment of the control environment and of

conditions and characteristics of the business that might indicate increased risk of fraud or error;

(c) obtain an understanding of the business, its organisational and commercial arrangements and the nature of its transactions, focusing on the substance of the arrangements and transactions, not just the form;

(d) if proposing to rely on the operation of controls to reduce the extent of their substantive procedures, evaluate the strengths and weaknesses of the internal control system, including any internal audit department. This will include an assessment of the potential for management override and the checks and balances that exist in order to guard against this. Attention should be paid to any areas of special weaknesses in the systems and to the adequacy of internal control procedures over those aspects of the business where there is specific risk of increased fraud or error;

(e) obtain from management an understanding of any events of which they are aware during the period involving dishonest or fraudulent conduct and any material weaknesses or breakdowns in the accounting records or controls and, where appropriate, obtain written representations;

(f) are alert throughout the conduct of the audit to audit evidence indicating unusual events or actions, such as
  – control overrides
  – unusual transactions
  – insubstantial responses to audit enquiries, delays or vague representations
  – unusual accounting judgements;

(g) obtain sufficient reliable audit evidence that puts appropriate emphasis on external evidence or evidence created by the auditors. Particular attention is paid to the quality of audit evidence generated by the company or by third parties with whom the company has a relationship.

27 Unless the audit reveals evidence to the contrary, the auditors accept representations as truthful and records and documents as genuine[1]. However, auditors plan and perform the audit with an attitude of professional scepticism, recognising that conditions or events may be found that indicate fraud or error may exist.

28 When conducting an audit where the risk assessment or the audit evidence obtained suggests that there may be fraudulent or dishonest conduct by directors or senior management, the level of professional scepticism and the degree to which evidence independent of the entity is sought is increased. In such circumstances,

[1] See SAS 440 – Management representations.

auditors place less emphasis on management representations and documents generated or provided by the entity.

Procedures when there is an indication that fraud or error may exist

29   When auditors become aware of information which indicates that fraud or error may exist, they should obtain an understanding of the nature of the event and the circumstances in which it has occurred, and sufficient other information to evaluate the possible effect on the financial statements. If the auditors believe that the indicated fraud or error could have a material effect on the financial statements, they should perform appropriate modified or additional procedures. (SAS 110.4)

30   The extent of such modified or additional procedures depends on the auditors' judgement as to

(a) the types of fraud or error indicated,
(b) the identity of the persons involved,
(c) the likelihood of the occurrence of fraud or error,
(d) the likelihood that a particular type of fraud or error could have a material effect on the financial statements, possibly including those of prior years, and
(e) the extent to which it is realistic to expect that further procedures are likely to clarify the position.

Unless circumstances clearly indicate otherwise, the auditors cannot assume that an instance of fraud or error is an isolated occurrence. If necessary, the auditors adjust the nature, timing and extent of their substantive procedures.

31   When evaluating the possible effect of dishonest or fraudulent conduct on the financial statements, the auditors consider its potential materiality. This includes an evaluation of

* the potential financial consequences, such as fines, penalties, damages, threat of expropriation of assets, enforced discontinuance of operations and litigation,
* whether the potential financial consequences require disclosure, and if so, the adequacy of any disclosure,
* whether breaches of laws and regulations may be involved, or
* whether the potential financial consequences are so series as to call into question the view given by the financial statements.

Such an evaluation may require the assistance of the entity's directors, legal advisers, bankers or other advisers.

32 As the assessment of the effect of dishonest or fraudulent conduct may involve consideration of matters which do not lie within the competence and experience of individuals trained in the audit of financial information, it may be necessary for auditors to obtain appropriate expert advice (whether through the entity or independently) in order to make their assessment of the possible effect on the entity's financial statements. Where this is the case, auditors are required to meet the Standards set out in SAS 520 'Using the work of an expert'.

33 **When the auditors become aware of, or suspect that there may be, instances of error or fraudulent conduct, they should document their findings and, subject to any requirement to report them direct to a third party, discuss them with the appropriate level of management. (SAS 110.5)**

34 Depending on the circumstances, the methods which auditors may decide to adopt to document their findings include copies of records and documents and making minutes of conversations. When discussing with management findings which indicate the possibility of fraud, they ensure so far as possible that there is no communication with any person who may be implicated in the events which they are investigating.

35 If the directors do not provide sufficient information to satisfy the auditors' concerns in relation to the suspected or actual error or fraudulent conduct, the auditors may consider it prudent to obtain legal advice about the application of law or regulations to the particular circumstances (including, for example, section 389A of the Companies Act 1985 – see paragraph 11 above) and the possible effects on the financial statements.

36 The auditors may need, with the entity's permission, to consult the entity's lawyer as to the possible legal consequences of any fraudulent conduct. However, where it is not possible to consult the entity's own lawyer, or it is not appropriate to rely on the entity's lawyer's opinion, or where the auditors so wish, or it is not clear what further action, if any, the auditors ought to take, they may obtain their own legal advice.

37 When adequate information about the suspected or actual error or fraud cannot be obtained, the auditors ensure that the board of directors is aware of the position, and consider the implications of the lack of audit evidence for their report on the financial statements (as required by SAS 110.9) and whether any obligation arises to report to third parties (see SAS 110.10, 110.11 and 110.12 below).

38   The auditors should consider the implications of suspected or actual error or fraudulent conduct in relation to other aspects of the audit, particularly the reliability of management representations. (SAS 110.6)

39   If the auditors consider that error or fraudulent conduct may have or has occurred, they re-evaluate their assessments of audit risk, reconsider whether their other audit procedures have been performed with an appropriate degree of professional scepticism and consider the validity of management representations. Factors affecting the auditors' risk assessment on discovering a possible instance of fraudulent conduct include

- any apparent failure of specific control procedures
- the level of management or employees involved, and
- the concealment, if any, of the act.

For example, a series of suspected or actual instances of error of fraudulent conduct which are financially immaterial may be symptomatic of management's probity and hence may throw doubt on the integrity of the financial statements and perhaps even the future prospects of the entity.

Reporting fraud or error

40   The action taken by auditors to report an event varies in relation to its nature and the gravity of its consequences. For example, if the suspected or actual error or fraud is likely to have a substantial effect on the financial statements but there is little firm evidence yet available, auditors nevertheless need to consider whether the matter requires inclusion in their report in accordance with the requirements of SAS 600 concerning either fundamental uncertainties or circumstances in which a qualified opinion is to be expressed. If the matter is fully documented but the effect is not material, then unless the auditors conclude that an apparently isolated incidence is part of a wider pattern calling into question the probity of the entity's management no reference need be made in the financial statements or in their report.

Reporting to management

41   The auditors should as soon as practicable communicate their findings to the appropriate level of management, the board of directors or the audit committee if

(a) they suspect or discover fraud, even if the potential effect on the financial statements is immaterial (save where SAS 110.12 applies), or
(b) material error is actually found to exist. (SAS 110.7)

42   In determining an appropriate representative of the entity to whom to report occurrences of apparent fraud or material error, the auditors need to consider all the circumstances. With respect to apparent fraud, the auditors report the matter to the appropriate higher level of authority within the entity which they do not suspect of involvement in the fraud. If the auditors suspect that members of senior management, including members of the board of directors, are involved, it may be appropriate to report the matter to the audit committee. Where no higher authority exists, or the auditors are precluded by the entity from obtaining sufficient appropriate audit evidence to evaluate whether fraud or error which is material to the financial statements has, or is likely to have, occurred, or if the auditors believe that the report may not be acted upon or are unsure as to the person to whom to report, they may wish to obtain legal advice.

43   Where the auditors determine that the matter involves error rather than suspected fraud, they will request the directors to make appropriate amendments to the financial statements. If such amendments are not made, the auditors need to consider whether their opinion on the financial statements ought to be qualified, as required by SAS 600.

Reporting to addressees of the auditors' report on the financial statements

44   Where the auditors conclude that the view given by the financial statement could be affected by a level of uncertainty concerning the consequences of a suspected or actual error or fraud which, in their opinion, is fundamental, they should include an explanatory paragraph referring to the matter in their report. (SAS 110.8)

45   Where the auditors conclude that a suspected or actual instance of fraud or error has a material effect on the financial statements and they disagree with the accounting treatment or with the extent, or the lack, of disclosure in the financial statements of the instance or of its consequences they should issue an adverse or qualified opinion. If the auditors are unable to determine whether fraud or error has occurred because of limitation in the scope of their work, they should issue a disclaimer or a qualified opinion. (SAS 110.9)

46   In determining whether disclosures concerning the matter are adequate, or whether an explanatory paragraph needs to be included in their report, auditors base their decision primarily on the adequacy of the overall view given by the financial statements. Steps taken to regularise the position, or the possible consequences of qualification, are not, on their own, grounds on which the auditors may refrain from qualifying their opinion or from including an explanatory paragraph reflecting a fundamental uncertainty.

47   When determining whether the directors have appropriately treated a possible or actual instance of dishonesty or fraud that may require disclosure in the financial statements, auditors have regard to whether the financial statements are free of material misstatements, whether shareholders require the information to enable them to assess the performance of the company and any potential implications for its future operations or standing. Corrections to the financial statements need to be made in respect of errors identified. Where a suspected or actual instance of dishonest or fraudulent conduct needs to be reflected in the financial statements, a true and fair view will require that sufficient particulars are provided to enable users of the financial statements to appreciate the significance of the information disclosed. This would usually require the full potential consequences to be disclosed and, in some cases, it may be necessary for this purpose that the financial statements indicate that dishonest or fraudulent conduct is or may be involved.

48   When considering whether the financial statements reflect the possible consequences of any suspected or actual dishonest or fraudulent conduct, auditors have regard to the requirements of SSAP 18 'Accounting for contingencies'. Suspected or actual dishonest or fraudulent conduct may require disclosure in the financial statements because, although the immediate financial effect on the entity may not be material, there could be future material consequences such as fines or litigation.

Reporting to third parties

49   Paragraphs 53 to 60 below give guidance to auditors on the circumstances in which to report to third parties who have a proper interest in receiving such information. In addition, auditors of financial institutions subject to statutory regulation, who are required to report certain information direct to the relevant regulator, have separate responsibilities. Guidance on these responsibilities is given in SAS 620 'The auditors' right and duty to regulators to report in the financial sector', and the associated Practice Notes.

50   Where the auditors become aware of a suspected or actual instance of fraud they should

(a) consider whether the matter may be one that ought to be reported to a proper authority in the public interest; and where this is the case,
(b) except in the circumstances covered in SAS 110.12, discuss the matter with the board of directors, including any audit committee. (SAS 110.10)

51   Where, having considered any views expressed on behalf of the entity and in the light of any legal advice obtained, the auditors conclude that the matter ought to be reported to an appropriate authority in the public interest, they should notify the directors in writing of their view and, if the entity does not voluntarily do so itself or is unable to provide evidence that the matter has been reported, they should report it themselves. (SAS 110.11)

52   When a suspected or actual instance of fraud casts doubt on the integrity of the directors auditors should make a report direct to a proper authority in the public interest without delay and without informing the directors in advance. (SAS 110.12)

53   Confidentiality is an implied term of the auditors' contract. The duty of confidentiality, however, is not absolute. In certain exceptional circumstances auditors are not bound by the duty of confidentiality and have the right or duty to report matters to a proper authority in the public interest. Auditors need to weigh the public interest in maintaining confidential client relationships against the public interest in disclosure to a proper authority. Determination of where the balance of public interest lies requires careful consideration. Auditors whose suspicions have been aroused need to use their professional judgement to determine whether their misgivings justify them in carrying the matter further or are too insubstantial to deserve reporting.

54 Examples of circumstances which may cause the auditors no longer to have confidence in the integrity of the directors include situations

- where they suspect or have evidence of the involvement or intended involvement of the directors in possible fraud which could have a material effect on the financial statements, or
- where they suspect or have evidence that the directors are aware of such fraud and, contrary to regulatory requirements or the public interest, have not reported it to a proper authority within a reasonable period.

55 Auditors are protected from the risk of liability for breach of confidence or defamation provided that

- in the case of breach of confidence
  - disclosure is made in the public interest, and
  - such disclosure is made to an appropriate body or person, and
  - there is no malice motivating the disclosure, and
- in the case of defamation
  - disclosure is made in their capacity as auditors of the entity concerned, and
  - there is no malice motivating the disclosure.

In addition, auditors are protected form such risks where they are expressly permitted or required by legislation to disclose information (see paragraph below).

56 'Public interest' is a concept that is not capable of general definition. Each situation must be considered individually. Matters to be taken into account when considering whether disclosure is justified in the public interest may include:

- the extent to which the suspected or actual fraud is likely to affect members of the public;
- whether the directors have rectified the matter or are taking, or are likely to take, effective corrective action;
- the extent to which non-disclosure is likely to enable the suspected or actual fraud to recur with impunity;
- the gravity of the matter; and
- the weight of evidence and the degree of the auditors' suspicion that there has been an instance of fraud.

57 When reporting to proper authorities in the public interest it is important that auditors only report to one which has a proper interest to receive the information.[2] Which body or person is the proper authority in a particular instance depends on the nature of the suspected or actual fraud. Proper authorities could include, in the United Kingdom, the Serious Fraud Office, the Crown Prosecution Service, police forces, the Securities and Investments Board and the Self Regulating Organisations it has recognised, the Recognised Professional Bodies recognised by the SIB under the Financial Services Act 1986, the International Stock Exchange, the Panel on Takeovers and Mergers, the Society of Lloyd's, the Bank of England, local authorities, the Charity Commission for England and Wales, the Scottish Office for Scottish Charities, the Inland Revenue, HM Customs and Excise and the Department of Trade and Industry. Comparable bodies in the Republic of Ireland could include the Garda Fraud Squad, the Revenue Commissioners, the Irish Stock Exchange and the Department of Enterprise and Employment. In cases of doubt as to the appropriate authority, auditors are advised to consult with their professional body. Auditors in the United Kingdom may wish to refer the facts to the Investigations Division of the Department of Trade and Industry with a view to investigation by that Division.

58   Auditors receive the same protection even if they only have a reasonable suspicion that fraud has occurred. Auditors who can demonstrate that they have acted reasonably and in good faith in informing an authority of an instance of fraud which they think has been committed would not be held by the court to be in breach of duty to the client even if, an investigation or prosecution having occurred, it were found that there had been no offence.

59   Auditors may need to take legal advice before making a decision on whether the matter should be reported to a proper authority in the public interest.

60   Auditors need to remember that their decision as to whether to report, and if so to whom, may be called into question at a future date, for example on the basis of

- what they knew at the time
- what they ought to have known in the course of their audit
- what they ought to have concluded, and
- what they ought to have done.

Auditors may also wish to consider the possible consequences if financial loss is occasioned as a result of fraud which they suspect (or ought to suspect) has occurred but decide not to report.

[2] See *Initial Services v Putterill* (1967) All England Law Report 3, page 145 and *Lion Laboratories Ltd v Evans* (1984) All England Law Report 2, page 417.

61 In addition to the duty of auditors of businesses in the financial sector to report direct to regulators in certain circumstances (see paragraph 49 above), auditors and others have a statutory duty to take the initiative to report to the appropriate authorities suspected money-laundering related to drug trafficking and terrorism.[3] A failure to report in these circumstances is itself a criminal offence.

Withdrawal from the engagement

62 The auditors may conclude that withdrawal from the engagement is necessary in certain circumstances, for example if they consider that the shareholders have not been given the information they require and see no opportunity for reporting such information to the shareholders whilst continuing as auditors. Factors that may affect the auditors' conclusion include the implications if the highest authority within the entity is suspected of involvement with the suspected or actual fraud, which may affect the reliability of management representations, and the effects on the auditors of continuing association with the entity. In reaching such conclusion, the auditors may need to seek legal advice.

63 Resignation by auditors is a step of last resort. It is normally preferable for the auditors to remain in place to fulfil their statutory duties, particularly where minority interests are involved. However, there are circumstances where there may be no alternative to resignation, for example where the directors of a company refuse to issue its financial statements or the auditors wish to inform the shareholders or creditors of the company of their concerns and there is no immediate occasion to do so.

64 Guidance for auditors on the circumstances of withdrawing from engagements is provided in ethical guidance issued by the accountancy bodies[4].

Overseas activities

65 Where any of the activities of a company or group are carried on outside the United Kingdom or the Republic of Ireland, the auditors

[3] See Criminal Justice Act 1993.
[4] Reference should be made to the appropriate section of the relevant guidance to members. For auditors of limited companies in Great Britain who cease to hold office, the requirements of section 394 of the Companies Act 1985 apply.

should take steps to ensure that the audit work in relation to the detection and reporting of any fraud and error is planned and carried out in accordance with the requirements of this SAS. (SAS 110.13)

66   The requirements of this SAS apply irrespective of whether the overseas activities are carried on by a subsidiary of a United Kingdom or Irish parent, a division of the company based overseas or employees operating from the United Kingdom or the Republic of Ireland.

Compliance with International Standards on Auditing

67   Compliance with this SAS and with relevant ethical guidance ensures compliance in all material respects with International Standard on Auditing 240 'Fraud and Error'.

Effective date

68   Auditors are required to comply with the Auditing Standards contained in this SAS in respect of audits of financial statements for periods ending on or after 30 June 1995. Adoption of the requirements when reporting on financial statements for financial periods ending before that date is encouraged.

Appendix 1 – Examples of conditions or events which may increase the risk of fraud or error occurring

Included below are examples of conditions or events which may increase the risk of either fraud or error, or in some cases both. It is not an exhaustive checklist of such conditions or events.

1   Previous experience or incidents which call into question the integrity or competence of management

- Management dominated by one person (or a small group) and no effective oversight board or committee.
- Complex corporate structure where complexity does not seem to be warranted.

- High turnover rate of key accounting and financial personnel.
- Personnel (key or otherwise) not taking holidays.
- Significant and prolonged under-staffing of the accounting department.
- Frequent changes of legal advisers or auditors.

2   Particular financial reporting pressures within an entity

- Industry volatility.
- Inadequate working capital due to declining profits or too rapid expansion.
- Deteriorating quality of earnings, for example increased risk taking with respect to credit sales, changes in business practice or selection of accounting policy alternatives that improve income.
- The entity needs a rising profit trend to support the market price of its shares due to a contemplated public offering, a takeover or other reason.
- Significant investment in an industry or product line noted for rapid change.
- Pressure on accounting personnel to complete financial statements in an unreasonably short period of time.
- Dominant owner-management.
- Performance-based remuneration.

3   Weaknesses in the design and operation of the accounting and internal controls system

- A weak control environment within the entity.
- Systems that, in their design, are inadequate to give reasonable assurance of preventing or detecting error or fraud.
- Inadequate segregation of responsibilities in relation to functions involving the handling, recording or controlling of the entity's assets.
- Indications that internal financial information is unreliable.
- Evidence that internal controls have been overridden by management.
- Ineffective monitoring of the operation of systems which allows control overrides, breakdown or weakness to continue without proper corrective action.
- Continuing failure to correct major weakness in internal control where such corrections are practicable and cost effective.

4   Unusual transactions

- Unusual transactions, especially near the year end, that have a significant effect on earnings.
- Complex transactions or accounting treatments.

- Unusual transactions with related parties.
- Payments for services (for example to lawyers, consultants or agents) that appear excessive in relation to the services provided.

5 Problems in obtaining sufficient appropriate audit evidence

- Inadequate records, for example incomplete files, excessive adjustments to accounting records, transactions not recorded in accordance with normal procedures and out-of-balance control accounts.
- Inadequate documentation of transactions, such as lack of proper authorisation, supporting documents not available and alteration to documents (any of these documentation problems assume greater significance when they relate to large or unusual transactions).
- An excessive number of differences between accounting records and third party confirmations, conflicting audit evidence and unexplainable changes in operating ratios.
- Evasive, delayed or unreasonable responses by management to audit inquiries.
- Inappropriate attitude of management to the conduct of the audit – eg time pressure, scope limitation and other constraints.

6 Some factors unique to an information systems environment which relate to the conditions and events described above

- Inability to extract information from computer files due to lack of, or non-current, documentation of record contents or programs.
- Large numbers of program changes that are not documented, approved and tested.
- Inadequate overall balancing of computer transactions transactions and data bases to the financial accounts.

Appendix 2 – Examples of offences under the Theft Act 1968[5]

The Theft Act 1968 (the Act) only applies to England and Wales. In Scotland, such matters are dealt with, if at all, under common law. In the Republic of Ireland, there is no such equivalent legislation. In Northern Ireland, the equivalent legislation is the Theft Act (Northern Ireland) 1969.

[5] References to the Theft Act 1968 also include references to the Theft Act (Northern Ireland) 1969.

Definitions within the Act

1   The basic definition of theft is to be found in the Act. Section 1 of the Act provides that

(a) a person is guilty of theft if he dishonestly appropriates property belonging to another with the intention of permanently depriving the other of it; and 'thief' and 'steal' shall be construed accordingly, and

(b) it is immaterial whether the appropriation is made with a view to gain, or is made for the thief's own benefit.

Theft is an arrestable offence, and punishable on conviction on indictment by imprisonment for a term not exceeding ten years.

2   The Act does not define dishonesty, that being a question of fact to be decided on the circumstances of each case. The Act does, however, provide for certain circumstances in which the appropriation of property belonging to another is not to be treated as dishonest. These include cases in which a person appropriating property does so in the belief that he has in law the right to deprive the other of it, or in the belief that he would have had the other's consent if the other had known of the appropriation and the circumstances of it.

Obtaining property, or pecuniary advantage, by deception

3   Under section 15 of the Act, a person who by any deception dishonestly obtains property belonging to another with the intention of permanentely depriving the other of it commits an arrestable offence. Obtaining property covers obtaining ownership, possession or control of it. 'Obtain' includes obtaining for another, or enabling another to obtain or retain. 'Deception' means any deception, deliberate or reckless, by words or conduct as to fact or law, including a deception as to the present intention of the person using the deception or any other person.

4   Under section 16 of the Act, a person who by any deception (defined as above) dishonestly obtains for himself or another any pecuniary advantage commits an arrestable offence. A pecuniary advantage within the meaning of section 16 is obtainable for a person where

(a) he is allowed to borrow by way of overdraft, or to take out any policy of insurance or annuity contract, or obtains an improvement of the terms on which he is allowed to do so, or

(b) he is given the opportunity to earn remuneration or greater remuneration in an office or employment, or to win money by betting.

5 The Theft Act 1978 creates a range of offences and replaces section 16(2)(a) of the Act. The offences created are

(a) dishonestly obtaining services from another by deception
(b) evading liability by deception. The offence is committed where a person by deception dishonestly secures the remission of a liability to make payment, or, with intent to make permanent default, dishonestly induces a creditor or person claiming payment on his behalf to wait for or forgo payment, or dishonestly obtains exception from or abatement of liability to make payment, and
(c) dishonestly making off without payment, where it is known that payment on the spot is required or expected, and with intent to avoid payment.

False accounting

6 Under section 17 of the Act, it is an arrestable offence

(a) dishonestly to destroy, deface, conceal or falsify any account or record or document made or required for any accounting purpose, or
(b) in furnishing information for any purpose dishonestly to produce or make use of any account or any record or document as aforesaid which, to the knowledge of the person producing or making use of it, is or may be misleading, false or deceptive in a material particular, with a view to gain for oneself or another or with intent to cause loss to another.

For this purpose, a person who make or concurs in making an entry which is or may be misleading, false or deceptive in a material particular, or who omits or concurs in omitting a material particular, is treated as falsifying the account or document.

7 Under section 34(2) of the Act, 'gain' and 'loss' are to be construed for the purposes of the Act as extending not only to gain or loss in money or other property, but also to any such gain or loss whether temporary or permanent; and 'gain' includes a gain by keeping what one has, as well as a gain by getting what one has not, and 'loss' includes a loss by not getting what one might get, as well as a loss by parting with what one has.

Liability of company officers for certain offences by company

8   Under section 18[6] of the Act, where the offences of obtaining property by deception, obtaining pecuniary advantage by deception or false accounting are committed by a body corporate and are proved to have been committed with the consent or connivance of any director, manager, secretary or other similar officer of the body corporate, or any person who was purporting to act in any such capacity, that person as well as the body corporate is guilty of the offence and is liable to be proceeded against and punished accordingly.

False statements by directors, etc

9   Under section 19 of the Act, where an officer of a body corporate or an unincorporated association (or person purporting to act as such), with intent to deceive members or creditors about its affairs, publishes or concurs in publishing a written statement or account which to that person's knowledge is or may be misleading, false or deceptive in a material particular, that person commits an arrestable offence.

Suppression, etc, of documents

10   Under section 20 of the Act, a person who dishonestly, with a view to gain whether personal or for another or with intent to cause loss to another, destroys, defaces or conceals any valuable security, any will or other testamentary document or any original document of, or belonging to, or filed or deposited in, any court of justice or any government department, commits an arrestable offence. Similarly, a person who dishonestly procures execution of a valuable security commits an arrestable offence. This applies in relation to the making, acceptance, endorsement, alteration, cancellation, or destruction in whole or in part of a valuable security, and in relation to the signing or sealing of any paper or other material in order that it may be made or converted into, or used or dealt with as a valuable security, as if that were the execution of a valuable security.

[6] There is no equivalent section in Northern Ireland legislation.

A valuable security means any document creating, transferring, surrendering or releasing any right to, in or over property, or authorising the payment of money or delivery of any property, or evidencing the creation, transfer, surrender or release of any such right, or the payment of money or delivery of any property, or the satisfaction of any obligation.

Example of an external auditor's inherent risk assessment

D

The items marked in bold are those areas particularly likely to have an impact on the risk of fraud. As you can see, this is a majority of the areas considered.

Risk factor	Low → High					Comments
	1	2	3	4	5	
Managerial issues						
Extent to which management comprises owner shareholders						
The financial position of the business						
The liquidity of the business						
Our assessment of the integrity of the management						
Extent of external use of the financial statements						
Management experience and knowledge to operate the business						
Extent of management turnover						
Emphasis on maintaining earning levels						

Risk factor	1	2	3	4	5	Comments
Management attitude about financial reporting						
Frequent changes of advisers						
Past experience as to adequacy of management control						
History of legal / regulatory breaches						
Remuneration levels appropriate to the nature and performance of the business						
Accounting environment						
Competence of accounting personnel						
Attitude of accounting personnel						
Likelihood of erroneous, inadequate or late financial information						
Degree to which material transactions or adjustments occur at or near the end of accounting periods						
Past evidence of window dressing						
Frequency and significance of hard to audit transactions						
Complex or new accounting policies						
Complexity of corporate and accounting structure relative to size of the business						
Disruptions or breakdowns in the accounting system						

Risk factor	1	2	3	4	5	Comments
Evidence that there are likely to be problems with the accounting records						
Business environment						
Nature of the industry – growth / decline, new / old						
Allegations and / or actions brought against company or management by third parties / regulators						
Changes in profitability / liquidity						
Compliance with terms of external finance						
Likelihood of disposal of a significant part of the business, or sale of interest by a significant investor						
Commercial threats to the business						
Intention to raise significant new finance						
Evidence of over trading						
Plans to make significant acquisitions / external investments						
Level of performance relative to business sector as a whole						
Audit issues						
Record of qualification						
Reporting of fundamental uncertainties, including going concern issues						

Risk factor	1	2	3	4	5	Comments
Relationship with senior management						
Expectation of difficulties in obtaining audit evidence						
Unusual or industry specialist transactions and practices which are hard to audit						
Possibility of money laundering						

Overall assessment	Minimal (1) Very Low (2) Low (3) Medium (4) High (5)

Explanation for assessment

Prepared By.................................... Date..

Example of an internal audit testing schedule

The following two documents are examples of the types of schedules that you might expect an internal audit department to use when completing their work. If work is badly recorded in an unstructured format it is likely to be difficult to reach proper conclusions about the state of controls checked. Using a format such as that below will help to ensure a methodical working pattern and recording of data.

Example of test for company with payroll contract

Control Objective That the payroll system is subject to a signed management contract with its payroll provider.
Evidence of Control Find signed copy of payroll contract.
Testing Purpose The purpose of the test is to ensure that an appropriate contract is in place for the company's payroll service

Test Period	Details of Test
Current year contract:	Determine: (1) That a signed contract is in place (2) That the contract includes a provision for payroll number expansion (3) That future accounting periods are covered (4) That appropriate performance indicators are in place (5) That appropriate control systems are embedded at the service provider

Test Outcomes

Test Evaluation / Conclusion

Matter for Management Attention

Auditor(s) Completing Test & Date	Reviewing Officer & Date

Example of company with agency staff

Control Objective

That the staff compliment is signed off as 'confirmed' prior to payments being made

Evidence of Control

Indicate whether control appear to operate

Testing Purpose

The purpose of the test is to ensure that all payroll payments to staff are confirmed prior to them being made.

Test Period	Details of Test
April 2001 – February 2002	(1) Obtain copies of schedules for the test period and ensure that all payment schedules have been duly 'authorised' as complete by the Finance Manager.

Test Outcomes

Test Evaluation / Conclusion

Matter for Management Attention

Auditor(s) Completing Test & Date	Reviewing Officer & Date

What to do if you suspect a fraud

(Provided by DS Lee Dinnell of the Hampshire Constabulary.)

Reporting cases to the police

Although the following is based upon a draft Memorandum of Understanding between ACPO and the newly formed NHS Counter Fraud Operational Services, it gives a good guide as to the information needed when referring matters to the police. Although many organisations will not have the luxury of an internal investigation department, there may be an investigation of a suspected fraud using either the internal staff available or an external consultant.

Referral of cases to the police

Ideally, cases that are referred to the police for investigation or prosecution will be made in the form of an evidential package, which should contain the information set out in the following table. There is a blank column to the right of the information required, so that you may use this as a checklist and cross-referencing tool should you have a suspected case of fraud that needs reporting.

Details required	Information/Document reference
A chronological summary of the allegations, including values of monies or goods involved and relevant dates.	
Full name and personal details, where known, of suspect/s.	
Status/job title where that person is/was employed or the relationship of that person to the business/company.	
All available details of any other parties suspected of involvement in the alleged criminal offences, including reasons for those suspicions.	
Full details of any investigations already undertaken.	
Names and contact details of all witnesses identified at the time of reporting to the police, including copies of any statements already taken.	
Details of any previous suspected offences or irregularities believed to have involved the suspected person/s.	
Details of any forensic examination which may have been undertaken or will need to be undertaken. (Material for or subject of a forensic examination must be preserved in a sterile state.)	
Copies of labelled and numbered documents supporting the allegation. The originals to be preserved and supplied on request.	

Details required	Information/Document reference
Copies of all statements, documents and any other material obtained from suspects.	
Details of any 'relevant' documents or other material which have been retained by a third party. (All such material will be retained in a durable and retrievable form.)	
To avoid confusion in cases which are to be undertaken as a joint investigation, or involving a parallel civil case, a written memorandum should be produced, showing at the outset the agreed roles and responsibilities of both parties.	

A request to the police accompanied by documentary evidence, which substantiates that there is a prima facie case, will serve to improve the efficiency of any investigation and enhance the probability of a police investigation being initiated and successfully completed.

Fraud Squads – National contact list

The list was compiled by the police in partnership with Experian.

Organisation	Postal Address	Telephone
An Garda Siochana	Garda Bureau of Fraud Investigation, 'C' Branch, Harcourt Square, Harcourt Street, Dublin 2.	00353 16771156
Avon & Somerset Constabulary	Fraud Squad, PO Box 37, Portishead, Bristol, BS20 8QJ	01275 818181
Bedfordshire Police	Fraud Squad, Woburn Street Police Station, Amptill, Bedfordshire MK45 2HX	01234 841212

Organisation	Postal Address	Telephone
Cambridgeshire Constabulary	Fraud Squad, PO Box 156, Huntingdon, Cambridgeshire PE18 8NP	01480 456111
Central Scotland Police	Fraud Unit, Police Office, Tullibody, FK10 2RF	01259 720592
Cheshire Constabulary	Fraud Unit, Charles Stewart House, 55 Museum Street, Warrington, Cheshire, WA1 1NE	01244 614868
City of London Police	Fraud Squad, 37 Wood Street, London, EC2P 2NQ	0171 601 2222
Cleveland Constabulary	Fraud Squad, PO Box 70, Ladgate Lane, Middlesbrough, Cleveland, TS8 9EH	01642 326326
Cumbria Constabulary	Commercial Fraud Unit, Police HQ, Carelton Hall, Penrith, Cumbria, CA10 2AU	01766 891999
Derbyshire Constabulary	Fraud Squad, 16 St. Mary's Gate, Derby, DE1 3JN	
Devon & Cornwall Constabulary	Fraud Squad, Devonport Police Station, Exmouth Road, Plymouth, Devon, PL1 4QH	01752 284501
Dorset Police	Commercial Branch, Police HQ, Winfrith, Dorset, T2 8DX	01929 462727
Dumfries & Galloway Constabulary	Criminal Investigations Department, Loreburn Street Police Station, Dumfries, DG1 1HP	01387 252112
Dun & Bradstreet Ltd	Customer Services Department, Holmers Farm Way, High Wycombe, Bucks, HP12 4UL	0161 228 7744
Durham Constabulary	Fraud Squad, Police HQ, Aykley Heads, Durham, DH1 5TT	0191 386 4929
Dyfed-Powys Police	Fraud Squad, Police HQ, PO Box 99, Carmarthen, Dyfed, SA31 2PF	01267 222 0202
Essex Police	PO Box 2, Police Headquarters, Springfield, Chelmsford, Essex, CM2 6DA	01245 491491
Fife Constabulary	Fraud Squad, Police Headquarters, Detroit Road, Glenrothes, Fife, KY6 2RJ	01592 418888

Organisation	Postal Address	Telephone
Gloucestershire Constabulary	Fraud Squad, Police HQ, Holland House, Lansdown Road, Cheltenham, Glos. GL51 6QH	01242 521321
Grampian Police	Fraud Squad, Police HQ, Queen Street, Aberdeen, AB9 1BA	01224 386000
Greater Manchester Police	Commercial Fraud Unit, Bradford park, 3 Bank Street, Clayton, Manchester, M11 4AA	0162 872 6657/8
Guernsey Police	Commercial Fraud Department, Police HQ, St. Peter Port, Guernsey, GY1 2QN	01481 725111
Hampshire Constabulary	Fraud Squad, Hamble Lane, Hamble, Southampton, Hampshire, SO31 4TS	01703 456464
Heddlu Gwent Police	Fraud Squad, Maindee Police Station, 81 Chepstow Road, Newport, Gwent, NP9 8BY	01633 843093
Hertfordshire Constabulary	Fraud Squad, Police HQ, Stanborough Road, Welwyn Garden City, Herts. AL8 6XF	01707 638183
Humberside Police	Fraud Section, Police HQ, Queens Gardens, Hull, HU1 3DJ	01482 597156
Isle of Man Constabulary	Fraud Squad, Police HQ, Glencrutchery Road, Douglas, Isle of Man, IM2 4RG	01624 631212
Kent County Constabulary	Fraud Squad, Police HQ, Sutton Road, Maidstone, Kent, ME15 9BZ	01622 690690
Lancashire Constabulary	Commercial Fraud Unit, PO Box 77, Hutton, Preston, Lancashire, PR4 5SB	017782 614444
Leicestershire Constabulary	Fraud & Commercial Branch, Hamilton Police Station, Colin Grundy Drive, Leics LE5 1FY	0116 222 2222
Lincolnshire Police	Fraud Squad, Police HQ, PO Box 999, Lincoln, LN5 7PH	01522 532222
Lothian & Borders Police	Company Fraud branch, Police HQ, Fettes Avenue, Edinburgh, EH4 1RB	0131 311 3131

Organisation	Postal Address	Telephone
Merseyside Police	Major Crime Unit – Fraud Wing, 222 Mather Avenue, Liverpool, L18 9TG	0151 777 3255
Metropolitan Police	Fraud Squad, Greenway House, 2 Richbell Place, Holborn London, WC1N 3LA	0171 230 1280
Ministry of Defence Police	Fraud Squad, Building 1071, MDP Wethersfield, Braintree, Essex, CM7 4AZ	01371 854476
Norfolk Constabulary	Fraud Squad, 1 Ferry Road, Norwich, Norfolk, NR1 1SU	01603 472423
North Wales Police	Fraud Branch, Police HQ, Glan Y Don, Colwyn Bay, Clwyd, LL20 8AW	01492 517171
North Yorkshire Police	Fraud Squad, County Police Office, Station Road, Tadcaster, North Yorkshire, LS14 9JR	01937 833213
Northamptonshire Police	Fraud Section, Police HQ, Wootton Hall, Northampton, NN4 0JQ	01604 700700
Northern Constabulary	Criminal Investigations Department, Police HQ, Perth Road, Inverness, IV2 3SY	01463 715555
Northumbria Police	Fraud & Commercial Squad, Sunderland Road, Felling, Tyne & Wear, NE10 9LQ	0191 454 7555
Nottinghamshire Constabulary	Fraud Squad, Century House, 428 Carlton Hill, Carlton, Nottingham, NG4 1QA	0115 953 3974
Royal Ulster Constabulary	Fraud Squad, RUC Strandtown, Brooklyn, Knock Road, Belfast, BT5 6LE	01232 650222
South Wales Constabulary	Fraud Squad, Police HQ, Bridgent, Glamorgan, CF31 3SU	01656 869470
South Yorkshire Police	Commercial Branch, Commerce Hse, Occupation Lane, Hackenthorpe, Sheffield, S12 4PQ	0114 220 2020
Staffordshire Police	Commercial Fraud Unit, Police HQ, Cannock Road, Stafford, ST17 0QG	01785 257717

Organisation	Postal Address	Telephone
States of Jersey Police	Commercial Branch, The Town Police Stn, Piquet Hse, 11 Royal Square, St. Helier, Jersey, JE2 4WA	01534 612612
Strathclyde Police	Fraud Squad, 923 Helen Street, Glasgow, G52 1EE	0141 532 2000
Suffolk Constabulary	Fraud Squad, Glenfield Court, Glenfield Avenue, Felixstowe, Suffolk, IP11 9JG	01473 383361
Surrey Police	Financial Investigation Unit, Mount Browne, Sandy Lane, Guildford, Surrey, GU3 1HQ	01483 571212
Sussex Police	Commercial Investigation Unit, Sussex House, Crowhurst Road, Hollingbury, Brighton, BN1 8AF	01273 859089
Tayside Police	Fraud Branch, PO Box 59, 4 West Bell Street, Dundee, DD1 9JU	01382 223200
Thames Valley Police	HQ Fraud Squad, Loddon Valley Police Stn, Rushey Way, Lower Earley, Reading, RG6 4PS	0118 918 1818
Warwickshire Constabulary	Fraud & Financial Unit, PO Box 4, Leek Wootton, Warwick, CV35 7QB	01926 415000
West Mercia Constabulary	Economic Crime Unit, Police HQ, PO Box 55, Hindlip Hall, Worcester, WR3 8SP	01905 723000
West Midlands Police	Fraud Squad, PO Box 52, Colmore Circus, Queensway, Birmingham, B4 6NQ	0121 626 5000
West Yorkshire Police	Fraud Squad, Laburnam Road, Wakefield, West Yorkshire, WF1 3QP	01924 375222
Wiltshire Constabulary	Police Headquarters, London Road, Devizes, Wiltshire, SN10 2DN	01380 722341

Criminal offences that may be appropriate for cases of fraud

Theft Act 1968

- Theft – dishonestly appropriating property belonging to another with the intention of permanently depriving the other of it.
- Obtaining property or pecuniary advantage by deception.

Theft Act 1978

- Dishonestly obtaining services from another by deception.
- Evading liability by deception.
- Dishonestly making off without payment where it is known that payment is required or expected on the spot and with intent to avoid payment.

False accounting (Theft Act 1978)

- To dishonestly destroy, deface, conceal or falsify any account or record or document made or required for any accounting purpose.
- In furnishing information for any purpose dishonestly to produce or make use of any account or any record or document, as above which, to the knowledge of the person producing or making use of it, is or may be misleading false or deceptive in a material particular, with a view to gain for oneself or another or with intent to cause loss to another.

Insolvency Act 1986

This act contains a number of Criminal Offences. Directors can be made liable for offences including:

- concealing the company's property to the value of £500 or more, or the concealment of any debt due to or from the company;
- the fraudulent removal of the company's property to the value of £500 or more;
- concealing, destroying, mutilating or falsifying any book or paper relating to the company's affairs;
- making or causing to be made any gift or transfer of the company's property with the intent to defraud creditors;
- failing to disclose or deliver up the company's property to the liquidator;
- making a material omission in any Statement of Affairs;
- making false representations to creditors;
- misuse of the company name.

Personal insolvency offences:

- non-disclosure of property to the Official Receiver or the Trustee;
- concealment or removal of property;
- concealment or falsification of books and papers;
- false statements or material omissions from statements;
- fraudulent disposal of property in the five years prior to bankruptcy;
- failure to keep proper accounts;
- absconding;
- fraudulent dealing with property obtained on credit, ie disposing of property in the 12 months prior to bankruptcy, that has not been paid for;
- gambling, if this has materially contributed to the insolvency;
- obtaining credit after bankruptcy of more than £250 or engaging in business in any name other than the name in which he was adjudged bankrupt, without disclosure.

Organisations that help with the pooling of data

CIFAS

Members of CIFAS are the major UK financial institutions – Banks, Building Societies, Retail Credit Grantors, Card Issuers etc. CIFAS has widened to include providers of Telecommunications Services and Insurance Companies.

The purpose of CIFAS is to prevent or limit fraud (crime) through members pooling information about specific incidents of fraud and attempted fraud. This exchange of data takes place on-line through participating agencies. Members have on-line access to at least one of the agencies, which are Equifax and Experian. In addition, because of the extensive use within the membership of the success-ful Hunter technology, MCL Software is also involved.

CIFAS data is used for one purpose only – the prevention and identi-fication of crime – and is not available for any other purpose.

Members of CIFAS are required to operate effective in house security procedures to enable fraud or attempted fraud to be identified and categorised according to agreed definitions. Basic information on such cases is then filed with their participating credit agency as a warning. The information is then transferred electronically between the agencies. When an address against which a warning has been entered is searched, by any other member, through any participating agency, the searching member is made aware of the warning, the fraud category, and the identity of the member filing the data. Additional 'Keys to Information' may also be provided. This indi-cates to the searching member the reason for filing and what further checks should take place. One of these is to contact the filing member for full details.

Once an application is identified as a further fraudulent attempt, the address is given a further CIFAS entry.

In certain circumstances, for example following the theft of ID documents, individuals may request a 'Protective Registration' of their address on CIFAS. This alerts members to the necessity to make further checks on the identity of any applicant using the address flagged. This may include contacting the CIFAS office to cross-check the information provided.

CIFAS membership involves both responsibilities and benefits. Members have a responsibility to contribute information by identifying, categorising and filing fraud cases on the database. In return for doing so they receive the benefit of system generated warnings previously filed by other members.

CIFAS has been consistently successful in protecting not only its membership but also the wider public from the effects of fraud.

Fraud healthcheck   I

This questionnaire is designed as a relatively quick way to achieve an overall picture of the level of fraud awareness and general controls within the organisation. In order to consider the more detailed question of controls and fraud prevention you will also need to consider the other areas discussed in the book.

General questions

Question	Answer	Comment
Is there a company fraud policy?		
Is fraud considered important at board level?		
Is fraud awareness training given to all directors (including non-executive directors)?		
Is the Combined Code on corporate governance followed (see Chapter 2 on Directors' Duties)?		
Is there an internal audit department, or an outsourced equivalent?		
Is there an audit committee?		

Question	Answer	Comment
Is fraud considered as part of an organisation-wide, risk review procedure?		
Is the risk review updated regularly and whenever there are indications of a major change in risk?		
Does suspected fraud always get reported to the police?		
Are staff involved in investigating suspected fraud fully trained in the requirements of PACE with regard to the requirements of evidence?		
Are civil as well as legal remedies sought to recover losses?		
Are employees clear as to what is allowed as a perk of the job and what is regarded as theft or fraud?		
Are references always taken up before staff are appointed?		
If agency/temporary staff are employed, are references taken up/checked with the agency?		
Where qualifications are claimed by applicants, are these checked to ensure that they are genuine?		
Are other controls with respect to staff recruitment in place (see Chapter 6, Payroll and expenses fraud)?		
Do internal controls operate as required by the organisation's policies?		
Are regular independent checks carried out to determine if controls operate correctly?		

Question	Answer	Comment
Is there a helpline for staff to ring regarding concerns on fraud?		
Is the helpline number widely publicised to staff?		
Are all staff trained in fraud awareness?		
Does someone in the organisation have the job of keeping up to date with the types of frauds that exist and the controls which can be implemented?		

Questions on the computer environment (general controls)

Question	Answer	Comment
Does access to computers always require a password?		
Are passwords hierarchical, only allowing access to areas required by the employee?		
Are passwords kept secret and not freely shared with colleagues or other third parties?		
Are passwords changed regularly with the system preventing the reuse of a password for a specified period?		
Are passwords a mix of letters and numbers (as these are more difficult to guess), especially for secure areas?		
Are only staff with special authority permitted to add any software or amend any software on the system and is this password controlled?		

Question	Answer	Comment
Are programmers/maintenance staff always separate from those using the applications who must not have authority to reprogram?		
Is all software backed up and kept off-site as well as on-site?		
Is all data backed up on a regular basis (at least daily and more often if there is a large volume of transactions)?		
Are back-ups kept off-site or at least in a fire proof safe?		
Are restore procedures checked regularly to ensure that they operate correctly?		
Is any software developed in-house properly developed and documented, including any amendments?		
Are all amendments to systems authorised at a senior level?		
Do all terminals have an auto-matic log-off after a set period (for sensitive systems such as finance, the log-off may need to be after just five minutes or so)?		
Does the organisation consider using new technology to fight fraud on a regular basis?		

Application controls

Application controls are the controls in existence in each individual application that operates on the computer system. They will therefore be varied but can be used to help ensure that fraud is prevented or detected. An example is given below in relation to a purchasing system.

Question	*Answer*	*Comment*
Can invoices only be entered for previously set up suppliers?		
Do only specific, senior members of staff have a password which allows them to add suppliers to the list?		
Are entries only accepted on the system when all relevant details have been completed (this may help to avoid dummy invoices being put on the system)?		
Where details of goods bought are input, are they matched with stock records to ensure that only goods received are paid for?		
Can invoices only be entered where authorised?		

Example fraud policy and response plan   J

Foreword

This document assumes that the organisation will designate or appoint an individual as the nominated officer whom staff may contact confidentially if they suspect a fraudulent act. To maintain openness and good corporate governance this individual will be independent of the organisation and will treat all contacts in accordance with the relevant legislation and the agreed protocol.

This fraud response policy needs to be read in conjunction with the organisation's memorandum and articles and related management and operational procedures.

An abridged version of this policy is available on the organisation's intranet. Full copies are available on request from human resources.

Managing the threat of fraud and corruption

Those charged with corporate governance are committed to managing risk, both real and potential, across the organisation.

The Board of Directors consider the management of fraud and corruption as a key element of its overall risk strategy.

This policy together with the policy on the 'Code of Business Conduct' is designed to both create an anti-fraud culture throughout the organisation and to provide guidance to staff of what to do in the case of a suspected fraud.

1. Managing the threat of fraud and corruption

1. Introduction

The board of directors has already implemented policies and procedures that reduce the likelihood of fraud occurring. These include Financial Regulations and documented financial procedures, which are reviewed on a regular basis and are overseen by a robust and effective Audit Committee.

The impact of Turnbull has meant that the responsibilities of Directors of listed companies has been widened to include formal risk assessment of the activities of the organisation and an annual statement by the Directors on the effectiveness of the system of internal controls.

The Directors regard this document as evidence that the organisation has proactively considered its risk of exposure to fraud and corruption and has installed management systems to deal with any occurrence.

This document is intended to provide direction and help to those officers and Directors who find themselves having to deal with suspected cases of theft, fraud or corruption. It gives a framework for a response and advice and information on various aspects and implications of an investigation. This document is not intended to provide direction on fraud prevention.

1.2 The organisation's values

The Code of Conduct of the organisation is underpinned by three core organisation values (public sector values).

Accountability: Everything done by those who work in the organisation must be able to stand the tests of external scrutiny, external audit, public judgements on propriety and professional codes of conduct.

Probity: Absolute honesty and integrity should be exercised in dealing with assets, staff, suppliers and customers.

Openness: The organisation's activities should be sufficiently public and transparent to promote confidence between the organisation and its staff and
its other shareholders.

All those who work in the organisation should be aware of, and act
in accordance with, these values.

Or private sector values

Honesty: The organisation and all its officers and employees
should act honestly at all times, in respect of their
dealings with or on behalf of the organisation.

Integrity: All officers and staff should be trustworthy.

Conflicts of Staff should make every effort to ensure that con-
interest: flicts of interest do not arise, or that where they do
appropriate officers are informed of the situation.

Confidentiality: Officers and employees should understand that
knowledge gained through the course of their
employment should be treated as confidential
unless there is a clear business case for its disclosure.

1.3 The Board of Directors' policy

The Board of Directors is committed to maintaining an honest, open
and anti-fraud culture within the organisation. It is also committed to
the elimination of any fraud and corruption within the organisation,
and to the rigorous investigation of any such cases.

The Directors wish to encourage anyone having reasonable suspicions of theft, fraud and corruption to report them to a designated
professionally qualified and INDEPENDENT adviser, namely

Insert name and contact details for designated person.
This may, for example, be the organisation's external auditors.

For these purposes 'reasonably held suspicions' shall mean any
suspicion other than those which are raised maliciously **and** found to
be groundless.

It is also the Board's policy, which will be rigorously enforced, that
no employee will suffer in any way as a result of reporting reasonably held suspicions.

1.4 Roles and responsibilities

Responsibility for theft, fraud and corruption management has been delegated by the Board of Directors to the Deputy Chief Executive. This officer shall also be responsible for informing third parties such as any relevant regulator, external audit or the police when appropriate. The Deputy Chief Executive shall inform the Chief Executive in all cases, inform the Audit Committee at the next available meeting and inform others on a strict 'need to know' basis.

The Deputy Chief Executive shall also seek advice from the independent specialist fraud investigator appointed by the organisation where the fraud and corruption exceeds or is estimated to exceed £50,000.

When, as part of an investigation, a member of staff is to be interviewed as a witness, then this interview will be undertaken by the independent fraud specialist but in accordance with the organisation's personnel procedures.

When, as part of an investigation, a member of staff is to be interviewed as a suspect, then this interview will be undertaken either by the independent fraud specialist in accordance with PACE 1984 (as amended) procedures and other relevant legislation or by the police.

When, as part of an investigation, an external individual/agency is to be interviewed, then this interview will be undertaken by the independent fraud specialist in the presence of an officer of the organisation.

When the independent fraud specialist is contacted by an internal or external 'whistle blower', then the latter will be treated in accordance with the legislation existent at the time of the investigation.

The Head of Human Resources shall advise those involved in the investigation in matters of employment law and in other procedural matters, such as disciplinary and complaints procedures, as requested.

Finally, the Board of Directors supports the view that all staff have a duty to protect the assets of the organisation including intellectual property rights, information, goodwill and property.

What to do when you suspect a fraud or corrupt practice – guidance for staff

The Directors wish to encourage anyone having reasonable suspicions of theft, fraud and corruption to report them to an appropriate officer within the organisation.

In the spirit of propriety and openness, the Directors have appointed a professionally qualified and INDEPENDENT adviser you can speak to if you wish, to discuss your concerns with someone outside the organisation.

It is also the Board's policy that no employee will suffer in any way as a result of reporting reasonably held suspicions.

2 Guidance to staff on fraud

As part of the Board of Directors' programme to enact all the elements of current best practice in corporate governance, this document is approved by the Board as outlining the organisation's policy and advice to employees in dealing with fraud or suspected fraud or other illegal acts involving dishonesty or damage to property.

2.1 The organisation's values

The Code of Conduct of the organisation is based on 3 fundamental premises: These are:

Accountability: Everything done by those who work in the organisation must be able to stand the tests of external regulatory scrutiny, external audit, public judgments on propriety and professional codes of conduct.

Probity: Absolute honesty and integrity should be exercised in dealing with assets, staff, suppliers and customers.

Openness: The organisation's activities should be sufficiently public and transparent to promote confidence between the organisation and its staff and its cohort.

All those who work in the organisation and attend the organisation as should be aware of, and act in accordance with, these values.

Or the following may be appropriate for the private sector

Honesty: The organisation and all its officers and employees should act honestly at all times, in respect of their dealings with or on behalf of the organisation.

Integrity: All officers and staff should be trustworthy.

Conflicts of   staff should make every effort to ensure that con-
interest: flicts of interest do not arise, or that where they do appropriate officers are informed of the situation.

Confidentiality: officers and employees should understand that knowledge gained through the course of their employment should be treated as confidential unless there is a clear business case for its disclosure.

Or insert organisation's own code of conduct

2.2   The Directors' policy

The Board of Directors is committed to maintaining an honest, open and anti-fraud culture within the organisation. It is also committed to the elimination of any fraud and corruption within the organisation, and to the rigorous investigation of any such cases.

The Directors wish to encourage anyone having reasonable suspicions of theft, fraud and corruption to report them to a Board designated professionally qualified and INDEPENDENT adviser, namely

Insert name and contact details for designated person.
This may, for example, be the organisation's external auditors.

For these purposes 'reasonably held suspicions' shall mean any suspicions other than those which are raised maliciously and found to be groundless.

It is also the Board's policy, which will be rigorously enforced, that no employee will suffer in any way as a result of reporting reasonably held suspicions.

You should be assured that there would be no recriminations against staff who report reasonably held suspicions. Victimising or deterring staff from reporting concerns is a serious disciplinary matter. Any contravention of this policy should be reported to the Deputy Chief Executive or Chairman of the Audit Committee.

Equally however, abuse of the process by raising malicious allegations could be regarded as a disciplinary matter.

Instructions to staff

If you believe you have good reason to suspect a colleague, contractor other person of a fraud or an offence involving the organisation (examples could include:

- theft of the organisation's property;
- abuse of/damage to the organisation's property;
- submitting fraudulent time and expense claims;
- setting up 'ghosts' ie a fictitious employee on the payroll;
- fictitious staff long-term sick claims;
- setting up a bogus company and arranging payments to that company;
- personal use of the organisation's facilities and utilities including computers;
- submitting false information on application forms and CVs;
- showing undue favour to contractors in procurement contracts;
- receiving 'unreasonable' inducements;
- selling intellectual property for personal gain;)

you should discuss it in the first place with your manager – unless you suspect the manager of involvement in the fraud, in which case you should go to the next more senior person. Alternatively you may first discuss the matter confidentially and anonymously with the organisation's nominated fraud officer.

If you and your manager or the organisation's nominated fraud officer decide between you that your suspicion may be justified, your manager (or nominated fraud officer) will report the matter to the Deputy Chief Executive. The organisation will then follow the fraud response plan to investigate and take appropriate action.

Under no circumstances should staff speak to representatives of the press, radio, TV or other third party unless expressly authorised by the Chief Executive.

Further information and a copy of the detailed response plan may be obtained from the office of the Deputy Chief Executive.

Fraud management response plan

The Directors will actively manage any suspected fraud and corruption carried out against the organisation in a structured, professional manner that is mindful of both the organisation's own policies and procedures and relevant legislation.

3.   The response plan

3.1   Introduction

The flowcharts in this section describe the organisation's intended response to a reported suspicion of fraud. The flowcharts are intended to diagrammatically describe the required procedure to follow that allow for evidence gathering and collation in a manner that will facilitate informed *initial* decisions by the organisation's Governing Board and its officers. Such a procedure will also ensure that evidence gathered will be admissible in any future criminal or civil actions.

Each situation is different, therefore the guidance in the flowcharts will need to be considered carefully in relation to the actual circumstances of each case before action is taken.

It should be added that under no circumstances should a member of staff speak, write or e-mail representatives of the press, TV, radio, or to another third party about a suspected fraud without the express authority of the Chief Executive. In such cases extreme care needs to be taken to ensure that nothing is done that could give rise to an action against the organisation for slander or libel.

In some cases, eg if a major diversion of funds is suspected, speed of response will be crucial to avoid financial loss. To facilitate this process the independently appointed fraud specialist will ensure that established lines of communication are in place with the appropriate regional police force.

Chart 1 – Reporting fraud

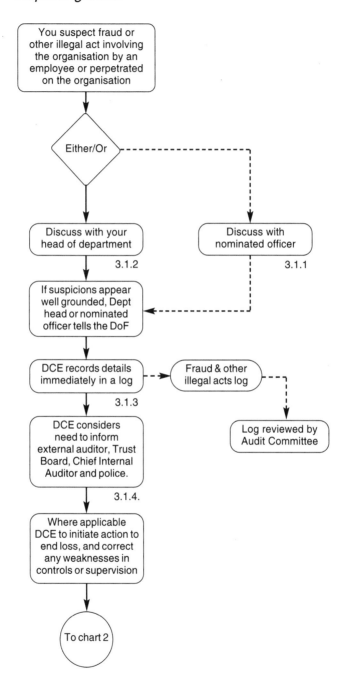

Chart 1 – Reporting fraud

3.1.1   Discussions with the nominated specialist fraud officer

The nominated specialist fraud officer can be contacted by any employee, and any other third party in strict confidence. The nominated officer is duty bound under criminal law to protect the source of his information and he/she will NOT disclose his source to any other party without your written consent. The nominated officer will be mindful of the organisation's policies and procedures and shall review and substantiate the source of your allegation before advising on his preferred course of action. The nominated officer will record the case in the organisation's Fraud Log, subject to the need to protect the identity of informants under the organisation's Whistle-Blowing Policy. The specialist fraud adviser to the organisation is:

Insert name and contact details for designated person.
This may, for example, be the organisation's external auditors.

3.1.2   Discuss with your head of department

An employee should normally discuss his/her suspicions with the head of department, unless circumstances dictate the use of the nominated fraud officer. The head of your department will then agree on the next course of action. If the suspicion seems well founded the head of department will inform the Deputy Chief Executive of the allegation.

If an employee suspects his/her department manager, the employee should report the suspicions to the Deputy Chief Executive or the independent nominated fraud specialist.

If the suspicion involves an executive director, the matter should be reported directly to the Chair of the Audit Committee.

3.1.3   The Deputy Chief Executive records details immediately in a log

The log will contain details of all reported suspicions, including those dismissed as minor or otherwise not investigated. It will also contain details of actions taken and conclusions reached. The Audit Committee will review this log at least once a year, which will report any significant matters to the Board of directors. The log WILL NOT contain the names of those officers making allegations who wish to remain anonymous.

3.1.4 Deputy Chief Executive considers the need to inform the Chief Executive, the Board of Directors, the Audit Committee, external audit, the nominated officer and the police.

The Deputy Chief Executive shall inform and consult the Chief Executive at the first opportunity in all cases of fraud and corruption. Where the loss exceeds or is estimated to exceed £50,000 the Deputy Chief Executive shall also advise the nominated fraud specialist.

Others will be advised on a need to know basis.

Chart 2 – Managing the investigation

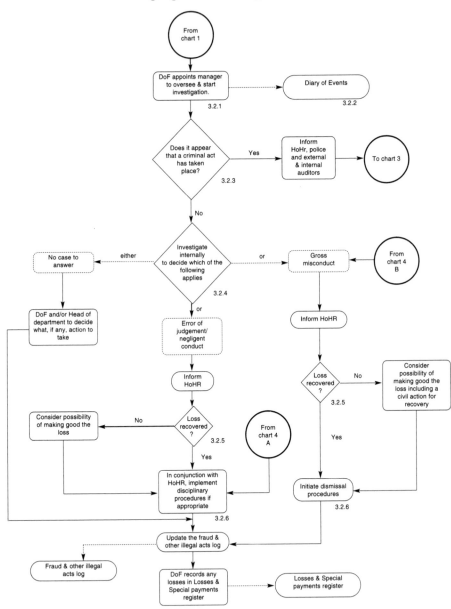

Chart 2 – Managing the investigation

3.2.1 Deputy Chief Executive appoints officer/agent to oversee investigation. Start investigation.

The circumstances of each case will dictate who will be involved and when. The following is intended to be general guidance to assist management in deciding the best course of action.

3.2.2 Diary of events

The Manager overseeing the investigation (referred to hereafter as the investigation manager) should initiate a Diary of Events to record the progress of the investigation.

3.2.3 Does it appear a criminal act has taken place?

In some cases this question may be asked more than once during an investigation. The answer to the question obviously determines if there is to be fraud investigation (or other criminal investigation). In practice it may not be obvious if a criminal act has taken place. If a criminal event is believed to have occurred the matter should be referred to the nominated fraud specialist for advice.

Section 4 gives further details of the commoner offences relevant to fraud.

3.2.4 Investigate internally

If it appears a criminal act has not taken place the next step should probably be an internal investigation to determine the facts, what if any disciplinary action is needed, what can be done to recover a loss and what may need to be done to improve internal control to prevent the event happening again.

Broadly, where no criminal act has taken place the event could have three outcomes.

The most serious would be where it is decided there was gross misconduct, this could involve dishonesty but not with a criminal intent. The outcome is likely to be dismissal if a member of staff is involved.

Less serious would be if it were decided that there was negligence or an error of judgment that caused the event. This is unlikely to lead to dismissal but might involve disciplinary procedures. (The chart here shows a link with Chart 4 where as a result of an investigation of suspected criminal activity it was considered there was sufficient evidence of gross misconduct to justify dismissal.)

Finally it may be concluded there is no case for an individual to answer.

In each case the investigation manager should consider what can be done to recover any loss and whether anything should be done to improve control to prevent the event happening again.

3.2.5 Recovering a loss

Where recovering a loss is likely to require a civil action it will probably be necessary to seek legal advice.

As a matter of policy where fraud and/or corruption has or there is reasonable grounds to suspect that an offence has taken place and a loss has been incurred, subject to the costs involved, the Governing Board will operate a 'triple tracking' approach to employees and a 'dual action' against external fraudsters.

The triple tracking will involve the following actions:

- disciplinary action against the employees in according with the organisation's Disciplinary Procedures,
- freezing of the employees assets and the instigation of civil recovery procedures,
- prosecution through the criminal courts.

The dual action approach involves the following:

- freezing of the external bodies assets and the instigation of civil recovery procedures,
- prosecution through the criminal courts.

The legal cost of any civil recovery will be considered at the outset by the Deputy Chief Executive. This officer will decide on a case by case basis on whether to seek redress via the civil court.

Where external legal advisers are used the investigation manager must ensure there is coordination between the various parties involved.

If the loss may be covered by insurance the investigation manager should inform the manager responsible for insurance matters.

3.2.6 Disciplinary/Dismissal procedures

The disciplinary procedures of the organisation have to be followed in any disciplinary action taken against an employee (including dismissal). This may involve the investigation manager recommending a disciplinary hearing to consider the facts, the results of the investigation (a formal report) and take appropriate action against the employee.

Where there are simultaneous criminal and and/or civil recovery actions also underway, then the evidence presented to the disciplinary hearing will need to be reviewed by appropriate College representatives and agents in the light of such pending actions.

Chart 3 – Gathering evidence

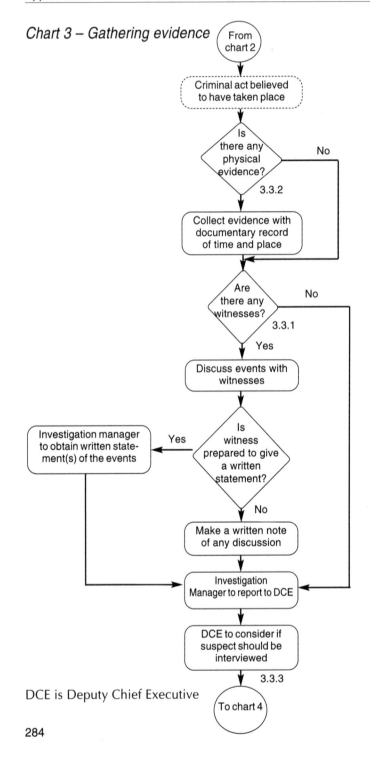

DCE is Deputy Chief Executive

Chart 3 – Gathering evidence

NB the chart cannot cover all the complexities of gathering evidence. Each case must be treated according to the circumstances taking professional advice if necessary.

3.3.1 Witnesses

If a witness to the event is prepared to give a written statement, it is best practice for the statement to be taken by an experienced investigator supported by an experienced member of staff, preferably from Personnel/HR. to take a chronological record using the witness's own words.

3.3.2 Physical evidence

Upon taking control of any physical evidence, it is very important that evidence is secured in an appropriate manner and that the continuity of evidence is maintained. A full and logical record must be made including the name of the securing officer, the time and place it is taken. If evidence consists of several items, for example many documents, each one should be tagged with a reference number corresponding to the written record.

3.3.3 Deputy Chief Executive to consider if suspect should be interviewed

The Deputy Chief Executive will consider the report (written or verbal) of the Investigation Manager and consider if the suspect should be interviewed. In this consideration he/she may consult others eg the Head of Human Resources, the Chief Executive and the police. If a crime is suspected, it is recommended that the police be consulted before any interview with the suspect takes place (see section 3.4.6).

Chart 4 – Interview procedure

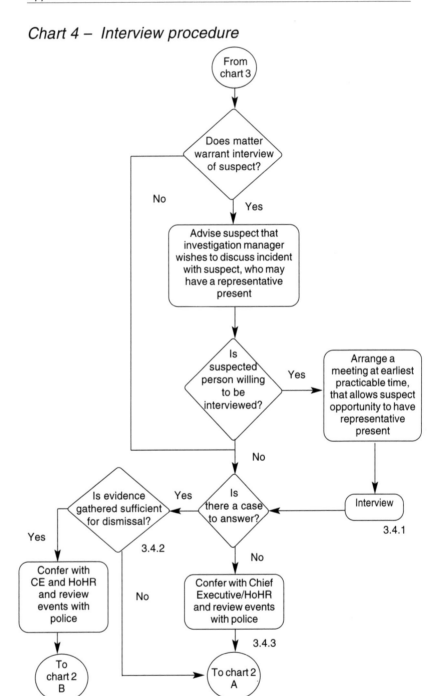

Chart 4 – Interview procedure

3.4.1 Interview

The requirements of the Police and Criminal Evidence Act (PACE) must be considered before any interview with a suspect is performed, since compliance with PACE determines whether evidence is admissible in criminal proceedings (see Sections 7 & 8). If in doubt about the requirement of PACE it is important to take specialist advice from your specialist fraud adviser.

3.4.2   Is evidence gathered sufficient for dismissal?

Under UK employment legislation dismissal must be for a 'fair' reason. The manner of dismissal must also be reasonable. It is therefore important that no employee should be dismissed without close consultation with the Head of Human Resources. The Head of Human Resources (HoHR) should be consulted about the provision of references for employees who have been dismissed or who have resigned following suspicions of a fraud. In all cases the organisation's disciplinary procedures should be followed (but see Section on 'triple tracking').

3.4.3   Review events with police

Whether or not the evidence gathered is thought sufficient for dismissal or prosecution, if there is evidence of fraud or another criminal offence, the Police should be consulted at this stage if they are not already involved.

3.4.4   Insurance

The possibility of recovering a loss through insurance should not be overlooked. There may be time limits for making a claim and in certain cases claims may be invalidated if legal action has not been taken.

3.4.5   More detailed investigation

The flowcharts cover the basics of reporting fraud, initial evidence gathering, interviewing, and management action. It will be necessary to decide whether further investigation is required, and if so, by what means it should be undertaken. The remainder of this chapter discusses some of the considerations in cases of fraud and corruption, with special regard to the often conflicting objectives of maximising control and minimising cost.

Points of good practice for any investigation include:

(1) Having an established line of communication with the local police or fraud squad.
(2) Identifying a manager responsible for the investigation. The manager should be independent of the area under investigation.
(3) Define the objectives of the investigation.
(4) Prepare an Operational Briefing.
(5) Define scope and timing of investigation and likely outputs.
(6) Seek advice where necessary from such sources as police, specialist investigators.
(7) Agree resources required for investigation.
(8) Define responsibilities.
(9) Budget and monitor resources used (costs and time).
(10) Monitor progress and inform as required.
(11) Consider lessons to be learned, eg how control can be improved.
(12) Draw up an action plan based on lessons learned.
(13) Keep proper records including a diary of events.

3.4.6 Involving the police

Some managers may mistakenly be reluctant to involve the police in the belief that:

- the are only interested if the alleged criminal offence is greater than a specific £ value; or that the police are not interested because of potentially complex issues involved that render little chance of a successful prosecution; or
- the organisation prefers to deal with the incident themselves, keeping it quiet while implementing dismissal and pursuing recovery through civil action; or
- that the police want hard evidence before they will pursue investigations, but when it is provided they advise that the rules of evidence have not been complied with; or
- the disciplinary process has to wait behind a police prosecution.

Protracted internal investigations often unnecessarily delay involving the police, thereby diminishing the value of cooperation with the police. However, properly organised investigations, conducted by accredited individuals supported by staff with an inside working knowledge, will be of great assistance to any subsequent police inquiry, and management should therefore not be discouraged from liaising with Police as soon as the issues involved are identified.

The decision to involve the police will include the following considerations:

(1) The requirements of this policy document.
(2) Whether the investigation requires further resources to conclude.
(3) The means to recover losses through civil actions.
(4) Prosecution of the perpetrator(s) through criminal action.
(5) Disciplinary action and dismissal of the perpetrator(s) (through formal disciplinary procedures).
(6) Procedures for the preservation of evidence.
(7) Management of public relations.
(8) Potential corporate seriousness of the malpractice.
(9) Whether the malpractice is fraud.
(10) Number and seniority of the persons involved.
(11) Apparent complexity of the case.
(12) Whether the malpractice is thought to be continuing.
(13) Involvement of individuals or organisations outside the organisation.
(14) Need to display deterrent action.

Additional advice

4. Investigation resource options

After completion of initial fact finding in accordance with procedures given in the flowcharts, the following options for resourcing an investigation are available to the organisation. These options are not mutually exclusive. In complex cases a number of different parties will need to be involved.

Action	Advantages	Disadvantages
No action required	No incremental cost	Fails to allay suspicions, deter or recover lost assets Clear message to staff that 'they can get away with it' Possible adverse publicity if suspicion eventually becomes public
Use spare capacity within the organi-sation to investigate	No incremental cost Entirely controlled by the Organisation	Lack of independence Lack of knowledge of PACE/ evidence gathering Little or no investigative experience May delay involving the police until it is too late.
Use Internal Audit to investigate	Sometimes good knowledge of investigations, PACE and evidence gathering Familiar with the Organisation Can be controlled by the Organisation	Cost Sometimes little knowledge of evidence gathering processes or PACE.
Use Personnel to assist in staff matters	Familiar with the Organisation Can be controlled by the Organisation Good knowledge of Organisation pro-cedures relating to employment and of relevant employment law	

Action	Advantages	Disadvantages
Use External Audit to investigate	Independent	Cost
	Knowledge of Investigative Procedures	Further from the control of the Organisation
	Familiar with the Trust	Possibly limited knowledge of evidence gathering processes and insufficient investigative expertise.
Use an external specialist consultancy to investigate eg specialist accredited fraud investigators, forensic specialists or lawyers	Independent	Cost
	Knowledgeable on the rules of evidence and evidence gathering processes, together with investigative expertise.	Lack of existing knowledge of the Organisation
	Can be controlled by the Organisation	
	Can advise on dealing with the media	
Call the Police	No incremental cost	Potentially little control over the investigation
	Independent	Goal tends to be gathering evidence for conviction, which may be different from the objective
	Good knowledge of PACE	Greater possibility of publicity, which may or may not be adverse
	Access to large resources	
	Powers extend beyond the confines of the Organisation	Possible lack off sensitivity to Organisation requirements
	Can assist with dealing with the media	Difficult to revoke

4.1   The law and its remedies

Criminal law may impose sanctions on the defendant for causing loss, while Civil law may assist the organisation to recover its loss.

In Civil law the method of concealment (in the case of fraud) is unlikely to be a key factor in the value of compensation or the drafting of the statement of claim.

In Criminal law, the nature of the deceit is highly relevant in the framing of charges, but the law is not primarily concerned with restitution or recovery of the proceeds of fraud or theft – although there are statutory powers to award compensation and to order restitution or forfeiture in some circumstances. However, criminal law now requires the financial benefits (to the villain) to be quantified as part of the investigation process. The proceeds direct, and indirect, can now be seized and dealt with by court of trial.

There is no reason why the criminal prosecution and civil process cannot be taken at the same time if the evidence supports such action. But there are dangers in unilateral uncoordinated action.

4.2   Civil law remedies

The following is a brief description of some of the commoner civil law remedies. It is not comprehensive and legal advice should be sought before action is taken.

4.3   Monies had and received

The claim will refer to funds of the plaintiff, which have been 'had and received' by the defendant at the plaintiff's expense – and will seek their recovery.

4.4   Interest

The plaintiff may be entitled to interest on the amount lost, and there are claims for interest under court rules and statute.

4.5   Tracing

Tracing is an equitable remedy for the recovery of assets. Its meaning is that the trail by which assets have been removed must be followed through the hands they pass through after leaving control of the plaintiff.

4.6 Freezing Order or Restraint Order

In some cases a court order can be used to freeze the assets of a person suspected of fraud or a person who has been convicted of a criminal offence in respect of their fraudulent activity. A Mareva Injunction (now known as a freezing order may be used in conjunction with criminal or civil proceedings. A Restraint Order can only be related to criminal proceedings, when it may be a simpler alternative to a Freezing Order where proceedings have been or are about to be instituted.

4.7   Damages for deceit

A defendant may become liable in tort to the plaintiff for damages arising out of the act, and if the plaintiff can establish this liability, there is entitlement to be put back into the position that would have been if the tortious act had not been committed. If successful, this claim may result in the award of damages beyond mere recovery of assets stolen.

4.8   Criminal law

The following are brief descriptions of some of the criminal offences most relevant in this context. It is not comprehensive, and legal advice should be sought before action is taken.

4.9   Theft

The misappropriation of Trust assets for gain or otherwise.

> Section 1 Theft Act 1968 A person who dishonestly appropriates property belonging to another with the intention of permanently depriving the other of it.

4.10 Fraud

English law does not specifically define fraud, however, Buckley J's description in *Re London and Globe Finance Ltd* encapsulates the two key ingredients: *'to defraud is to deprive by deceit'* thereby underlining the two essential elements in fraud:

- deception or concealment, and
- deprival or loss to the victim.

The following are the most frequently used definitions:

> Section 15 Theft Act 1968 A person who by any deception dishonestly obtains property belonging to another with the intention of depriving the other of it.

> Section 16 Theft Act 1968 A person who by any deception dishonestly obtains for himself or another any pecuniary advantage.

This offence is committed where a person obtains employment or increased remuneration, for example by falsely stating qualifications or professional history.

> Section 17(1) Theft Act 1968 (False Accounting) A person who dishonestly with a view to gaining for himself or another or with intent to cause loss to another
> (a) destroys, defaces, conceals or falsifies any account or any record or document made or required for any accounting purpose.
> or
> in furnishing information for any purpose produces or makes use of any account or any such record or document as aforesaid, which to his knowledge is or may be misleading, false or deceptive in any material particular.

This is a very wide ranging offence dealing with fraudulent transactions.

In criminal law, every individual element of the statutory wording must be proved beyond reasonable doubt. The essential different between theft and criminal deception is reflected in the two terms 'appropriates' and 'by deception obtains'.

Under s 15, for 'deception' to be proved it must be established that the proposition on which the victim acted was false and that the defendant knew the proposition to be false. Secondly, this section requires evidence of the obtaining ownership, possession or control of property and includes obtaining for another person or enabling another person to obtain or retain property.

Essentially, s 15 is used in circumstances where ownership of the property concerned has been gained by the accused with the consent of the owner.

4.11   Corruption

The definition (in the context of the Prevention of Corruption Acts) is: the offering, giving, soliciting or acceptance of an inducement or reward which may influence the action of any person.

4.12   Damage

Relates to arson, vandalism or sabotage of property, including computer systems and records.

> S1(1) Criminal Damage Act 1971 Any person who without lawful excuse destroys or damages any property belonging to another intending to destroy or damage such property, or being reckless as to whether any such property would be destroyed or damaged.

There are many other offences dealing with criminal activity.

4.13   Evidence

For the purpose of criminal proceedings, the admissibility of evidence is governed by the Police and Criminal Evidence Act (PACE). For non-criminal (ie civil or disciplinary) proceedings, PACE does not apply, but should nevertheless be regarded as best practice. Interview procedure is covered in the next section.

The collection of evidence must be coordinated if several parties are involved in an investigation, eg internal audit, police and solicitors. Evidence gathering requires skill and experience and professional guidance should be sought where necessary. There is a considerable amount of case law concerning the admissibility of evidence.

Documentary evidence should be properly recorded, it will need to be numbered and include accurate descriptions of when and where is was obtained and by and from whom. In criminal actions evidence on or obtained from electronic media needs a document confirming its accuracy.

4.14 Interviews

The approach taken in an interview situation depends on who is doing the interview, what the purpose is and the likely outcome.

In the first instance the interview is likely to be conducted by a manager whose purpose is to find out the facts. The manager has the right to ask an employee to account for his actions in respect of that employment. For this reason it is important to involve Human Resources before interviewing a suspect if the manager is not experienced in such situations.

It should be a gross misconduct/dismissal offence if the employee refuses to answer questions about his/her actions as an employee. If the employee, knowing the criminal law, refuses to answer on the grounds that he/she might incriminate himself, that is his/her right, and if he/she asks that questions he/she should be told so. He/she can still be dismissed.

This interview should not be under caution. However, in certain circumstance a caution by an appropriately qualified officer under PACE, may need to be given especially. It should be noted that if a manager starts the interview with a caution, he/she is telling the suspect that he/she does not have to answer legitimate management questions (but the judge will instruct the jury that inferences may be made for any refusal to answer reasonable questions).

An interview under caution should not be considered unless it is conducted by an appropriately qualified officer. Where an arrest is likely the police need to be involved in the process.

If the question of an interview under caution arises during a disciplinary procedure, then the requirement of PACE must be met from the point of caution.

All interviews must be conducted fairly. In particular comments such as 'if you do not tell me the truth you will get the sack' will render any evidence obtained inadmissible under Section 78 PACE.

Interviews conducted by inappropriately trained managers may be admissible in a criminal trial at the discretion of the trial Judge Section 78 PACE. The question of fairness will always be a crucial point. Having said that, current criminal case law is moving towards absolute exclusion of such interviews in a criminal process. This should not deter management from carrying out an internal interview to find out what happened. It is the right of the organisation to do so.

The Human Resources Department should be advised of interviews taking place and consulted, particularly for interviews of witnesses, if advice is required on the procedure to be followed.

It should be noted that investigations carried out prior to an individual being charged are open to a discovery motion by that individual's defence.

4.15 Interview procedure

Where an interview takes place under caution the following is a summary of the procedure to be followed. This procedure should not however be regarded as authoritative and interviewers should ensure they understand the requirements of PACE fully before initiating an interview.

It is important that the suspected individual is advised of the reason for requesting the interview, and told that anything he/she says may be used as evidence against him/her. This verbal statement *must* be given as follows:

> 'You do not have to say anything, but it may harm your defence if you do not mention, when questioned, something which you may wish to rely on later in court. The Court may make an inference from your refusal to speak. Anything you do say may be given in evidence.'

It is also critical that the suspect(s) be told that he/she is not under arrest, and may leave the interview at any time.

There should be a second person with the interviewer, ideally from Human Resources, who will make a contemporaneous record of all that is said by the questioner and suspect. The suspect must be advised he/she has a right to legal representation. In addition, if the suspected person has a representative present, this person may also wish to make a written record. A tape recorder may be used for recording the interview provided this is done overtly.

Once the interview is over, the suspected person should be given an opportunity to read the written record and be asked to initial any crossings out or alteration as well as sign the bottom of each page in acknowledgment of its accuracy. (If they are unable to read, their representative, or in his/her absence the writer, should read the record back). Should the suspect decline to sign the record, a note to that effect should be made at the conclusion of writing (on the last page), signed by the writer.

All persons present in the interview should be listed at the header to the record, and all should sign to acknowledge the accuracy of what was said.

5. Your independent adviser

Detailed advice on the workings of PACE and other relevant legislation should be sought from your specialist fraud adviser.

For specialist advice of fraud and corruption contact:

Insert name and contact details for designated person.
This may, for example, be the organisation's external auditors.

HM Treasury Model Fraud Policy Statement: Short Version K

Introduction

The department requires all staff at all times to act honestly and with integrity and to safeguard the public resources for which they are responsible. Fraud is an ever-present threat to these resources and hence must be a concern to all members of staff. The purpose of this statement is to set out your responsibilities with regard to the prevention of fraud.

What is fraud?

No precise legal definition of fraud exists; many of the offences referred to as fraud are covered by the Theft Acts of 1968 and 1978. The term is used to describe such acts as deception, bribery, forgery, extortion, corruption, theft, conspiracy, embezzlement, misappropriation, false representation, concealment of material facts and collusion. For practical purposes fraud may be defined as the use of deception with the intention of obtaining an advantage, avoiding an obligation or causing loss to another party.

Responsibilities

The department is responsible for:

(a) developing and maintaining effective controls to prevent fraud;
(b) carrying out vigorous and prompt investigations if fraud occurs;

(c) taking appropriate legal and/or disciplinary action against perpetrators of fraud;

(d) taking disciplinary action against supervisors where supervisory
failures have contributed to the commission of the fraud

Managers are responsible for:

(e) identifying the risks to which systems and procedures are
exposed;

(f) developing and maintaining effective controls to prevent and
detect fraud;

(g) ensuring that controls are being complied with.

Individual members of staff are responsible for:

(h) acting with propriety in the use of official resources and in the
handling and use of company funds whether they are involved
with cash or payments systems, receipts or dealing with contractors or suppliers;

(i) reporting details immediately to their line manager (or next most
senior manager) if they suspect that a fraud has been committed
or see any suspicious acts or events.

Ethics and conduct of staff

Civil Servants are servants of the Crown and owe a duty of loyal
service to the Crown as their employer. As stewards of public funds
civil servants must have, and been seen to have, high standards of
honesty, propriety and integrity in the exercise of their duties. Staff
should not receive gifts, hospitality or benefits of any kind from a
third party which might be seen to compromise their personal judgement or integrity.

HM Treasury Model Fraud
Policy Statement: Long Version L

Introduction

The department requires all staff at all times to act honestly and with integrity and to safeguard the public resources for which they are responsible. Fraud is an ever-present threat to these resources and hence must be a concern to members of staff. The purpose of this statement is to set out your responsibilities regarding both the prevention of fraud and the procedures to be followed where a fraud is detected or suspected.

Definitions

In law there is no specific offence of fraud; many of the offences referred to as fraud are covered by the Theft Acts of 1968 and 1978. The term is used to describe such acts as deception, bribery, forgery, extortion, corruption, theft, conspiracy, embezzlement, misappropriation, false representation, concealment of material facts and collusion. For practical purposes fraud may be defined as the use of deception with the intention of obtaining an advantage, avoiding an obligation or causing loss to another party.

Obviously fraud can be perpetrated by persons outside as well as inside an organisation. The criminal act is the attempt to deceive and attempted fraud is therefore treated as seriously as accomplished fraud.

Computer fraud is where information technology equipment has been used to manipulate progams or data dishonestly (for example, by altering substituting or destroying records, or creating spurious records), or where the use of an IT system was material factor in the perpetration of fraud. Theft or fraudulent use of computer time and resources is included in this definition.

The department's responsibilities

The department's responsibilities are set out in Chapter 37 of *Government Accounting:*

> 'Departments should develop and maintain effective controls to prevent fraud and to ensure that if it does occur it will be detected promptly. If fraud occurs departments must carry out a vigorous and prompt investigation. They should take the appropriate legal and/or disciplinary action in all cases where that would be justified; and they should make any necessary changes to systems and procedures to ensure that similar frauds will not happen again. Investigation should consider as a matter of course whether there has been a failure of supervision; and appropriate disciplinary action should be taken where supervisory failures have occurred. Departments should establish systems for recording and subsequently monitoring all discovered cases of fraud.'

Although [the Accounting Officer] bears overall responsibility and is liable to be called to account for specific failures, these responsibilities fall directly on line management and many involve *all* of the department's staff.

Line managers' responsibilities

Line managers are responsible for ensuring that an adequate system of internal control exists within their areas of responsibility and that controls operate effectively. The responsibility for the prevention and detection of fraud, therefore, rests primarily with managers. There is a need for all managers to assess the types of risk involved in the operations for which they are responsible; to review and test the control systems for which they are responsible regularly; to ensure that controls are being complied with; and to satisfy themselves that their systems continue to operate effectively.

[Internal Audit] is available to offer advice and assistance on control issues as necessary. In terms of establishing and maintaining effective controls it is generally desirable that:

(a) there is a regular rotation of staff, particularly in key posts;
(b) wherever possible, there is a separation of duties so that control of a key function is not vested in one individual;
(c) backlogs are not allowed to accumulate; and
(d) in designing any new system, consideration is given to building in safeguards against internal and external fraud.

Fraud response plan

The department has prepared a fraud response plan which can act as a checklist of actions and a guide to follow in the event of fraud being suspected. It covers:

• How to conduct preliminary enquiries
• Who to report to
• How to secure the evidence
• When and how to contact the police
• How to prevent losses
• How to initiate recovery action.

Fraud detection

Line managers should be alert to the possibility that unusual events or transactions could be symptoms of fraud or attempted fraud. Fraud may also be highlighted as a result of specific management checks or be brought to management's attention by a third party. Additionally, irregularities occasionally come to light in the course of audit reviews.

Irrespective of the source of suspicion, it is for line management to undertake an initial enquiry to ascertain the facts. This enquiry should be carried out as speedily as possible after suspicion has been aroused; prompt action is essential. The purpose of the initial enquiry is to confirm or repudiate the suspicions which have arisen so that, if necessary, further investigation may be instigated. [Internal Audit] is available to offer advice on any specific course of action which may be necessary.

The factors which gave rise to the suspicion should be determined and examined to clarify whether a genuine mistake has been made

303

or an irregularity has occurred. An irregularity may be defined as any incident or action which is not part of the normal operation of the system or the expected course of events. Preliminary examination may involve discreet enquiries with staff or the review of documents. It is important for staff to be clear that any irregularity of this type, however apparently innocent, will be analysed.

If initial examination confirms the suspicion that a fraud has been perpetrated, then to prevent the loss of evidence which may provide essential for subsequent disciplinary action or prosecution, management should take steps to ensure that all original documentation is preserved in a safe place for further investigation. Additionally, the department may suspend any officer involved pending the outcome of an investigation. Suspension itself does not imply guilt; it is another safeguard to prevent the removal of destruction of evidence.

Staff responsibilities

Every member of staff has a duty to ensure that public funds are safeguarded, whether they are involved with cash or payments systems, receipts, stocks or dealings with contractors or suppliers. Staff should alert their line manager where they believe the opportunity for fraud exists because of poor procedures or lack of effective oversight. In addition it is the responsibility of every member of staff to report details immediately to [their line manager or next most senior person] if they suspect that a fraud has been committed or see any suspicious acts or events. Staff should also assist in any investigations by making available all relevant information and by co-operating in interviews.

Personal conduct

As stewards of public funds civil servants must have, and be seen to have, high standards of personal integrity. Staff should not accept gifts, hospitality or benefits of any kind from a third party which might be seen to compromise their integrity. The department subscribes to the seven principles of public life set out in the Nolan Committee's first report, *Standards in Public Life.*

Disciplinary action

After proper investigation the department will take legal and/or disciplinary action in all cases where it is considered appropriate. Departmental policy generally in relation to proven frauds or suspected frauds which come to light, whether perpetrated by a member of staff or by persons external to the organisation, is that the case will be referred to the police at the earliest possible juncture. The department will co-operate fully with police enquiries and these may result in the offender(s) being prosecuted. Steps should be taken to attempt to recover any losses resulting from the fraud. A civil action against the perpetrator may be appropriate. The investigations described above will also consider whether there has been any failure of supervision. Where this has occurred appropriate disciplinary action will be taken against those responsible.

Learning from experience

Where a fraud has occurred management must take any necessary changes to systems and procedures to ensure that similar frauds will not recur. The investigation may have pointed up where there has been a failure of supervision, breakdown or an absence of control. Internal Audit is available to offer advice and assistance on matters relating to internal control, if considered appropriate.

Conclusion

The circumstances of individual frauds will vary. But it is important that all are vigorously and promptly investigated and that appropriate action is taken. To repeat, the department views fraud very seriously.

Useful websites and bibliography

Organisations with anti-fraud information

URL	Organisation
www.ncis.co.uk	General details about the National Criminal Intelligence Service, including contact details.
www.police.uk	Details of all UK police forces, locations, contact points etc.
www.cityoflondon.gov.uk/citypolice	Pictures of suspects, information about city-based crimes.
www.usps.gov/websites/depart/inspect/consmenu.htm	Information on chain letters, pyramids and similar scams on the US Post Office Consumer Fraud site.
www.hmso.gov.uk	Government bills, statutory instruments, etc.
www.official-documents.co.uk	Access to official reports published by various Government Departments.

URL	Organisation
www.thecentralregister.co.uk	Provides a list of persons prohibited under the Financial Services Act 1986 from carrying on a business regulated under FSA 1986 and being employed by a company which is regulated under FSA 1986 (50p per search).
www.TruSecure.com	Security alerts, the latest information on viruses, computer security, helplines and forums.
www.gocsi.com	Computer Security Institute Testimony, surveys, guidebooks and other educational literature on computer security from an international information security organisation.
www.bbb.org	Better Business Bureau
www.cardwatch.org.uk	Card fraud information site
www.fraud.org.uk	Umbrella site with lots of fraud information.
www.companieshouse.gov.uk	Basic information on current and recently dissolved companies, previous company names, incorporation details, Liquidator's names and disqualified directors.

URL	Organisation
www.hmce.gov.uk	Customs website with information on avoiding and reporting fraud.
www.asb.org.uk	UK accounting standards body with information on UITFs and where to get the standards.
www.apb.org.uk	UK Auditing Practices Board site with information on how to get auditing standards.
www.abi.org.uk	Association of British Insurers.
www.apacs.org.uk	Organisation responsible for automatic payment systems – BACS, CHAPS, DDs etc.
www.sfo.gov.uk	Serious Fraud Office – includes case studies of frauds.
www.londonstockexchange.com	Information on investments and markets.
www.fsa.gov.uk	Financial Services Authority – a huge amount of information, including money laundering regulations.
www.investorwords.com	Contains huge glossary of financial terms to help understand complex financial documents.

URL	Organisation
www.scambusters.org	Common scams to be wary of, many from a personal rather than corporate fraud point of view, but useful nonetheless.
www.fbi.gov/hq/cid/fc/sitemap/sitemap.htm	FBI's site with warning information on fraud.
www.met.police.uk/police/mps/so/so6.htm	Metropolitan Police fraud information site.
www.icaew.co.uk/library/index.cfm?AUB=TB2I_31352	Institute of Chartered Accountants' library link to all things to do with fraud and money laundering.
www.acca.co.uk	Association of Chartered Certified Accountants – lots of fraud articles.
www.cima.org.uk	Excellent fraud information, including a detailed guide to civil recovery.
www.cipfa.org.uk	Chartered Institute of Public Finance Accountants' website, including some fraud information from the public sector viewpoint.
www.theiia.org	The Institute of Internal Auditors' website, with information on role of internal auditors with regard to fraud and other aspects.
www.fsa.gov.uk/pubs/speeches/sp17.html	Speech on fraud.
www.uk-fraud.info/welcome.htm	National Working Group on Fraud – fraud reduction website.

URL	Organisation
www.charitycommission.gov.uk	Information on charities including warnings on fraud and information on risk analysis
www.e-buyersguide.com	E-buyers guide.
www.inventorfraud.com	National Inventor Fraud Centre.
www.europa.eu.int	The European Union's website. Lots of information about the EU including fraud and laws and regulations.

Companies providing anti-fraud and security products

URL	Organisation
www.carratu.com	Staff vetting and security company.
www.necho.com	Expense management system provider.
www.captura.com	Expense management system provider.
www.concur.com	Expense management system provider.
www.cevas.com	Accounts outsourcing and expense management software.
www.networksecurity.co.uk	Supplier of security equipment including CCTV and perimeter security.
www.sas.com	Data mining and fraud detection software.

URL	Organisation
www.cybersource.com	Fraud protection software on credit card transactions etc.
www.bio4.co.uk	Biometrics security products such as face, iris and fingerprint technology.
www.nochex.com	E-money website.
www.digicash.com	E-cash company now owned by Infospace.
www.geocities.com	Security company providing tags for retail companies among other products.
www.sophos.com	Virus and intrusion detection software, including firewalls.
www.mcafee.com	Virus and intrusion detection software, including firewalls.
www.symantec.com	Virus and intrusion detection software, including firewalls.
www.graydon.co.uk	Credit reference company.
www.dandb.com	Credit reference and corporate information company.
www.eliashim.com	Smart card and anti-virus products and downloads.
www.tis.com	Details about firewall technology and products, background on internet security scanners and job opportunities in computer security.

URL	Organisation
www.i2.com	E-business solutions.
www.sctc.com	Technical and product information about firewalls.
www.securid.com	Information about smart cards and other advanced security products.
www.equifax.co.uk	Supplier of credit reports, including anti-fraud information.
www.blandy.co.uk	Firm of solicitors that provides litigation services.
www.cvdfk.com	Firm of chartered accountants that provides fraud awareness training.

Articles and other information about fraud

URL	Organisation
news.bbc.co.uk/hi/english/static/in_depth/business/2002/enron/timeline/default.stm	Detailed articles about the Enron collapse.
www.bbc.co.uk	Search for fraud for lots of information and articles.
www.ft.com	FT website with all sorts of financial information.
www.telegraph.co.uk	Telegraph website with news and articles – search for fraud to find relevant articles.

URL	Organisation
www.guardian.co.uk	Some fraud articles.
www.thetimes.co.uk	Lots of fraud articles.
www.skynews.co.uk	Articles on fraud.

Search engines

URL	Organisation
www.altavista.com/	Helps find answers and other relevant sites.
www.lycos.com	Helps find answers and other relevant sites.
www.webcrawler.com	Searches other search engines to find answers.
www.vivisimo.com	Metasearch engine, US based but extensive search results that will return lots of fraud information.
www.ask.co.uk	Natural English search engine.
www.yahoo.com	Helps find answers and other relevant sites.

Utilities

URL	Organisation
babelfish.altavista.com	Provides a reasonably good translation service for French, German, Spanish, Italian and Portuguese.
www.royalmail.co.uk	Postcode and address checker.

URL	Organisation
www.infospace.co.uk	People, e-mail and telephone numbers.
uk.multimap.com	Street level maps of UK (and USA).
www.192.com	The ability to reverse search on a telephone number (not ex-directory).
www.illumine.co.uk	Mindmapping software.

Bibliography

Money Laundering: *Guidance notes for Chartered Accountants* – The Institute of Chartered Accountants in England and Wales, Technical release 15/99

Fraud Watch – A guide for Business – Ian Huntington & David Davies (KPMG), Accountancy Books

Fraud: Risk and Prevention – City of London Police, Metropolitan Police & Ernst & Young (A business guide on types of fraud, recognising the warning signs, minimising the risk and dealing with fraud.)

Managing Risk on the Net – What Internet Merchants need to know – CyberSource Corporation, 2000

Preventing Corporate Embezzlement – Paul Shaw & Jack Bologna, Butterworths Heinemann

The Fraud Advisory Panel – Third Annual Report 2000/2001

Auditing Standards and Guidance for Members – The Institute of Chartered Accountants in England and Wales, 2001

Fighting Public Sector Fraud and Corruption in London – The Annual Report of the Public Sector Steering Group, 1999/2000

Fraudstop – The City of London Police in partnership with Coopers & Lybrand, November 1995

Fraud – The Centre for Retail Research
(Estimated annual UK fraud costs 1998/1999.)

Managing the Risk of Fraud – A guide for managers
(Short and long versions of the Model Fraud Policy Statement.)

Press Releases – British Retail Consortium, 27 June 2001

Strategic Risk Management Framework – The Charity Commission
for England and Wales

Cybercrime survey 2001 – CBI The voice of business
(Making the information superhighway safe for business.)

Fighting fraud: a guide for SME – The Fraud Advisory Panel

*Acceptance Criteria & Guidelines for the Reporting of Suspected
fraudulent Insurance claims to the Police* – In association with the
Chief Police Officers and the Association of British Insurers.
August 1999

*Raising Standards & Upholding Integrity: The Prevention of
Corruption* – The Home Office, June 2000

Fraud Risk Management – A guide to good practice – CIMA

A guide to civil recovery – CIMA

Securing your Web Site for Business – VeriSign
(A step-by-step guide for secure online commerce.)

Index

Accounting standards, 3.40–3.42
Accounts
manipulation of, 3.35–3.39
illustration of, 3.46–3.50
methods, 3.44
Advance fee fraud, 8.6–8.11
Agency staff fraud, 6.8, 6.9
Alcohol
watering down, 7.4
Audit Committee, 2.14–2.16
Auditors, 2.14–2.16
external—
approach adopted by,
App C general procedures
required, 12.9–12.14
indication of fraud,
12.15–12.18, App C
materiality, 12.3, 12.4
non-audit companies, 12.25
overseas activities, App C
professional scepticism, 12.7,
12.8
public sector, in, App C
reporting fraud in audit report,
12.19–12.24, App C
responsibility, 12.1, 12.2,
App C
risk assessment, 12.6–12.8,
App D

withdrawal from engagement,
App C
internal—
advantages over external, 13.9
audit process—
diagram, 13.1
performing, 13.4
planning, 13.3
report, 13.7
schedule, 13.6, App E
substantive test, 13.5
walk through test, 13.5
corporate governance, role in,
13.10
risk review output, 13.2

Backhanders' fraud, 4.4–4.8
Bad debt write-offs, 5.4
Bank fraud
example of, 7.80
Bell Cablemedia case, 4.8
Biometrics, 11.1–11.3
Bribery, 4.2, 4.3

Cadbury Report, 2.6, 2.7
Charity Commission
action against fraud, 7.18
strategic risk management
framework, App B
Charity fraud, 7.16

charity collection
boxes/envelopes, thefts from,
7.21
Charity Commission—
action taken by, 7.18
strategic risk management
framework, App B
charity shops, frauds in, 7.19,
7.20
donations sent to charity, theft of,
7.22
examples, 7.17
grant fraud, 7.23
manipulation of charity accounts,
7.24, 7.25
CIFAS, App H
Conviction, 1.12
Corporate fraud
contingency plans on
discovering, 14.1–14.2
controls against, 3.20–3.23, 3.36
internal controls, 3.29–3.34
criminal offences, App G
directors' duties in prevention,
2.1–2.3
directors' policy, App J
employee fraud. *See* EMPLOYEE
FRAUD
evidence, gathering, 14.8–14.11,
App J
external fraud. *See* EXTERNAL FRAUD
guidance to staff, App J
healthcheck, App I
interview procedure, App J
investigation—
information available,
14.18–14.19
leading, 14.4
managing, App J
'modus operandi', of, 14.16,
14.17
resource options, App J
legal proceedings—
enforcement and recovery of
assets, 14.28–14.35
interim orders, 14.21–14.26
judgment or final orders, 14.27
management fraud. *See*
MANAGEMENT FRAUD
meaning, 1.25

offender, identification of,
14.12–14.14
organisation's values, App J
policy and response plan, App J
publicity, dealing with, 14.5, 14.6
recovery of funds, 14.15
remedies, App J
reporting, App J
reporting cases to police, App F
reports to be made, 14.7
risk factors. *See* RISK FACTORS
useful websites, *See* WEBSITES
whistle-blowing, 3.27
Corporate governance, 2.4
accountability and audit, 2.7
annual report, disclosures in, 2.7
audit committee and auditors—
code provisions, 2.15, 2.16
principle, 2.14
Cadbury Report, 2.6, 2.7
code provisions, 2.8, 2.9
directors' duties, 2.7
general requirements, 2.7
internal control, 2.10, 3.34
code provisions, 2.12, 2.13
principle, 2.11
Turnbull Report, 3.33, App A
principles, 2.5
unlisted companies and other
organisations, 2.17, 2.18
Credit note fraud, 5.5
Crime prevention
access control, 1.18
deflecting offenders, 1.24
environmental design, 1.20
increase chance of getting
caught, 1.22
reduce payoff, 1.16
removing means, 1.17
rule setting, 1.21
surveillance and monitoring, 1.19
target hardening, 1.14
target removal, 1.15
ten points, 1.13
Criminal offences, App G

Data mining, 11.7–11.10
Debtor fraud, 5.1
bad debt write-offs, 5.4
credit note fraud, 5.5
forged credit rating, 5.10

insolvent debtors, 5.9
invoice factoring, 5.11, 5.12
long firm fraud, 5.6–5.8
teeming and lading, 5.2, 5.3
Dentists, 7.56, 7.57
Directors' duties, 2.1–2.3, 2.7, App
C, App J
Double invoice fraud, 4.17, 4.18
Dummy employees, 6.4, 6.5
Dummy invoices, 4.10–4.15

E-business fraud, 7.26
computer fraud, 7.27
firewalls, 7.51
Internet fraud, 7.27, 7.32
credit card fraud, 7.43–7.46
data alteration, 7.36
digital certificates, 7.39
identity theft, 7.47, 7.48
secure servers, 7.38
security breaches, 7.49
server IDs, 7.40
spoofing, 7.33
unauthorised action, 7.35
unauthorised disclosure, 7.34
virus scanners, 7.51
E-money services, 11.14–11.16
Employee fraud
example, 1.31, 1.32
meaning, 1.30
**Enforcement and recovery of
assets**, 14.28
attachment of earnings, 14.32
bankruptcy and corporate
insolvency procedures,
14.33–14.35
charging orders, 14.30
stop orders, 14.30
third party debt, 14.31
warrant of execution, 14.29
Enron case, 3.36, 3.37
Ernst & Young
research by, 1.8
Expenses fraud, 6.6, 6.7
External fraud
example, 1.34, 1.35
meaning, 1.33

Financial Reporting Review Panel,
3.43
Firewalls, 7.51

Forged credit rating, 5.10
Fraud
causes, 1.11
convictions achieved, 1.12
cost to UK economy, 1.1
Ernst & Young, research by, 1.8
Euromonitor Consultancy, 2000
survey conducted by, 1.10
impact of KPMG, survey by, 1.9
meaning, 1.5, App J
model fraud policy statement—
long version, App L
short version, App K
offences, 1.6
reporting cases to police, App F
technology for fighting—
access to computer systems,
checking identity for, 11.6
biometrics, 11.1–11.3
e-money services, 11.14–11.16
Nike's Internet shop, 11.10
PIN numbers, 11.13
signatures, 11.4, 11.5
surveillance, 11.11
webcards, 11.12
useful websites, *See* WEBSITES
Fraud Squads
national contact list, App F

GP fraud, 7.58

Holiday insurance fraud, 7.88
Hotel sector fraud, 7.2
consumable stocks, 7.5
misappropriating takings by not
recording occupancy, 7.3
watering down alcohol, 7.4
Household insurance fraud, 7.88

Insolvency fraud, 9.1
Insolvency Service Civil Recovery
Scheme, 9.5
Phoenix companies, 9.2–9.4
recent developments in dealing
with, 9.5
**Insolvency Service Civil Recovery
Scheme**, 9.5
Insolvent debtors, 5.9
Insurance fraud
holiday insurance, 7.88
household insurance, 7.88

industry campaigns against, 7.89
motor insurance, 7.81–7.87
Interim orders, 14.21
delivery up of goods, order for, 14.24
information about property or assets, order for, 14.25
Mareva-type injunctions, 14.23
search and seizure orders, 14.22
third parties, court orders in relation to, 14.26
Internet fraud, 7.27, 7.32
credit card fraud, 7.43–7.46
data alteration, 7.36
digital certificates, 7.39
identity theft, 7.47, 7.48
secure servers, 7.38
security breaches, 7.49
server IDs, 7.40
spoofing, 7.33
unauthorised action, 7.35
unauthorised disclosure, 7.34
Investigation
information available, 14.18–14.19
leading, 14.4
managing, App J
'modus operandi', of, 14.16, 14.17
resource options, App J
Investment businesses, 7.65–7.66
computerised systems, 7.75, 7.76
control objectives, 7.74
control systems, 7.71–7.73
documentation of systems and controls, 7.77
example of bank fraud, 7.80
internal audit and compliance departments, 7.78
objectives of rules, 7.67–7.70
risk of fraud and error, 7.79
Investment fraud
advance fee fraud, 8.6–8.11
online scams, 8.2
Prime Bank frauds, 8.3, 8.4
pyramid investment schemes, 8.5
Invoice factoring, 5.11, 5.12

KPMG
survey by, 1.9

Legal proceedings
enforcement and recovery of assets, 14.28
attachment of earnings, 14.32
bankruptcy and corporate insolvency procedures, 14.33–14.35
charging orders, 14.30
stop orders, 14.30
third party debt, 14.31
warrant of execution, 14.29
interim orders, 14.21
delivery up of goods, order for, 14.24
information about property or assets, order for, 14.25
Mareva-type injunctions, 14.23
search and seizure orders, 14.22
third parties, court orders in relation to, 14.26
judgment or final orders, 14.27

Management fraud
accounting standards, 3.40–3.42
Enron case, 3.36, 3.37
examples, 1.28, 1.29
Financial Reporting Review Panel, 3.45
manipulation of accounts, 3.35–3.39
illustration of, 3.46–3.50
methods, 3.44
meaning, 1.27
Manufacturing fraud, 7.14
stock fraud, 7.15
Mareva injunction, 14.23
Maxwell, Robert, 3.6
Mind-mapping, 3.24
Model fraud policy statement
long version, App L
short version, App K
Money laundering, 10.1, 10.2, 10.6
avoidance of organisation being used for, 10.27
cyberlaundering, 10.24
future developments, 10.28
integrating, 10.9
layering, 10.8

legal responsibilities for
accountants and other
professionals, 10.25, 10.26
methods, 10.12–10.23
placing, 10.7
primary legislation, 10.3
secondary legislation, 10.4, 10.5
warning signs, 10.10, 10.11
Motor insurance fraud, 7.81–7.87

NOCHEX, 11.14

Optician fraud, 7.55–7.57

PAYE fraud, 6.3
Payroll fraud, 6.1, 6.2
dummy employees, 6.4, 6.5
PAYE fraud, 6.3
Phoenix companies, 9.2–9.4
PIN numbers, 11.13
Prime Bank fraud, 8.3, 8.4
Procurement fraud, 4.1
backhanders' frauds, 4.4–4.8
bribery, 4.2, 4.3
double invoice fraud, 4.17, 4.18
dummy invoices, 4.10–4.15
stock theft and cover up, 4.16
supply frauds, underdelivery, 4.9
VAT fraud, 4.11, 4.12
Professional firms fraud, 7.62,
7.63
investment businesses, 7.65–7.66
computerised systems, 7.75,
7.76
control objectives, 7.74
control systems, 7.71–7.73
documentation of systems and
controls, 7.77
example of bank fraud, 7.80
internal audit and compliance
departments, 7.78
objectives of rules, 7.67–7.70
risk of fraud and error, 7.79
Public sector fraud, 7.52, 7.53
dentists, 7.56, 7.57
GP frauds, 7.58
indications such frauds are
happening, 7.59
optician frauds, 7.55–7.57
solicitors frauds, 7.60, 7.61
Pyramid investment schemes, 8.3

Retail fraud, 7.6, 7.7
cash taken and explained as
errors in giving change, 7.10
cheque fraud, 7.12
credit card fraud, 7.13, 11.10
not scanning items, 7.9
refunds fraud, 7.11
replacing barcodes, 7.8
Risk factors, 3.1
assessing, 3.18–3.24
complex structure for no business
reason, 3.14
cultural risks, 3.5
dominant CEO, 3.6
lack of anti-fraud policy, 3.17
lack of board support for
controls, 3.11
low staff morale, 3.7
mind-mapping, 3.24
organisational risks, 3.3
performance related pay, 3.16
personnel risks, 3.2
results at any cost, 3.16
risk register, 3.22
special purpose vehicles with
unclear association to main
entity, 3.15
staff with expensive lifestyle not
supported by salary, 3.10
staff keeping tasks when
promoted, 3.9
staff not taking holidays, 3.8
structural risks, 3.4
subsidiaries or branches with
geographical spread, 3.13
Treasury or IT controls not
understood, 3.12

Search and seizure orders, 14.22
Signatures, 11.3
Solicitors fraud, 7.60, 7.61
Stock fraud, 7.15
Supply fraud, underdelivery, 4.9

Teeming and lading, 5.2, 5.3
Turnbull report, 3.33
summary of, App A

Underdelivery
supply frauds, 4.9
Unlisted companies, 2.17, 2.18

VAT fraud, 4.11, 4.12
Virus scanners, 7.51

Webcards, 11.12
Websites
   articles and other information
   about fraud, App M

companies providing anti-fraud
and security products, App M
organisations with anti-fraud
information, App M
search engines, App M
utilities, App M
Whistle-blowing, 3.27

*Brings you the full text of new Accountancy
standards within days of their release*

UK & International GAAP*Plus* Online

World-class financial reporting -constantly updated at the click of a mouse

With the changeover for listed companies
from UK GAAP to International Accounting
Standards getting closer, there has never
been a greater need for rapid access to a
single source of all Accounting Standards –
both UK and International.

Every subscriber to **UK & International
GAAP*Plus* Online** will get instant access to:

■ The full text of UK & International GAAP
■ The full text of all UK Accounting Standards
■ The full text of all International Accounting Standards
■ Ernst & Young's UK Model Financial Statements
■ Ernst & Young's IAS Model Financial Statements
■ Over 20 full sets of FTSE Company Accounts
■ 12 full sets of accounts for Companies reporting under IAS
■ UK Companies Legislation

This unique online service is updated as soon as financial reporting changes happen,
bringing you the full text of a new Accounting Standard – both UK and International -
within days of their release.

Practical Advice based on Real Sets of Company Accounts

It is vital that you are aware of the many and complex implications of *FRS17, FRS18* and
FRS19. **UK & International GAAP*Plus* Online** will not only bring the full text of these
standards direct to your desktop, but also will show how to implement them using extracts
from real sets of company accounts.

Enhanced coverage of UK GAAP...Forward Planning for IAS

With links to all UK Financial Reporting and Accounting Standards, **UK & International
GAAP*Plus* Online** ensures you have all the latest material on pensions, benefits, deferred
taxation and many other complex new requirements at your fingertips.

The assisted search function is useful if you don't know where to find what you're looking for -
simply type in a search word or term to locate every piece of relevant information on this subject.

Each section of commentary includes links through to the relevant underlying authorities in
UK GAAP or International Accounting Standards, which means you'll have access to all the
information you need within a matter of seconds.

Launch Date: January 2002   **Product Code:** UKGO   **Price:** £225 exVAT

How To Order

To order, please contact LexisNexis Butterworths Tolley
Customer Service Dept: Lexis Nexis Butterworths Tolley,
FREEPOST SEA 4177, Croydon, Surrey CR9 5WZ
Telephone: 020 8662 2000   Fax: 020 8662 2012

Butterworths Tolley, 35 Chancery Lane, London WC2A 1EL
A division of Reed Elsevier (UK) Ltd
Registered office 25 Victoria Street London SW1H OEX
Registered in England number 2746621
VAT Registered No. GB 730 8595 20